Excel

ADVANCED SKILLS

MATHS

YEAR 6

AGES 11–12

START MATHS

Get the Results You Want!

Damon James

Contents

Unit 1 Numbers to one million
page 19

1 A number can be written in **words or digits**. e.g. one thousand, eight hundred and forty-six is 1846. To write in digits, write the values in place value. If there is no digit for a certain place then a zero is written, e.g. 4016.

Note: numbers can also be written with decimals, e.g. 421.89 is four hundred and twenty-one, point eight nine.

2 For a **place value chart**, each number is written in the column of place. If there is no value, a zero is written.
Note: U = units, T = tens, H = hundreds, Th = thousands, TTh = tens of thousands and HTh = hundreds of thousands.

3 To find the **value** of a certain digit, look at the place of that digit and this gives the value, e.g. the 8 in 2185 is in the tens place, so has a value of 8 tens. This could be written in words or as a number, e.g. 8 tens, eighty or 80.

4 Determine the **counting patterns** of units, tens, hundreds, thousands etc. by looking at the value of the units, tens, hundreds, thousands place. Complete the pattern or write the missing numbers in the spaces. This also applies to decimals by examining the values in the tenths, hundredths etc. places.

Unit 2 Place value
page 19

1 An abacus is read as the number of discs above each letter. U = units, T = tens, H = hundreds, Th = thousands, TTh = tens of thousands and HTh = hundreds of thousands.

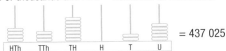 = 437 025

This also applies to decimals by showing the decimal point and then the Tths = tenths and Hths = hundredths.

2 See Unit 1 No. 2

3 < means **less than** and > means **greater than**. So 2481 < 2569 reads as 2481 is less than 2569, which is true.
0.9 > 0.6 reads 0.9 is greater than 0.6 which is also true.

4 Numbers can be described with approximations or statements, e.g. 49 861 is 'roughly fifty thousand' as 49 861 rounds to 50 000.

Unit 3 Numbers greater than one million
page 20

1 and 4 See Unit 1 No. 3

2 **Ordering numbers** can be determined by looking at the first digits of the same place value, e.g. millions and comparing. If the digits are the same, then look at the next number working left to right and so on. e.g. 1 632 488 is larger than 1 623 691 by comparing the values of the tens of thousands.

Note: **ascending order** means smallest to largest and **descending order** means largest to smallest.

3 **Rounding** means giving an approximate answer. To round a number to the **nearest million**, examine the number in the hundreds of thousands position. If it is 5 or greater, the number is rounded up to the nearest million. If it is less than 5, the number is rounded down to the nearest million.
e.g. 6 243 817 as the number in the hundreds of thousands position is 2, then the number is rounded down to 6 000 000.

Unit 4 Number patterns (1)
page 20

1 See Unit 3 No. 2; 2 see Unit 1 No. 4

3 A table can be completed by looking at the number pattern (see Unit 1 No. 4) and then the grid is filled in.

4 A **rule** is a simplified way of expressing a process.
e.g. × 5 means each number is multiplied by 5.
This can also be applied to number patterns.

Unit 5 Expanding numbers
page 21

1 To **write the number from the expanded form**, take the first digit of each number in the equation and put it in order of place.
e.g. 60 000 + 2 000 + 600 + 90 + 2 gives the digits 6, 2, 6, 9 and 2 so the number is 62 692. Note: if there is no digit in a certain place, then a zero is written.

2 To **expand a number**, break the number into its components of hundreds of thousands, tens of thousands and so on. Write as an addition equation.
e.g. 69 321 = 60 000 + 9000 + 300 + 20 + 1

3 – 4 The **number of tens** is all of the numbers in the tens place and to the left.
e.g.   72 has 7 tens
       139 has 13 tens
       483 215 has 48 321 tens
The same idea applies to hundreds, thousands, and so on.
e.g. 36 142 has 36 thousands.

Unit 6 Positive and negative numbers
page 21

1 – 2 A **negative number** is a number less than zero and is represented by a '−' sign. e.g. −4, −$\frac{1}{2}$, −0.6

3 See Unit 1 No. 4

4 **Simple equations** can be completed by thinking about the numbers on a number line, and the effect of the operation.
e.g. 3 − 4 =

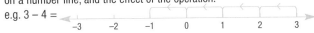

Unit 7 Addition review
page 22

1 When **adding larger numbers**, it is possible to ignore the zeros, add the familiar numbers and then put on the ignored zeros.
e.g.   700 + 200   add 7 + 2 = 9
                      then put two zeros on
       700 + 200 = 900

2 Either of the following three strategies could be used:
- The **split strategy**: where the numbers are expanded into their place values and numbers of the same value are added together.
  e.g. 26 + 37 = (20 + 30) + (6 + 7)
                = 50 + 13
                = 63
- The **compensation strategy**: where the number is rounded to the nearest 5 or 10, the rounded numbers are added and then the difference from the rounding is added or subtracted.
  e.g.   24 + 39:   24 + 40 = 64
  As 39 is rounded up 1, so the answer is counted back by 1.
       So 24 + 39 = 63

The **jump strategy**: where we start with the first number and then expand the second number into its components, and each component is added from largest to smallest.
e.g.   340 + 57 = 340 + 50 + 7
                = 390 + 7
                = 397

3 To **estimate** is to make a sensible guess. This can be completed by rounding to the **nearest hundred** and then using one of the strategies of No. 2 to add.

4 To add vertically, start at the right and add the numbers together. Write in the units and carry any tens. Then move to the tens, hundreds etc. through to the left carrying as necessary.
e.g.

$$\begin{array}{r} 6\ 4\ 8 \\ +\ 2\ 1\ 9 \\ \hline 8\ 6\ 7 \end{array}$$

Unit 8   Adding to 999 999   *page 22*

1 and 2 **Adding three or more numbers** is the same as adding two numbers. (See Unit 7 No. 4). With quantities don't forget the units!

3 Examine each solution and **find the missing number** by counting on or subtracting. Write the answer in the box.

e.g.

Note: this also applies to subtraction and multiplication.

4 Additions can be completed with **number and word equations**.

Unit 9   Adding large numbers   *page 23*

1 – 4 See Unit 8 Nos 1 – 2

Unit 10   Subtraction review   *page 23*

1 – 2 **Subtraction** is the process of taking one quantity away from another. It can be completed with numbers or words. Trading occurs when a subtraction such as 5 – 9 cannot be completed so a 'ten' needs to be traded.

e.g.
$$\begin{array}{r} {}^{5}\cancel{6}\ {}^{1}3 \\ -\ \ 2\ 9 \\ \hline 3\ 4 \end{array}$$
A trade from the 6 makes 13 – 9.

3 See Unit 8 No. 3

4 **Difference** also means subtraction.

Unit 11   Mental strategies for subtraction   *page 24*

1 When **subtracting larger numbers**, it is possible to ignore the zeros, subtract the familiar numbers and then add on the ignored zeros.
e.g. 640 – 320:   64 – 32 = 32   then add back zero
So 640 – 320 = 320.

2 and 4 Either of the following 2 strategies could be used.
- The **jump strategy**: where the second number is expanded, then each place value from greatest to least (left to right) is subtracted from the first number.
  e.g. 96 – 25 = 96 – 20 – 5 = 76 – 5
  $$= 71$$
- The **compensation strategy**: where the first number is rounded (and/or the second) to the nearest 5 or 10, then the numbers subtracted. Finally the difference is counted back or on.
  e.g. 63 – 19 is about 65 – 20 = 45
  As 63 is rounded up by 2 to 65, count back 2.
  As 19 was rounded up 1 to 20 and then subtracted, count on 1.
  Overall, count back 1.
  So, 63 – 19 = 44

3 See Unit 10 Nos 1 – 2 or when **subtracting from numbers with zeros** it is easier to make the numbers end with a 9, so 2000 becomes 1999 as it is easier to subtract from.
e.g.   300 – 72
    is about 299 – 72 = 227   then count on by 1
    so 300 – 72 = 228

Unit 12   Rounding numbers   *page 24*

1 – 4 See Unit 3 No. 3

1 For a number ending in 1, 2, 3 or 4 it is rounded down to the **nearest ten**, and for a number ending in 5, 6, 7, 8 or 9 it is rounded up to the nearest ten, e.g. 724 is rounded down to 720.

2 If the numbers being considered are from 0 to 49, they are rounded down to the **nearest hundred** and if they are from 50 to 99, they are rounded up to the nearest hundred.
e.g. 486 is rounded up to 500.

3 – 4 If the numbers being considered are from 0 to 499, they are rounded down to the nearest thousand, and if they are from 500 to 999, they are rounded up to the nearest thousand.
e.g. 3251 is rounded down to 3000.

Unit 13   Subtraction to 999 999   *page 25*

1 Subtraction can be completed with **larger numbers**. See Unit 10 Nos 1 – 2.
2 See Unit 12 Nos 3 and 4
3 Don't forget the **units and quantities**!
4 See Unit 10 No. 4

Unit 14   Subtracting large numbers   *page 25*

1 See Unit 10 Nos 1 – 2
2 and 4 see Unit 13 No. 3
3 See Unit 10 No. 4

Unit 15   Estimation   *page 26*

1 – 3 See Unit 7 No. 3
1 and 3 See Unit 12 No. 2
4 Addition and subtraction are **inverse operations**. This means they are opposite or reverse operations, and they undo each other.
e.g.   24 – 10 + 10 = 24   or   24 – 10 = 14
                                14 + 10 = 24

Unit 16   Multiplication tables (1)   *page 26*

1 – 2 and 4 **Multiplication** is the total number in the groups or rows. It can be described with a number sentence such as 3 × 4 = 12 or
$$\begin{array}{r} 3 \\ \times\ \ 4 \\ \hline 1\ 2 \end{array}$$
or in words.

Product, groups of, times and **lots of** all mean multiply.
Note: 0 × anything = 0 and 1 × anything = itself.

3 **Missing numbers** can be found by inverse operations.
e.g.
$$5 \times \square = 25$$
$$25 \div 5 = \square$$
$$\square = 5$$
so 5 × 5 = 25
or by saying '5 multiplied by what equals 25?'

Unit 17   Multiplication tables (2)   *page 27*

1 – 3 See Unit 16 Nos 1 – 2 and 4
4 The total number of days in one **week** is 7.

Unit 18   Multiplication review   *page 27*

1 – 2 and 4 See Unit 16 Nos 1 – 2 and 4
3 See Unit 16 No. 3

Unit 19   Multiplication of tens, hundreds and thousands (1)   *page 28*

1 See Unit 16 No. 1
2 – 4 To multiply by **groups of tens, hundreds and thousands**, start at the right and multiply to the left carrying as required.
e.g.
$$\begin{array}{r} 6\ 0 \\ \times\ \ \ 3 \\ \hline 1\ 8\ 0 \end{array}$$

Note: it is possible to multiply the familiar numbers first, such as 3 x 6 = 18 and then add the required number of zeros:
1 for tens so 60 × 3 = 180
2 for hundreds so 600 × 3 = 1800
3 for thousands so 6000 × 3 = 18 000

Unit 20 Multiplications of tens, hundreds and thousands (2) *page 28*

1 See Unit 19 Nos 2 – 4
2 – 4 When numbers are multiplied that **both have tens**, e.g. 30 × 20, then multiply the familiar numbers first so 3 × 2 = 6. Then count the number of zeros in the question, in this case 2, and add these to the end of the answer. So 30 × 20 = 600.
Note: this applies to hundreds and thousands, and so on.
4 Don't forget the **units of quantities**!

Unit 21 Multiplications of tens, hundreds and thousands (3) *page 29*

1 and 3 See Unit 20 Nos 2 – 4
2 When **multiplying by 1 ten** add 1 zero, so 42 x 10 = 420
When **multiplying by 1 hundred** add 2 zeros, so 42 x 100 = 4200
When **multiplying by 1 thousand** add 3 zeros, so 42 x 1000 = 42 000
4 See Unit 16 Nos 1, 2 and 4

Unit 22 Multiplication *page 29*

1 – 4 **Larger numbers** can be multiplied by working right to left:

```
   1
  4 6 1     Multiply 3 by 1 = 3
×     3     Multiply 3 by 6 = 18, write the 8 and carry the 1.
-------     Multiply 3 by 4 = 12, add the 1 = 13.
1 3 8 3     Write 13 to complete the answer, 1383.
```

Unit 23 Multiplication by 2-digit numbers *page 30*

1 – 4 With **multiplication by 2-digit numbers**, work right to left multiplying by the units value and then the tens.

```
e.g.      2 4 8
×           2 6
       ---------
        1 4 8 8    (248 × 6)
      + 4 9 6 0    (248 × 20)
       ---------
        6 4 4 8    total
```

Note: this is the same as expanding the two-digit number into its tens and units, e.g. 26 = 20 + 6, and completing two multiplications and then adding them together.
1 See Unit 7 No. 3

Unit 24 Extended multiplication (1) *page 30*

1 – 2 See Unit 20 Nos 2 – 4
3 See Unit 19 Nos 2 – 4
4 See Unit 23 Nos 1 – 4

Unit 25 Extended multiplication (2) *page 31*

1 – 4 See Unit 23 Nos 1 – 4
4 Don't forget the **$ sign**!

Unit 26 Extended multiplication (3) *page 31*

1 – 2 and 4 See Unit 23 Nos 1 – 4
3 To find the missing numbers, look at the end number of the first part of the answer 4, then work backwards to find what × 2 = 4?

```
e.g.          3 2
       ×     
            -------
              6 4    (32 × 2)
        + 1 9 2 0    (32 × 6)
            -------
          1 9 8 4    Missing number is 62
```

Unit 27 Extended multiplication (4) *page 32*

1 – 4 See Unit 23 Nos 1 – 4
Don't forget the **$ and units**!

Unit 28 Multiples, factors and divisibility *page 32*

1

Divisor	Divisibility test
2	The number must be **even**, e.g. ends in 0, 2, 4, 6 or 8.
3	The **sum of the digits** must be divisible by 3. e.g. 126: 1 + 2 + 6 = 9 which is divisible by 3.
4	The **number made by the last two digits** must be divisible by 4, e.g. for 124, 24 which is divisible by 4.
5	The **last digit must be 0 or 5**.
8	The **number made by the last three digits** must be divisible by 8, e.g. for 4128, 128 which is divisible by 8.
9	The **sum of the digits** must be divisible by 9, e.g. for 108, 1 + 0 + 8 = 9.
10	The **last digit must be a 0**.

2 – 3 A **factor** is a number which divides evenly into another number, e.g. 6 is a factor of 12. A number may have many factors, e.g. 1, 12, 2, 6, 3 and 4 are all factors of 12.
4 A **multiple** is the product of a number's factors, so 12 is a multiple of 3 and 4. e.g. The first 3 multiples of 3 are:
1 × 3 = 3, 2 × 3 = 6, 3 × 3 = 9 so 3, 6, 9.

Unit 29 Multiplication strategies *page 33*

1 – 2 See Unit 20 Nos 2 – 4
3 **Using doubles** means doubling a number and is the same as multiplying by 2. Doubling a number twice is the same as multiplying by 4. Doubling a number three times is the same as multiplying by 8.

```
e.g.      20 × 2 = 40
          20 × 4 = 20 × 2 × 2
                 = 40 × 2 = 80
          20 × 8 = 20 × 2 × 2 × 2
                 = 40 × 2 × 2 = 80 × 2 = 160
```

4 See Unit 23 Nos 1 – 4

Unit 30 Estimating products *page 33*

1 – 4 See Unit 12 Nos 1 – 2 and Unit 20 Nos 2 – 4
2 – 4 See also Unit 23 Nos 1 – 4

Unit 31 Division practice *page 34*

1 – 4 **Division** is the sharing or grouping of a number or quantity into equal amounts. **Groups of** and **sharing** also mean division.
Division can be written as 18 ÷ 9 = 2 or 9)18 with quotient 2.
To find the missing digit, the **inverse operation** multiplication, can be used.
e.g. 24 ÷ ☐ = 4   4 x 6 = 24
then 24 ÷ 6 = 4

Unit 32 Division review *page 34*

1 See Unit 31 Nos 1 – 4
2 and 4 When a division or grouping is made, and there are some items or an amount left over, these are called **remainders**. The abbreviation for remainder is r, e.g. 13 ÷ 5 = 2 groups and remainder 3 which can be written as 2 r 3. The number of shares is also called the **quotient**.
3 When **dividing larger numbers** that include zeros, the zero can be ignored and the familiar division completed, then the zero can be added back onto the end.
e.g. To calculate 120 ÷ 4,   12 ÷ 4 = 3
Then 120 ÷ 4 = 30

Unit 33   **Division with remainders**   page 35

1 See Unit 32 Nos 2 and 4

2 **Division** can be completed working left to right. Remember if it is not possible to divide the first digit, move to divide the first two digits.

e.g.

$$\begin{array}{r} \quad\; 6\,2 \\ 4\,\overline{)\,2\,4\,8} \end{array}$$

3 – 4 Remainders can also be found completing larger divisions. See Unit 32 Nos 2 and 4.

Unit 34   **Division with remainders – fractions**   page 35

1 – 4 Remainders of division equations can be expressed as a **remainder** (r), as a **fraction** of the **divisor** (the number dividing) or a **decimal**. To find the remainder as a fraction, complete the division as per usual (see Unit 33 No. 2) and then the remainder is written over the divisor.

e.g.

$$\begin{array}{r} 54 \quad r\;1 = 54\tfrac{1}{5} \\ 5\,\overline{)\,271} \end{array}$$

Note: a fraction should always be written in its simplest form.

Unit 35   **Division with zeros in the answer**   page 36

1 See Unit 33 No. 2 and Unit 34 Nos 1 – 4

2 Complete the division as usual (see Unit 33 No. 2). If a **number cannot be divided into**, then a zero is written above.

e.g.

$$\begin{array}{r} 2\,0\,6 \\ 4\,\overline{)\,8\,2\,4} \end{array}$$

3 See Unit 33 No. 2 and Unit 34 Nos 1 – 4

4 See Unit 33 No. 2 and Unit 34 Nos 1 – 4 and don't forget the **units and quantities**.

Unit 36   **Division with zeros in the divisor**   page 36

1 and 3 Remember when **dividing by 10**, move the decimal point one place to the left.

e.g. $3\,2\,0 \;\div\; 10 \;=\; 32$

     and $4\,6\,8 \;\div\; 10 \;=\; 46.8$

2 See Unit 5 Nos 3 – 4

4 The number of **millimetres in 1 centimetre is 10**. Therefore to change millimetres to centimetres we divide by 10 and change the units to cm.

Unit 37   **Division by numbers with zeros**   page 37

1 See Unit 36 Nos 1 and 3

2 When **dividing by 100** move the decimal point two places to the

e.g. $4\,6\,0\,0 \;\div\; 100 \;=\; 46$

3 and 4 See Unit 36 Nos 1 and 3, then divide the familiar numbers.

e.g.

$$80\,\overline{)\,480}$$

Divide both numbers by 10 first giving:

$$\begin{array}{r} 6 \\ 8\,\overline{)\,48} \end{array}$$

Note: a decimal answer is possible. The decimal point is written in the answer above the decimal point in the question and the division is continued as usual. Only calculate to two or three decimal places.

Unit 38   **Division of numbers larger than 999**   page 37

1 and 3 See Unit 33 No. 2 (don't forget units!)

2 See Unit 34 Nos 1 – 4

4 To find the **missing number**, use the inverse operation, multiplication, working right to left.

e.g.

$$\begin{array}{r} 4\,2\,1 \\ 3\,\overline{)\,1\,2\,6\,3} \end{array} \qquad \begin{aligned} 3 \times 1 &= 3 \\ 3 \times 2 &= 6 \\ 3 \times 4 &= 12 \end{aligned}$$

Unit 39   **Extended division**   page 38

1 – 3 **Extended division** is the same as short division except more steps need to be completed. It is set out with each smaller division and the subtractions visible.

e.g.

$$\begin{array}{r} 2\,1 \\ 12\,\overline{)\,2\,5\,2} \\ -\,2\,4 \downarrow \\ \hline 1\,2 \\ -\,1\,2 \\ \hline 0 \end{array} \quad \begin{aligned} ②\times 12 &= 24 \\ ①\times 12 &= 12 \end{aligned}$$

Note: the circled numbers are the same as the answer.

There may be a remainder resulting from an extended division and this is written as a remainder or a fraction.

4 See Unit 38 No. 4. Note: if there is a **remainder**, this needs to be added to the last number of the multiplication.

e.g.

$$\begin{array}{r} 2\,1\;r\,2 \\ 6\,\overline{)\,1\,2\,8} \end{array} \quad \begin{aligned} 2 \times 6 &= 12 \\ 1 \times 6 &= 6,\;\; 6 + 2 = 8 \end{aligned}$$

Unit 40   **Averages (1)**   page 38

1 – 2 and 4 The **average** is the sum of all the numbers or totals divided by how many numbers or totals.

e.g.

The average of 41, 50 and 62

$$\frac{41 + 50 + 62}{3}$$

$$= \frac{153}{3} = 51$$

Note: **mean** is another name for the average.

3 The **average speed** is found by dividing the total distance travelled by the time taken.

e.g. 6 hours to drive 426 km,

therefore $\dfrac{426}{6} = 71$ so 71 km/h.

Don't forget: units are very important!

Unit 41   **Averages (2)**   page 39

1 See Unit 34 Nos 1 – 4

2 – 4 See Unit 40 Nos 1 – 2 and 4

Unit 42   **Inverse operations and checking answers**   page 39

1, 3 and 4 See Unit 15 No. 4

2 – 4 Multiplication and division are **inverse operations**.

e.g. $12 \times 2 \div 2 = 12$

   or $12 \times 2 = 24$

     $24 \div 12 = 2$ or $24 \div 2 = 12$

Unit 43 Number lines and operations   page 40

1 – 4 A **number line** is a line marked with numbers in order over an interval.

e.g.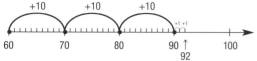

Operations (+, −, × and ÷) can be performed on a number line, using the jump strategy.

e.g.

$$+10 \quad +10 \quad +10$$

60   70   80   90 ↑   100
                      92

+1 +1

Therefore 60 + 32 = 92.

Unit 44 Order of operations (1)   page 40

1 – 4 The **order of operations** is the order in which the different operations should be completed. This is known as BODMAS or PEDMAS. Questions with ×, ÷ only should be worked left to right. Complete the brackets first then multiplication and division, and finally addition and subtraction.

B	brackets	P	parenthesis
O	over	E	exponents
D	division	D	division
M	multiplication	M	multiplication
A	addition	A	addition
S	subtraction	S	subtraction

e.g. $3 \times 4 - (2 + 1) = 12 - 3 = 9$
but without brackets: $3 \times 4 - 2 + 1 = 11$

Unit 45 Order of operations (2)   page 41

1 – 4 See Unit 44 Nos 1 – 4

Unit 46 Order of operations (3)   page 41

1 – 4 See Unit 44 Nos 1 – 4

Unit 47 Order of operations with decimals and fractions   page 42

1 – 4 The same rules apply with decimals and fractions, for order of operations, see Unit 44 Nos 1 – 4

Unit 48 Number patterns (2)   page 42

1, 3 and 4 See Unit 4 No. 3
2 See Unit 4 No. 4

Unit 49 Number patterns (3)   page 43

1 See Unit 1 No. 4
2 See Unit 4 No. 4
3 – 4 See Unit 4 No. 3

Unit 50 Mixed operations   page 43

1 See Unit 7 No. 2 and Unit 11 Nos 2 and 4
2 – 3 See Unit 44 Nos 1 – 4
4 See Unit 15 No. 4 and Unit 42 Nos 2 – 4

Unit 51 Zero in operations   page 44

1 See Unit 44 Nos 1 – 4
2 See Unit 7 No 4 and Unit 10 Nos 1 – 2
3 See Unit 19 Nos 2 – 4 and Unit 33 No. 2
4 See Unit 8 No. 3

Unit 52 Equations   page 44

1 and 3 To find the **value of the letter** or symbol or box, use inverse operations (see Unit 15 No. 4 and Unit 42 Nos 2 – 4).

e.g. $60 = x \div 2$
Say what divided by 2 equals 60?
Answer is 120.
Therefore $x = 120$

2 and 4 To find the **value of the letter or missing amount**, calculate the answer of the completed equation and then use inverse operations (See Unit 15 No. 4 and Unit 42 Nos 2 – 4).

Unit 53 Binary numbers   page 45

1 – 4 The **binary system** is used by computer programmers.
Binary notation:

	2^4 sixteen	2^3 eight	2^2 four	2^1 two	2^0 one
5 (4 + 1)			1	0	1
25 (16 + 8 + 1)	1	1	0	0	1

Unit 54 Operations with money   page 45

1 There are 6 different **coins**: $2, $1, 50c, 20c, 10c and 5c and 5 different **notes**: $100, $50, $20, $10 and $5 in **the Australian Money System**. Money is rounded to the **nearest 5c**.
Amounts ending in 1 or 2 are rounded down to the nearest 10c, amounts ending in 3 or 4 are rounded up to the nearest 5c, amounts ending in 6 or 7 are rounded down to the nearest 5c and amounts ending in 8 or 9 are rounded up to the nearest 10c.
e.g. $3.58 is rounded up to $3.60.

2 **Adding and subtracting money** is like normal addition (see Unit 7 No. 4) and subtraction (see Unit 10 Nos 1 – 2) except the decimal point needs to be lined up first and then carried through into the answer. Don't forget the $ and c signs!

3 **Multiplication with money** is like normal multiplication (see Unit 19 Nos 2 – 4), except the decimal point is ignored until the end of the calculation, when the total number of decimal places needs to be counted from the question and this needs to be counted back in the answer.

e.g. $4.22
    ×   3
        $12.66

There are two decimal places in the question, therefore two decimal places in the answer.
With **division**, the decimal point needs to be lined up first in the answer with that in the question, and then the division is completed as usual (see Unit 33 No. 2). Note: only decimal answers are given and these are to only two decimal places.

4 **Change** is the left over amount of money owed back to the person after the purchase. It can be found by counting on.
e.g. The change from $5.00 after spending $2.60 is 40c which makes $3.00 and $2.00 makes $5.00.
Therefore the total change is: $2.00 + 40c = $2.40

Unit 55 Equations with numbers and words   page 46

1 and 4 Letters or symbols can be used to represent values. They can then be used in equations. Inverse operations can be used to **find the values of these letters** or symbols.

e.g. $M + M + M = 30$
As each letter is the same, it must represent the same value.
As there are 3 Ms then $3 \times M = 30$
                    $M = 10$

Try: $10 + 10 + 10 = 30$ ✓
2 Equations written in words can be rewritten with just numbers and solved.
3 See Unit 44 Nos 1 – 4

Unit 56 **Substituting values** page 46
1 – 2 See Unit 52 Nos 1 and 3
3 See Unit 15 No. 4 and Unit 42 Nos 2 – 4
4 See Unit 55 No. 2

Unit 57 **Number sentences (1)** page 47
1 – 2 See Unit 52 Nos 1 and 3
3 See Unit 52 Nos 2 and 4
4 See Unit 55 No. 2

Unit 58 **Number sentences (2)** page 47
1 – 2 See Unit 52 Nos 1 and 3
3 – 4 See Unit 55 No 2

Unit 59 **Number sentences (3)** page 48
1 – 2 See Unit 52 Nos 1 and 3
3 See Unit 55 No. 2
4 See Unit 52 Nos 2 and 4

Unit 60 **Square and cube numbers** page 48
1 – 3 A **squared number** is the number that results from multiplying another number by itself.
e.g. $3^2 = 3 \times 3 = 9$
A **cubed number** is the number that results from multiplying another number by itself twice more.
e.g. $2^3 = 2 \times 2 \times 2 = 8$
Note: it is not 3 times the number as $2 \times 3 = 6$
4 **Square and cubed numbers** can be used in calculations. Find the value of the squared and cubed numbers first, and then complete the equation as normal.

Unit 61 **Working with numbers** page 49
1 See Unit 2 No. 3 and Unit 5 Nos 1 – 2
2 **Immediately after** means to count on by 1.
Immediately before means to count back by 1.
Greater than and more than means to count on.
Less than means to count back.
3 To add on 10 000, add 1 to the tens of thousands place, carrying as necessary.
4 A **tree diagram** allows us to break a number into its factors (see Unit 28 Nos 2 – 3) in a graphical way.
e.g.

The factor tree is stopped when **prime factors** (factors which are prime numbers or numbers that are only divisible by one and themselves) are reached on each of the branches.

Unit 62 **Change of units** page 49
1 and 4 To **change between length units**
  10 mm = 1 cm
  100 cm = 1 m
  1000 m = 1 km
2 and 4 To **change between weight units**
  1000 g = 1 kg
  1000 kg = 1 tonne
3 and 4 To **change between time units**
  60 s = 1 min
  60 min = 1 h
  24 h = 1 day

Unit 63 **Negative numbers** page 50
1 – 3 See Unit 6 Nos 1 – 2
4 See Unit 43 Nos 1 – 4

Unit 64 **Prime and composite numbers** page 50
1, 3 and 4 **Prime numbers** are numbers that are only divisible by 1 and themselves, e.g. 3, 5, 7. Note: 1 is not a prime number.
Composite numbers are numbers which have factors other than 1 and themselves, e.g. 12, 10, 90.
2 See Unit 28 No. 1

Unit 65 **Fractions** page 51
1 – 3 The **numerator** is the top number part of a fraction (over the line). It shows how many parts out of a whole. The **denominator** is the bottom number part of the fraction (below the line). It shows how many parts are in the whole.
e.g. $\frac{3}{5}$ is 3 out of 5 equal parts.
Fractions can be represented with diagrams where the fraction is the shaded/coloured part.
e.g. $\frac{3}{4}$ is represented by:

 or or

4 The **fraction of a group** can also be represented with a diagram:
$\frac{3}{4}$ is represented by or or

Unit 66 **Fraction of a group (1)** page 51
1 – 4 The **fraction of a group** can be found by dividing the number of the group by the denominator of the fraction and then multiplying by the number of required groups (the numerator).
e.g. $\frac{1}{5}$ of 10 $10 \div 5 = 2$ and $2 \times 1 = 2$
  $\frac{2}{5}$ of 15 15 7 5 = 3 and 2 x 3 = 6

Unit 67 **Fraction of a group (2)** page 52
1 – 4 See Unit 66 Nos 1 – 4. Note: to find how much more, subtract the fraction from 1 and solve as usual.

Unit 68 **Equivalent fractions (1)** page 52
1 – 3 An equivalent fraction is a fraction that has the same value or amount.
e.g. all of the following fractions are equal to $\frac{1}{2}$.
$\frac{1}{2} = \frac{2}{4} = \frac{3}{6} = \frac{4}{8} = \boxed{} = \boxed{} = \bigcirc = \bigcirc\bigcirc$
An equivalent fraction can be found by using the idea of 'what is done to the bottom is done to the top'. The numerator and denominator are always multiplied or divided.
e.g.
$\frac{4}{5} = \frac{8}{10}$ both the denominator and numerator are multiplied by 2
$\frac{90}{100} = \frac{9}{10}$ both the denominator and numerator are divided by 10
4 When **comparing fractions**, it is easier to first make the fractions over the same denominator by either multiplying or dividing the fraction. Then they can easily be compared. See Unit 2 No. 3.

Unit 69 **Equivalent fractions (2)** page 53
1 – 4 See Unit 68 Nos 1 – 3

Unit 70 **Equivalent fractions (3)** page 53
1, 2 and 4 See Unit 68 Nos 1 – 3
3 See Unit 68 No. 4

Unit 71   **Improper fractions and mixed numbers**   page 54

1 An improper fraction is a fraction that is larger than one. The numerator is larger than the denominator.

e.g. $2\frac{1}{2}$ is ◯◯◯ or $\frac{5}{2}$

A **mixed number** is a number written as a whole number with a fraction, e.g. $1\frac{3}{4}$ or ▢ ▢▢

2 and 4 It is possible to simplify improper fractions to mixed numbers by dividing the denominator into the numerator to find how many whole numbers there are and the remainder is written as a fraction.

e.g. $\frac{9}{4}$ = 2 whole with 1 left over

      $= 2\frac{1}{4}$

3 A **mixed number can be written as an improper fraction** by multiplying the denominator by the whole number and adding the numerator. This total is placed over the denominator.

e.g.   For $2\frac{1}{4}$

      $2 \times 4 + 1 = 9$

So, $2\frac{1}{4} = \frac{9}{4}$

Unit 72   **Using fractions**   page 54

1 See Unit 68 No. 4

2 Fractions with the **same denominator** can be added.

e.g. $\frac{1}{5} + \frac{1}{5} = \frac{2}{5}$ (as 1 + 1 = 2)

Fractions with **different denominators** can be **added** by first making the denominators the same (see Unit 68 Nos 1 – 3), then the fractions are added as usual.

e.g. $\frac{1}{2} + \frac{3}{4}$

Making the denominator the same: $\frac{2}{4} + \frac{3}{4}$

Now add 2 + 3 = 5

The answer is $\frac{5}{4}$.

Note: if the answer is an improper fraction it should be simplified.

e.g. $\frac{5}{4} = 1\frac{1}{4}$

3 Fractions with the **same denominator** can be **subtracted**.

e.g. $\frac{9}{10} - \frac{3}{10} = \frac{6}{10} = \frac{3}{5}$

Fractions with **different denominators** can be **subtracted** by first making the denominators the same (see Unit 68 Nos 1 – 3), then the fractions are subtracted as usual.

e.g. $\frac{7}{10} - \frac{2}{5}$

Making the denominator the same: $\frac{7}{10} - \frac{4}{10}$

Now subtracting: 7 – 4 = 3

The answer is $\frac{3}{10}$.

4 To **multiply fractions**

The numerators are multiplied together and then the denominators are multiplied together. If there is a whole number, then put the whole number over 1, so $2 = \frac{2}{1}$ and $3 = \frac{3}{1}$.

e.g. $5 \times \frac{1}{2} = \frac{5}{1} \times \frac{1}{2} = \frac{5}{2}$

The fraction is then simplified if necessary: $\frac{5}{2} = 2\frac{1}{2}$

Unit 73   **Fraction addition**   page 55

1, 3 and 4 See Unit 72 No. 2

2 A number line can be used to **add fractions**.

e.g. $\frac{1}{2} + \frac{1}{2} = 1$

(number line from 0 to $1\frac{1}{2}$ with $\frac{1}{2}$ arc)

Unit 74   **Fraction subtraction**   page 55

1 See Unit 68 Nos 1 – 3

2 – 4 See Unit 72 No. 3 (don't forget that **difference** means subtraction).

Unit 75   **Fraction addition and subtraction**   page 56

1 See Unit 71 No. 3

2 See Unit 71 Nos 2 and 4

3 See Unit 72 No. 2

4 See Unit 72 No. 3

Unit 76   **Fraction multiplication (1)**   page 56

1 See Unit 71 Nos 2 and 4

2 See Unit 71 No. 3

3 – 4 **Repeated addition** is the process where a number multiplied many times can be expressed as an addition equation.

e.g. $3 \times 6 = 6 + 6 + 6 = 18$

This also applies to fractions.

e.g. $3 \times \frac{1}{5} = \frac{1}{5} + \frac{1}{5} + \frac{1}{5} = \frac{3}{5}$

Note: the multiplication and the addition equations give the same answer.

Unit 77   **Fraction multiplication (2)**   page 57

1 See Unit 68 Nos 1 – 3

2 See Unit 76 Nos 3 – 4

3 – 4 See Unit 72 No. 4

Unit 78   **Fraction multiplication (3)**   page 57

1 See Unit 76 Nos 3 – 4

2 See Unit 72 No 4

3 When **multiplying two fractions** together, the numerators are multiplied together and then the denominators are multiplied together.

e.g. $\frac{4}{5} \times \frac{1}{3} = \frac{(4 \times 1)}{(5 \times 3)} = \frac{4}{15}$

If required, the answer should be simplified.

Note: the denominators do not need to be the same.

4 See Unit 72 No. 4 (don't forget units or quantities!)

Unit 79   **Fraction multiplication (4)**   page 58

1 See Unit 71 No. 3

2 – 3 See Unit 66 Nos 1 – 4

4 See Unit 78 No. 3

Unit 80   **Decimal place value – thousandths**   page 58

1 See Unit 2 No. 1

2 A **decimal** is part of a whole and can be written in numbers or words, e.g. 4.28 = four point two eight or four units and twenty-eight hundredths.

3 See Unit 1 No. 3

4 To write a **fraction as a decimal**, the number of zeros in the denominator of the fraction indicates the number of decimal places.

e.g. $\frac{4}{10}$ has one decimal place and is 0.4

      $\frac{3}{100}$ has two decimal places and is 0.03

      $\frac{321}{100}$ has two decimal places and is 3.21

Note: if the number is less than one, then a zero is written in front of the decimal point.

e.g. 0.21

Unit 81   Decimal addition   page 59

1 – 3 **Decimal addition** is the same as regular addition. Tens, units, tenths, hundredths and so on all need to line up in the correct place value columns. The easiest way is to line up the decimal point first.

e.g.
```
    6 . 2 1      The decimal point position
  + 3 . 4 8      also continues in the answer.
    9 ↓ 6 9
```

Trading is treated in the same way.

e.g.
```
      1
    4 . 6
    2 . 8
  + 1 . 3
    8 . 7
```

Note: any missing digits can have zeros added to keep the columns consistent.

e.g.
```
    4 . 2 1     becomes      4 . 2 1
  + 3 . 6      ⟶          + 3 . 6 0
                              7 . 8 1
```

3 and 4 See Unit 54 No. 2

Unit 82   Decimal subtraction   page 59

1 – 2 and **4** **Decimal subtraction** is the same as regular subtraction. Tens, units, tenths, hundredths and so on all need to line up in the correct columns. The easiest way is to line up the decimal point first.

e.g.
```
    8 . 9       The decimal point position
  - 2 . 4       also continues in the answer.
    6 ↓ 5
```

Trading is treated in the same way.

e.g.
```
      3 . 15
    4̸ . 6̸ 3
  - 2 . 8 9
    1 ↓ 7 4
```

Note: any missing numbers can have zeros added to keep the columns consistent.

e.g.
```
    4 1 . 6 9       becomes       3   8 1
                                4̸ 1 . 6̸ 9̸ 0
  - 2 8 . 3 5 1     ⟶          - 2 8 . 3 5 1
                                1 3 . 3 3 9
```

3 See Unit 54 No. 2

Unit 83   Decimal multiplication   page 60

1 – 4 When **multiplying decimals**, multiplication is completed as usual except the decimal point is ignored until the end of the calculation. Then the total number of decimal places in the question is counted and this is the number of decimal places required for the answer.

e.g.
```
      6 . 8 1      Two decimal places in question,
    ×       3      so two decimal places in answer.
    2 0 . 4 3
```

Therefore the answer is 20.43
Note: don't forget to include any units and signs.

Unit 84   Decimal division   page 60

1 – 4 **Decimal division** by a whole number is completed as usual. The decimal point in the answer is lined up above the decimal point in the question.

e.g.
```
      1 2 . 6
  3 ) 3 6 . 9
```

If the division doesn't go, such as 3 ÷ 6, then a zero is written as in normal division.
Note: don't forget any units and signs. Also, only state answers to two decimal places for money and quantities.

Unit 85   Multiplication and division of decimals (1)   page 61

1 When **multiplying by 10**, move the decimal point one place to the right, e.g. $6.39 \times 10 = 63.9$

2 When **multiplying by 100**, move the decimal point two places to the right, e.g. $4.28 \times 100 = 428$

When **multiplying by 1000**, move the decimal point three places to the right, e.g. $26.391 \times 1000 = 26\ 391$

Note: a zero is added if there are not enough places to move the decimal point.
e.g. $4.2 \times 100 = 420$

3 When **dividing by 10**, move the decimal point one place to the left, e.g. $42.8 \div 10 = 4.28$

4 When **dividing by 100**, move the decimal point two places to the left, e.g. $32.19 \div 100 = 0.3219$

When **dividing by 1000**, move the decimal point three places to the left, e.g. $483.3 \div 1000 = 0.4833$

Note: a zero is added if there are not enough places to move the decimal point.
e.g. $4.38 \div 100 = 0.0438$

Unit 86   Multiplication and division of decimals (2)   page 61

1 – 2 See Unit 22 Nos 1 – 4 and Unit 85 Nos 3 and 4
3 – 4 See Unit 31 Nos 1 – 4 and Unit 85 Nos 3 and 4

Unit 87   Fractions and decimals   page 62

1 See Unit 80 No. 4

2 To write a **decimal as a fraction**, first count the number of decimal places. This needs to be the number of zeros in the denominator, then the number needs to be written as the numerator.
e.g. 0.31 has two decimal places, therefore the denominator is 100. The answer is $\frac{31}{100}$.

3 To **convert fractions** that do not have a denominator of 10, 100 or 1000, first find the equivalent fraction (see Unit 68 Nos 1 – 3) of the fraction over 10 or 100 or 1000, and then convert as usual (see Unit 80 No. 4).
e.g. $\frac{4}{5} = \frac{8}{10} = 0.8$

4 Decimals can be represented on a **hundreds square**.

e.g.

is $\frac{65}{100}$ or 0.65

Unit 88   Rounding decimals   page 62

1 – 2 and 4 Rounding decimals is the same as rounding whole numbers. See Unit 12. Numbers **rounded to one decimal place** only have one number after the decimal point. Numbers **rounded to two decimal places** have two numbers after the decimal point.

3 To **round to the nearest whole number**, any number with a **decimal of 0.5 or greater rounds up**, e.g. 2.53 becomes 3. Any number with a **decimal of less than 0.5 rounds down**, e.g. 47.46 becomes 47 (see Unit 7 No. 3 also for estimation).

4 See Unit 81 Nos 1 – 3 and Unit 82 Nos 1 – 2 and 4

Unit 89 Percentages (1)
page 63

1 and 3 Percentage means out of 100. It is represented with the percentage sign %. Therefore 20% is 20 out of 100 or twenty percent or 0.2.

To express a **decimal as a percentage**, express the decimal as a fraction over 100, e.g. $0.3 = \frac{30}{100}$ and then write as a percentage, e.g. 30%.

2 and 3 To express a **percentage as a decimal**, express the percentage as a number out of 100 and then write as a decimal.
e.g. $15\% = \frac{15}{100} = 0.15$

4 To **compare fractions, decimals and percentages**, express the amounts in the same format, e.g. all fractions or all decimals or all percentages and then compare.
e.g. $\frac{52}{100}$, 50%, 0.58

All expressed as decimals: 0.52, 0.50, 0.58 Now the largest can be identified: 0.58

Unit 90 Percentages (2)
page 63

1 – 2 To find a **percentage of a quantity or number**, express the percentage as a fraction or decimal and then multiply by the number.

e.g. $\quad 10\%$ of $50 = \frac{10}{100} \times 50$
$$= \frac{500}{100}$$
$$= 5$$
or 10% of $50 = 0.1 \times 50$
$$= 5$$

Note: don't forget the **units**!

3 See Unit 89 No. 4

4 To find the **discount** (the reduced amount), find the percentage of the amount.
e.g. 10% discount of $200 is $\frac{10}{100} \times \$200 = \$20$

Unit 91 Percentages (3)
page 64

1 Remember $25\% = \frac{1}{4}$, $\quad 20\% = \frac{1}{5}$, $\quad 50\% = \frac{1}{2}$
See also Unit 90 Nos 1 – 2

2 – 3 See Unit 90 Nos 1 – 2

4 See Unit 90 No. 4. The **discounted price** is the original price minus the discount.
e.g. Given the discount is $20 and the original price of $200, then the discounted price is $200 – $20 = $180.

Unit 92 Fractions, decimals and percentages
page 64

1 See Unit 89 Nos 1 and 3

2 See Unit 89 No. 2

3 To express a **fraction as a percentage**, write the fraction as a fraction over 100. Then the percentage is the value of the numerator.
e.g. $\frac{4}{10} = \frac{40}{100} = 40\%$

4 See Unit 89 No. 4

Unit 93 Money in shopping
page 65

1 See Unit 54 No. 1

2 See Unit 54 No. 4

3 See Unit 54 Nos 2 – 3

4 See Unit 54 Nos 1 – 2

Unit 94 Money in banking
page 65

1 – 2 A **deposit** is the amount put into an account, such as cash, cheque or salary and it is added.

A **withdrawal** is the amount taken out of the account, that is cash, cheques or loans and it is subtracted.

The **account** gives a running total of the deposits, withdrawals and the total amount.

Interest is the amount earned by having the money in the account and it is added also.

3 – 4 Different countries have **different currencies** (or money). One Australian dollar is worth different amounts in different countries, e.g. 1 Australian dollar = 83 Canadian cents, € is a Euro and is used in Europe.

This information can be used to find what items cost in different countries or what they are worth in Australian money.
e.g. a $25 hat is worth $25 in Australia but is worth
$25 \times 0.83 = \$20.75$ in Canada (so it seems cheaper).

Unit 95 Symmetry
page 66

1 – 3 **Symmetry** is when one half of the shape is a **reflection** of the other half. So when folded on the line (axis) of symmetry, the two halves fit exactly.
e.g.

line (or axis) of symmetry

Note: a shape may have more than one line of symmetry.
e.g.

4 **Rotational symmetry** is when the tracing of a shape matches, after the shape is rotated part of a full turn.
e.g.

Unit 96 Rotational symmetry
page 66

1, 3 and 4 See Unit 95 No. 4

2 The number of times a shape matches its original position as it is rotated in one revolution is known as the **order of rotational symmetry**.
e.g.

The shape has rotational symmetry of order 4.

Unit 97 Diagonals, parallel and perpendicular lines
page 67

1 **Perpendicular lines** are straight lines which meet or cross at 90° (or right angles).

2 – 4 **Parallel lines** are straight lines that remain the same distance apart, never meeting.

Diagonals of a shape go from one corner of a shape to other corners except the neighbouring corners.

e.g. A square has two diagonals.

4 See Geometry Unit on page 18

Unit 98 · Parallel, horizontal and vertical lines · page 67

1 and 4 See Unit 97 Nos 2 – 4

2 and 3 **Horizontal lines** are straight lines that are perfectly level, like the horizon.

Vertical lines are straight lines at right angles to the horizontal.

3 See Unit 97 Nos 1 – 4

Unit 99 · Angles · page 68

1 – 2 An **angle** is the amount of turn between two straight lines (**arms**) fixed at a point (**vertex**).

An angle can be measured using a **protractor**. The centre of the protractor is placed at the vertex of the angle and the baseline is placed on one of the angle's arms. Then the scale is read around to the other arm.

e.g.

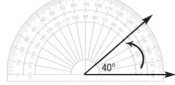

Note: for an angle facing left, it is possible to use the other scale. Be careful to always start from 0°.

3 An **acute angle** is between 0° and 90°.

e.g.

or

4 An **obtuse angle** is between 90° and 180°.

e.g.

or

Unit 100 · Reading angles (1) · page 68

1 and 4 A **reflex angle** is between 180° and 360°. e.g.

e.g.

2 and 4 A **straight angle** measures exactly 180°.

e.g.

3 See Unit 99 Nos 1 – 2

4 See Unit 99 Nos 1 – 2 and 3 and 4. Note: a **revolution** is equal to 360°.

e.g.

Unit 101 · Reading angles (2) · page 69

1 See Unit 99 Nos 1 – 2

2 and 4 For **angles larger than 180°**, the protractor can be turned around (don't flip) to measure the amount of angle below the line and this is then added to 180° to give the angle.

e.g.

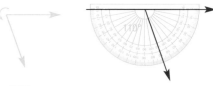
180°

180° + 110° = 290°

or the smaller angle can be measured and subtracted from 360°.

e.g. 360° − 70° = 290°

3 See Unit 99 Nos 3 and 4 and Unit 100 Nos 1 – 2

Note: a **right angle** is equal to 90°. It is often indicated with a small square.

e.g.

Unit 102 · Drawing angles · page 69

1, 3 and 4 To **draw an angle with a protractor**, draw a horizontal line and label one end with a dot.

Place the centre of the protractor on this dot and the baseline along the horizontal line.

protractor

Read around on the scale to the desired value and mark.

e.g.

• 40°

Join the vertex and this point to complete the second arm.

40° Label the angle.

2 See Unit 99 Nos 3 – 4 and Unit 100 Nos 1, 2 and 4

4 To **draw a reflex angle**, draw the line of 180° and then add the appropriate angle to complete the angle by turning the protractor around (don't flip it).

e.g.

260°

80°

Or subtract the given angle from 360° to find the angle. To draw given 260°, 360° − 260° = 100°. Draw 100°.

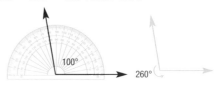
100°
260°

Label the outside of the angle instead of the inside.

Unit 103 — Angle facts
page 70

1 A **straight angle** is 180°, so if one angle is known then the other can be found by counting on to 180° (or subtracting from 180°).

2 **Adjacent angles** are angles that have a common ray.

3 The **sum of all angles in a triangle is 180°**. That means the three angles in a triangle always add up to 180°. Therefore if two angles are known, then the third can be found by counting on to 180° (or subtract the total of the two known angles from 180°).

e.g. $60° + 70° = 130°$
       $180° - 130° = 50°$
The missing angle is 50°

4 **Missing angles** can be found using angle facts.

e.g. To find a:
$30° + 150° = 180°$ (straight angle)
And $150° + a = 180°$ (**supplementary angles** i.e. angles that add up to 180°)
So $a = 30°$
This can also be completed via observations as the lines are parallel, so the angles in the same position must be equal.

Unit 104 — 3D objects
page 70

1 – 2 A **3D object** (solid) has three dimensions; length, breadth and height (depth). See Geometry Unit on page 18
A **prism** is a solid shape with two identical bases and all other faces are rectangles. A prism takes its name from its base. e.g. triangular prism
A **pyramid** is a 3D shape with a polygon as a base and triangular faces that meet at a vertex.

3 A **cross-section** is the shape (face) that is seen when a 3D object is cut through.

4 A **face** is the flat surface of a 3D shape.
An **edge** is where 2 surfaces meet.
A **vertex** (corner) is a point where edges meet.

Unit 105 — Drawing 3D objects
page 71

1 – 4 3D objects are constructed of familiar 2D shapes. See Geometry Unit on page 18

Unit 106 — Properties and views of 3D objects
page 71

1 – 2 See Unit 104 Nos 1, 2 and 4. **A surface is** the outer surface of an object. The surface may be flat or curved.
Different shapes will be seen from different **views**.

are different views of a cylinder.

3 – 4 A **stack** is a pile of 3D objects. In this case all objects in each stack are the same.

Unit 107 — Cylinders, spheres and cones
page 72

1 – 4 A **cone** is a 3D object with a circular base and a curved surface that meets at a vertex.
A **cylinder** is a 3D object with one curved surface and two equal circles as faces.

A **sphere** is a 3D object that is perfectly round like a ball.
2 See Unit 104 Nos 1, 2 and 4 and Unit 106 Nos 1 – 2

Unit 108 — Parallelograms and rhombuses
page 72

1 – 4 A **parallelogram** is a special quadrilateral which has two sets of parallel sides. Also, opposite sides and opposite angles are equal.

Note: a rectangle, square, rhombus and diamond are all parallelograms.

3 – 4 A **rhombus** is a parallelogram with 4 equal sides and equal opposite angles.

Unit 109 — Geometric patterns
page 73

1 – 4 A **pattern** is a repeated design or recurring sequence. These patterns are based on geometric shapes. For Nos 1 – 3, as well as counting the number of sides, it is possible to devise a rule so the number of sides does not need to be counted each time.

e.g. For rectangles,
the total number of sides = $4 \times n$
where n = the number of rectangles.

Unit 110 — Circles
page 73

1 – 4 A **circle** is a 2D shape which is bounded by a line which is always the same distance from the centre.
The **centre** is the exact middle of the circle.

The **radius** is the distance from the centre of the circle to the circumference of the circle.

The **diameter** is a straight line passing through the centre of a circle, joining two points on the circumference.

The **circumference** is the distance (perimeter) around a circle.

The **arc** is part of the circumference of a circle.

The **sector** is a section bounded by two radii and an arc on the circle.

A **semicircle** is half the inside of a circle.

Concentric circles are circles with a common centre.

Unit 111 — Nets and 3D objects
page 74

1 See Unit 104 No. 4 and Unit 106 Nos 1 – 2 and Geometry Unit (page 18)
2 See Unit 106 No. 2
3 – 4 A **net** is the flat pattern which can be used to make a 3D object. There should be no overlaps.
e.g.

Unit 112 **Scale drawings** page 74

1 – 4 A **scale** is used to tell how large an object or item on a map or diagram really is. A scale such as 1 cm : 100 cm reads as 1 cm on the diagram represents 100 cm (1 m) in real life, e.g. the actual item is 100 times larger than in the diagram.
For a scale of 1 cm: 100 cm
4 cm : 4 × 100 cm or 4 cm : 400 cm or 4 cm : 4 m

Unit 113 **Scale drawings and ratios** page 75

1 – 4 See Unit 112 Nos 1 – 4

Unit 114 **Tessellation and patterns** page 75

1 A **tessellation** is a repeating pattern of one or more identical shapes that fit together without any gaps or overlaps.
2 A **reflection** (flip) is a shape or object as seen in a mirror.
e.g.

Z | Ƨ

3 A **translation** (slide) is to move a shape or object left/right or up/down without rotating it.
e.g.

Z → Z   move right

Z
↑   move up
Z

4 A **rotation** (turn) turns a shape or object about one point in either a clockwise or anti-clockwise direction.
e.g.

is a clockwise rotation around the black dot.

Unit 115 **Compass directions** page 76

1 – 4 A **compass** is an instrument that shows direction.
Its points are:

```
        N
  NW         NE

W              E

  SW         SE
        S
```

where N = north, S = south, W = west and E = east.

Unit 116 **Maps (1)** page 76

1 – 2 and 4 See Unit 115 Nos 1 – 4
3 **Distance** is the length between two points (objects or locations).

Unit 117 **Maps (2)** page 77

1 – 2 Coordinates (grid references) are used to show position on a grid. They are represented by pairs of letters or numbers.
e.g. (A, 2) or (6, 3) or (B, C)
The first coordinate is the horizontal or x-value and the second coordinate is the vertical or y-value.
3 See Unit 112 Nos 1 – 4
4 See Unit 115 Nos 1 – 4

Unit 118 **Maps (3)** page 77

1 – 2 See Unit 98 Nos 2 – 3
3 See Unit 117 Nos 1 – 2

Unit 119 **Coordinates (1)** page 78

1 – 2 See Unit 117 Nos 1 – 2
3 – 4 See Unit 115 Nos 1 – 4

Unit 120 **Coordinates (2)** page 78

1 – 2 See Unit 117 Nos 1 – 2
3 See Unit 115 Nos 1 – 4
4 See Unit 116 No. 3

Unit 121 **Analog time** page 79

1 and 3 **Time** is the space between one event and the next. It is measured on a clock.
Analog time is represented with a clock that has a 'clock face dial', numbers, an hour hand, a minute hand and sometimes a second hand. To move between each number on the clock, the minute hand takes 5 minutes.

7 o'clock

half past 3

When the minute hand is pointing to the 6, it is stated as **half past** and when the minute hand is pointing to the 12, it is stated as **o'clock**.
2 When the minute hand is pointing to the 3, it is stated as **quarter past** and when the minute hand is pointing to the 9, it is stated as **quarter to**.

quarter to 12

quarter past 7

4 To find a certain amount of **time after a certain time**, count on (by hours and then groups of 5 minutes would be the easiest) remembering to change between am and pm as you cross between midday and midnight.

Unit 122   Digital time page 79

1   **Digital time** is represented on a digital clock, which has numbers that show the time in hours and minutes.

2 – 3   On a digital clock, the time is read as so many minutes past the hour, e.g. 7:35 is 35 minutes past 7. It can also be expressed as time to, e.g. 7:35 is 25 minutes to 8. 12:00 is noon or midday.

am means ante meridiem. It is any time in the morning between midnight and midday, e.g. 7 am or 9:32 am

pm means post meridiem. It is any time in the afternoon or evening between midday and midnight, e.g. 8:45 pm or 11 pm.

4   See Unit 121 No. 4

Unit 123   Digital and analog time page 80

1 – 2   See Unit 121 Nos 1 and 3

3 – 4   See Unit 121 Nos 1 and 3, and Unit 122 Nos 2 – 3

Unit 124   24-hour time (1) page 80

1 – 4   **24-hour time** uses all 24 hours of the day and is expressed with 4 digits. am or pm is not needed. For am times, the time is expressed the same except times between 1 and 9:59 am have a 0 written in front. e.g. 9:30 am is 0930 hours. Times between 10:00 am and 11:59 pm remain the same, e.g. 10:52 am becomes 1052 hours. For pm times, 12 is added to the normal time, e.g. 2 pm becomes 1400 hours.

Thus to write 24-hour time as pm time, 12 is subtracted from the time. e.g. 1930 hours becomes 7:30 pm.

Unit 125   24-hour time (2) page 81

1 – 3   See Unit 124 Nos 1 – 4

4   See Unit 121 No. 4 and Unit 124 Nos 1 – 4

Unit 126   Stopwatches page 81

1 – 3   A **stopwatch** allows accurate measurement of time intervals. It gives time in minutes, seconds and hundredths of a second. e.g. 03:40:06 reads as 3 minutes, 40.06 seconds.

4   See Unit 62 Nos 3 – 4

Unit 127   Timelines page 82

1 – 4   A **timeline** is a diagram (like a number line—see Unit 43 Nos 1 – 4) used to show the length of time between events.

Unit 128   Timetables page 82

1, 3 and 4   A timetable is a table where times are organised for when different events happen. They are used in schools, on public transport and in hospitals. They can be in am/pm time or 24-hour time.

2   See Unit 124 Nos 1 – 4

Unit 129   Time zones (1) page 83

1   See Unit 124 Nos 1 – 4

2 – 3   **Time zones** are the different times that occur in different states and territories.

In **Australia** there are 3 time zones:

- Eastern Standard (EST)
- Central Standard (CST), which is $\frac{1}{2}$ hour behind Eastern Standard Time
- Western Standard (WST), which is 2 hours behind Eastern Standard Time

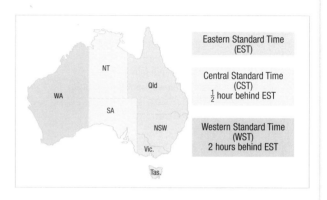

4   In summer NSW, ACT, Vic. Tas. and SA have **daylight savings**. This is where the clocks are moved forward one hour on the last Sunday in October and moved back on the last Sunday in March.

Unit 130   Time zones (2) page 83

1   Time zones apply **around the world**.

On maps there are imaginary lines running North and South called **meridians of longitude**. As the Earth rotates on its axis, each meridian will face the sun directly in turn. It takes 24 hours for the Earth to complete one rotation. In 24 hours the Earth rotates 360 degrees, therefore in one hour, the Earth turns through 15 degrees.

Time is measured from Greenwich in England. So when it is noon in Greenwich it is 10:00 pm at places of longitude 150°E (reading on the map).

2 – 3   To find the new **times at the different longitudes**, count on or count back by the appropriate time difference.

4   To find the **time at Greenwich**, locate the time on the line of longitude on the map, and the difference will need to be added or subtracted to the time at Greenwich.

Unit 131 Travelling speed   page 84
1 and 4 See Unit 40 No. 3
1 and 4 To find the **distance travelled**, multiply speed by the time.
3 and 4 To find the **time taken**, divide the distance travelled by the speed.

Unit 132 Length in millimetres and centimetres   page 84
1 Length is the distance from one end to the other, or how long something is. It is measured with a ruler or a tape. Units include millimetres (mm) for very small lengths such as the length of an ant, centimetres (cm), metres (m) and kilometres (km) for longer lengths such as the distance between two cities.
Decimal form is used to express different values in a simplified form.
e.g. 49 mm = 4.9 cm   (decimal form)
and 2 m 34 cm = 2.34 m   (decimal form).
2 It is possible to **convert between the different units**.

$$10 \text{ mm} = 1 \text{ cm}$$
$$100 \text{ cm} = 1 \text{ m}$$
$$1000 \text{ mm} = 1 \text{ m}$$
$$1000 \text{ m} = 1 \text{ km}$$

e.g. 2 m = 200 cm
3 When **comparing lengths**, convert all of the lengths to the same units such as centimetres, and then compare.
4 When **adding or subtracting lengths**, convert all to the same units such as centimetres, and then complete the operation.

Unit 133 Length in metres   page 85
1 See Unit 132 No. 1
2 – 4 See Unit 132 No. 2

Unit 134 Length in kilometres (1)   page 85
1 – 3 See Unit 132 No. 2
4 See Unit 132 No. 1

Unit 135 Length in kilometres (2)   page 86
1 See Unit 132 No. 1
2 – 3 See Unit 132 No. 2
4 The **table** is read by finding the first location on the vertical column, then finding the second location on the horizontal column and recording the number in kilometres where the two lines meet.
e.g. Brisbane to Alice Springs is 1966 km.

	Adelaide	Alice Springs	Brisbane
Adelaide		1320	1622
Alice Springs	1320		1966
Brisbane	1622	1966	

Unit 136 Converting lengths (1)   page 86
1 – 2 See Unit 132 No. 1
3 – 4 See Unit 132 No. 2

Unit 137 Converting lengths (2)   page 87
1 – 2 See Unit 132 No. 1
3 – 4 See Unit 132 No. 2

Unit 138 Perimeter (1)   page 87
1 and 4 **Perimeter** is the distance around the outside of a shape.
e.g.

$$P = 4 + 1 + 4 + 1$$
$$= 10$$
Perimeter is 10 cm.

2 and 4 To find the **perimeter** of a regular shape, multiply the side length by the number of sides.
Note: sides of equal length are indicated by the dash on the sides.
e.g.

3 Length is the longer distance of an object.
Breadth is the width from side to side of the object.
Perimeter of a rectangle is found by adding 2 × length and 2 × breadth.

Unit 139 Perimeter (2)   page 88
1 See Unit 138 No. 3
2 See Unit 138 Nos 2 and 4
3 See Unit 138 Nos 1 and 4
4 If the perimeter is known, it is possible to work backwards to **find the side lengths**.
e.g. For a square of perimeter 40 cm, as each side length is the same, divide 40 cm by 4 so, each side length is 10 cm.

Unit 140 Area in cm²   page 88
1 – 3 **Area** is the size of the surface of a shape. It is measured in square units, e.g. square cm (cm²) or square m (m²) for larger areas. The area of a rectangle can be calculated by multiplying the length by the breadth. The length is the longer side of the rectangle.

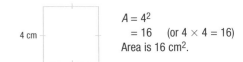

e.g. $A = 4 \times 2$
       $= 8$
So the area is 8 cm².
4 The **area of a square** can be found by squaring the side length.
e.g.

$A = 4^2$
$= 16$ (or $4 \times 4 = 16$)
Area is 16 cm².

Unit 141 Area in m²   page 89
1 – 3 See Unit 140 Nos 1 – 4
4 **Area of non-regular shapes** can be found by dividing the shapes into squares and rectangles. The area of each of these shapes is found and then all the areas are added together to find the total area.
e.g.

$4 \times 5 = 20$

$2 \times 2 = 4$

Total area = 20 + 4
          = 24
The total area is 24 m².

1 – 3 The **area of a triangle** is half the area of the related square or rectangle.

e.g.   Area rectangle = 4 × 3
              = 12
      Area triangle = $\frac{12}{2}$
              = 6

4 cm

3 cm

Area of the triangle is 6 cm².

4 The area of a triangle can also be found using the formula:

Area = $\frac{1}{2}$ base × perpendicular height

So $A = \frac{1}{2} b \times h$

e.g. $A = \frac{1}{2} b \times h$

  $= \frac{1}{2}(2 \times 5)$

  $= \frac{1}{2} \times 10$

  $= 5$

Area is 5 cm².

5 cm

2 cm

1 – 2 See Unit 142 Nos 1 – 3
3 – 4 See Unit 142 No. 4

1 – 4 A **hectare** is used to measure large areas such as a farm or a national park.

1 hectare (ha) = 10 000 m²
Therefore 2 ha = 20 000 m² and 40 000 m² = 4 ha.

1 – 4 A **square kilometre** is used to measure very large areas such as the area of a country.

It is equal to 1000 m × 1000 m = 1 000 000 m²
Therefore 1 km² = 100 ha
     so 5 km² = 500 ha and 600 ha = 6 km²

1 – 4 See Unit 145 Nos 1 – 4

1 – 4 **Mass** is the amount of matter in an object. It is measured in **grams** (g) for lighter objects and **kilograms** (kg) for heavier objects.

  1 kg = 1000 g
   so 4 kg = 4000 g and 1600 g = 1.6 kg
Note: mass can be written as 2 kg 100 g or 2100 g or 2.1 kg.

1 – 4 A measurement for very large masses is **tonnes**.
1 tonne = 1000 kg
  so 3 t = 3000 kg

1 Measuring devices such as scales and weight balances are used to measure mass.
2 – 4 See Unit 148 Nos 1 – 4

1 – 4 **Capacity** is the amount a container can hold. It is measured in litres (L) for larger capacities and millilitres (mL) for smaller capacities.

        1 litre = 1000 millilitres
          e.g. 3 L = 3000 mL
      and 2 500 mL = 2.5 L
Note: capacity can be written as 1 L 350 mL or 1350 mL or 1.35 L.
1 cm³ displaces 1 mL of water.
Therefore 50 mL would be displaced by 50 cm³ and 110 cm³ would displace 110 mL.
Note: 1000 cm³ = 1 L of water.

1 – 4 See Unit 150 Nos 1 – 4

1 – 2 1 litre of water = 1 kg
2 – 4 1 mL of water = 1 g

1 – 4 See Unit 150 Nos 1 – 4

1 – 3 A **cubic centimetre** (centicube) is a standard unit for measuring volume.
Volume of a prism can be calculated by multiplying the length by the breadth by the height.
The **length** is the longer side of the base.
The **breadth** is the shorter side of the base.
The **height** is the 'tallness' of the prism.
Its units are cubic centimetres (cm³).
e.g.

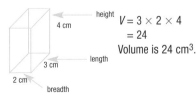

height
4 cm
length
3 cm
2 cm
breadth

$V = 3 \times 2 \times 4$
  $= 24$
Volume is 24 cm³.

4 See Unit 150 Nos 1 – 4

1 – 3 A **cubic metre** is a measurement for large volumes. Its abbreviation is m³.
4 See Unit 154 Nos 1 – 3

Unit 156   **Volume (1)**   page 96

1 See Unit 155 Nos 1 – 3
2 – 4 **Volume** can be found by counting the number of cubes or completing the calculation (see Unit 154 Nos 1 – 3).

Unit 157   **Volume (2)**   page 97

1 See Unit 15 Nos 1 – 3 and Unit 155 Nos 1 – 3
3 **Volumes of cubes** can be found by cubing the side length, as all side lengths are equal.
e.g.

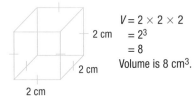

$$V = 2 \times 2 \times 2$$
$$= 2^3$$
$$= 8$$
Volume is 8 cm³.

3 To find the **volume of an irregular shape**, either count the cubes or separate the shape into blocks which make rectangular prisms and cubes. Then find the volume of each block and add the volumes together to find the total volume.
4 See Unit 154 Nos 1 – 3

Unit 158   **Arrangements (1)**   page 97

1, 3 and 4 **Chance** is the probability or likelihood of something happening. It can be described with words such as certain, impossible, likely, unlikely or equal chance.
It can also be described with a **scale** between 0 and 1, where 0 = impossible, 1 = certain and 0.5 = equal chance.

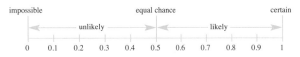

2 An **arrangement** is the way different objects are organised in different orders.
e.g. The numbers 1, 2 and 3 can be arranged the following ways: 123, 132, 213, 231, 312 and 321.

Unit 159   **Arrangements (2)**   page 98

1, 3 and 4 See Unit 158 Nos 1, 3 and 4
2 **Chance** can be described with a **fraction**, **decimal** or **percentage**, where 1 = certain, $\frac{1}{2}$ = equal chance and 0 = impossible.

Unit 160   **Predicting**   page 98

1 – 4 A **prediction** is a statement made about what could happen/be discovered based on existing data or information.
e.g. To predict how many children will ...
Look at the total number of sets of results and then how many need to be predicted for.
You have 10 sets of information, but want to predict about 20, so each piece of information will be doubled.
e.g. Of 10 children:

Eye colour	Blue	Green	Brown	Grey
Number	4	1	4	1

To predict how many children out of 20 will have brown eyes:
$2 \times 4 = 8$, so predict 8 children.

Unit 161   **Tables and graphs**   page 99

1 – 2 A **picture graph** is a graph which uses pictures to represent quantities.
e.g.

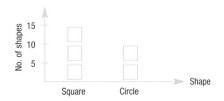

Note: one picture may represent many items. e.g. ☐ = 5 shapes
A **tally** is the process of using marks to record counting.
Note: ⅢⅡ represents a group of 5.
e.g.

	Tally	**Total**
△	ⅢⅡ IIII	9
○	ⅢⅡ III	8

Information recorded as a tally in a table is often called a **tally table** or **tally sheet**.
3 – 4 A **bar chart** or **column graph** uses bars or columns to show the number of items or objects so that they can be compared.
e.g.

Unit 162   **Bar graphs (divided)**   page 99

1 – 4 A **divided bar graph** uses a bar which is divided into sections to represent information.
e.g.

red	blue	green

By measuring the length of each part of the bar, the fraction or value of each section of the whole can be determined.

Unit 163   **Pie charts**   page 100

1 – 4 A **pie graph** uses a circle divided into sections where each section represents part of the total.
e.g.

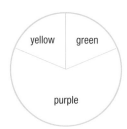

Unit 164 — Mean, median and graphs
page 100

1 – 3 The **mean** is another name for the average.
See Unit 40 Nos 1 – 2 and 4.

4 The **median** is the middle term of all of the data when the data is written in ascending order.

$$\overrightarrow{\hspace{1cm}}\quad \overleftarrow{\hspace{1cm}}$$

e.g. 2, 4, 6, 8, 10.
The median is 6.
If there is an **even number of terms**, then the median lies between the two centre terms.

$$\overrightarrow{\hspace{1cm}}\!\!>\!\!<\overleftarrow{\hspace{1cm}}$$

e.g. 2, 4, 6, 8, 10, 12.
Halfway between 6 and 8 is 7.
So the median is 7.

Unit 165 — Bar graphs and pie charts
page 101

1 and 4 See Unit 162 Nos 1 – 4
2 – 3 See Unit 163 Nos 1 – 4

Unit 166 — Line graphs
page 101

1 – 4 A **line graph** joins points which represent the data with lines.
e.g.

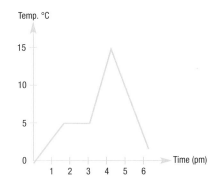

Unit 167 — Tally marks and graphs
page 102

1 See Unit 161 Nos 1 – 2
2 – 3 See Unit 161 Nos 3 – 4
4 See Unit 165 Nos 1 – 4

Unit 168 — Reading graphs
page 102

1 See Unit 161 Nos 3 – 4
2 and 4 See Unit 166 Nos 1 – 4
3 See Unit 163 Nos 1 – 4

Unit 169 — Collected data
page 103

1 – 2 See Unit 166 Nos 1 – 4
3 See Unit 161 Nos 1 – 2
4 See Unit 161 Nos 3 – 4

Unit 170 — Addition and subtraction practice
page 103

1 and 3 See Unit 7 No. 4
2 See Unit 10 Nos 1 – 2
4 See Unit 8 No 3

Unit 171 — Multiplication and division practice
page 104

1 and 3 See Unit 22 Nos 1 – 4
2 See Unit 37 Nos 3 – 4
4 See Unit 33 No. 2

Unit 172 — Fractions practice
page 104

1 See Unit 68 Nos 1 – 3
2 See Unit 66 Nos 1 – 4
3 See Unit 72 No. 2 and Unit 72 No. 3
4 See Unit 78 No. 3

Unit 173 — Decimals practice
page 105

1 See Unit 81 Nos 1 – 4
2 See Unit 82 Nos 1 – 2 and 4
3 See Unit 83 Nos 1 – 4
4 See Unit 85 Nos 3 – 4

Unit 174 — Problem solving – inverse operations
page 105

1 – 4 See Unit 52 Nos 1 – 4

Unit 175 — Problem solving – money
page 106

1 – 4 See Unit 54 Nos 1 – 4

Unit 176 — Problem solving
page 106

1 – 2 See Unit 132 Nos 1 – 4
3 See Unit 147 Nos 1 – 4
4 See Unit 158 No. 2

Geometry Unit

2-dimensional shapes

isosceles triangle

equilateral triangle

right-angled triangle

scalene triangle

square

rectangle

rhombus

parallelogram

trapezium

kite

Note: quadrilaterals have 4 sides.

pentagon

hexagon

heptagon

octagon

nonagon

decagon

circle

oval

semicircle

3-dimensional objects

sphere

cone

cylinder

hemisphere

cube

square prism

rectangular prism

triangular prism

pentagonal prism

hexagonal prism

triangular pyramid (or tetrahedron)

square pyramid

rectangular pyramid

pentagonal pyramid

hexagonal pyramid

Numbers to one million

1. Write each of the following in **numerals**:

   a. five hundred and twenty-one thousand, seven hundred and two _____

   b. nine hundred thousand, five hundred and seventy-six

   _____

   c. two hundred and fifty thousand, eight hundred and twenty

   _____

   d. six hundred and eleven thousand, four hundred and sixty-five _____

   e. one hundred and eight thousand, two hundred and thirty-nine _____

   f. ninety-five thousand, eight hundred and ninety-one

   _____

2. Write each of the numbers from question 1 as figures in the **place value chart**:

	HTh	TTh	Th	H	T	U
a						
b						
c						
d						
e						
f						

3. Write the **value** of each of the underlined digits:

   a. 617 4<u>8</u>2 _____   b. 987 05<u>6</u> _____

   c. <u>7</u>32 517 _____   d. 46<u>8</u> 190 _____

   e. 8<u>7</u>5 215 _____   f. 104 6<u>2</u>1 _____

4. Complete each of the **number series**:

   a. 458 957, _____, _____, _____, 450 957

   b. 742 015, _____, _____, _____, 742 415

   c. 907 116, _____, _____, _____, 907 156

   d. 842 105, _____, _____, _____, 882 105

   e. 123 467, _____, _____, _____, 523 467

   f. 821 046, _____, _____, _____, 861 046

5. Write seven hundred and ninety-eight thousand, four hundred and sixty-two in **numerals**.

   _____

6. Write seven hundred and ninety-eight thousand, four hundred and sixty-two in figures in the **place value chart**:

HTh	TTh	Th	H	T	U

7. Write the **value** of the underlined digit in 107 9<u>4</u>6 _____

8. Complete the **number series**:

   110 724, _____, _____, _____, 110 764

9. Write the following number in **words**:

   110 793 _____

Place value

1. Draw the beads on the **abacus** to represent each of the following numbers:

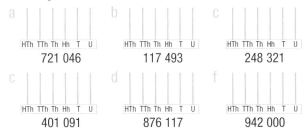

   a. 721 046   b. 117 493   c. 248 321

   c. 401 091   d. 876 117   f. 942 000

2. Write the numbers of the place value chart in **words**:

	HTh	TTh	Th	H	T	U
a		8	0	4	1	1
b		9	0	0	0	0
c	1	7	0	2	4	1
d	9	9	8	6	4	2
e	3	8	4	0	6	1
f	8	7	0	4	0	0

   a. _____

   b. _____

   c. _____

   d. _____

   e. _____

   f. _____

3. Use **< or >** to complete the number statements:

   a. 48 169 ☐ 49 102   b. 710 385 ☐ 79 041

   c. 87 946 ☐ 3249   d. 107 259 ☐ 110 300

   e. 4246 ☐ 9872   f. 871 104 ☐ 872 106

4. **Match** the expressions with the numerical information:

   a. slightly over nineteen thousand   51 010

   b. approximately two hundred thousand   24 879

   c. roughly fifty thousand   456 285

   d. slightly less than ninety thousand   198 921

   e. almost twenty-five thousand   19 221

   f. more than four hundred and fifty thousand   89 270

5. Draw the beads to show 871 960 on the **abacus**:

6. Write the number of the place chart in **words**:

HTh	TTh	Th	H	T	U
2	7	0	8	5	0

   _____

7. Use **< or >** to complete the number statement:

   231 805 ☐ 241805

8. **Match** the expression with the numerical value:

   almost thirty-two thousand

   31 795   302 176   39 821   320 985

9. How many **thousands** are there in each of the following numbers?

   a. 4689 _____   b. 23 921 _____

   c. 204 307 _____   d. 219 850 _____

Numbers greater than one million

1. Write the **value** of the 5 in each of the following:

   a 1 072 315 _____   b 5 162 409 _____

   c 9 875 211 _____   d 4 573 429 _____

   e 1 115 216 _____   f 1 050 943 _____

2. Arrange each set of numbers in **ascending order**:

   a 1 243 819, 1 346 721, 1 308 925

   _____

   b 2 487 905, 2 711 809, 2 635 921

   _____

   c 4 246 385, 4 105 907, 4 365 111

   _____

   d 8 051 987, 7 621 505, 7 921 300

   _____

   e 5 296 837, 5 121 352, 5 021 486

   _____

   f 7 932 481, 6 842 859, 8 110 425

   _____

3. Round each number to the **nearest million**:

   a 1 738 501 _____   b 6 219 850 _____

   c 992 106 _____   d 1 346 080 _____

   e 8 319 467 _____   f 4 511 909 _____

4. Write the **place value** of each of the underlined digits, then its **value** in the chart:

	Number	Place value	Total value
a	3<u>9</u>8 421		
b	<u>8</u> 710 486		
c	2 198 <u>7</u>04		
d	3 94<u>7</u> 825		
e	<u>2</u>1 843 211		
f	4<u>2</u>7 806 921		

5. Write the **value** of the 5 in 2 158 706: _____

6. Arrange the set of numbers in **ascending order**:

   2 196 380, 2 085 921, 2 127 460

   _____

7. Round 3 248 691 to the **nearest million**.

   _____

8. Write the **place value** of the underlined digit, then its **total value** in the chart:

Number	Place value	Total value
1 <u>4</u>38 216		

9. Is each of the following numbers **closer to** 50 000 000 or 60 000 000?

   a 53 107 915 _____

   b 54 681 999 _____

   c 58 702 117 _____

Number patterns (1)

1. Complete each of the **number patterns**:

   a 4, 6, 8, _____, _____

   b 40, 60, 80, _____, _____

   c 109, 118, 127, _____, _____

   d 421, 411, 401, _____, _____

   e 4, 8, 16, _____, _____

   f 916, 904, 892, _____, _____

2. Write the **rule** for each number pattern in question 1:

   a _____   b _____

   c _____   d _____

   e _____   f _____

3. Complete each of the following **tables**:

   a

1st No.	4	5	6	7	8
2nd No.	36	45	54		

   b

1st No.	26	36	46	56	66
2nd No.	45	55	65		

   c

1st No.	1.5	2.5	3.5	4.5	5.5
2nd No.	15	25	35		

   d

1st No.	7	17	27	37	47
2nd No.	35	85	135		

   e

1st No.	46	56	66	76	86
2nd No.	38	48	58		

   f

1st No.	64	54	44	34	24
2nd No.	80	70	60		

4. Write the **rule** which relates the second number to the first number for each of the number patterns in question 3.

   a _____   b _____

   c _____   d _____

   e _____   f _____

5. Complete the **number pattern**: $6\frac{1}{4}$, $8\frac{1}{2}$, $10\frac{3}{4}$, ____, ____

   _____

6. Write the **rule** for the number pattern in question 5:

   _____

7. Complete the table:

1st No.	100	90	80	70	60
2nd No.	20	18	16		

8. Write the **rule** for the number pattern in question 7.

   _____

9. Look at the **square numbers**:

   a Write the **rule** to give the number of dots in each diagram. _____

   b What would be the **10th term** in the pattern?

   _____

Expanding numbers

1 Write the **numeral** for each of the following:

a 100 000 + 40 000 + 2 000 + 500 + 60 + 1 _____

b 200 000 + 90 000 + 5 000 + 600 + 20 + 9 _____

c 400 000 + 50 000 + 3 000 + 700 + 80 +5 _____

d 600 000 + 8 000 + 90 + 6 _____

e 800 000 + 70 000 + 800 + 7 _____

f 900 000 + 50 000 + 2 000 + 3 _____

2 Write each of the following in **expanded notation**:

a 56 409 _____

b 213 847 _____

c 462 001 _____

d 896 325 _____

e 1 224 387 _____

f 1 905 621 _____

3 How many **tens** are there in each of the following?

a 4 283 _____

b 9 172 _____

c 48 632 _____

d 27 485 _____

e 213 689 _____

f 724 998 _____

4 How many **thousands** are there in each of the following?

a 4 639 _____

b 21 486 _____

c 92 327 _____

d 847 986 _____

e 123 428 _____

f 1 428 376 _____

5 Write 400 000 + 20 000 + 9 000 + 20 + 6 as a **numeral**.

_____

6 Write 4 632 589 in **expanded notation**.

_____

7 How many **tens** are there in 4 326 849?

_____

8 How many **thousands** are there in 468 725?

_____

9 Use **< or >** to make the statements true.

a 4 320 146 ☐ 4 000 000 + 300 000 + 20 000 + 1000 + 400 + 60

b 100 000 + 40 + 6 + 200 + 7000 ☐ 170 246

Positive and negative numbers

1 Order each set of numbers from **smallest to largest**:

a 5, 10, 6, 7, 0, −1, 9, −3

_____

b 8, −2, −3, −7, 0, 1, 4, 2

_____

c −2, −5, −8, 10, 1, 5, -4, 0

_____

d 14, 13, −10, 0, −6, 1, 2

_____

e −10, −5, 0, 1, 3, 5, −4, −2

_____

f −4, 3, 2, 8, 0, −1, −3, 5

_____

2 Circle the **larger** number in each pair:

a 10, 4   b −1 , 5

c 0, −5   d 11, −2

e −1, −5   f 0, −3

3 Complete the **number sequences**:

a 2, 4, 6, _____, _____, _____

b 0, 3, 6, _____, _____, _____

c 10, 8, 6, _____, _____, _____

d 5, 3, 1, _____, _____, _____

e 6, 3, 0, _____, _____, _____

f −2, 0, 2, _____, _____, _____

4 Complete the following **equations**:

a 1 − 3 = _____

b 5 − 10 = _____

c −1 + 2 = _____

d −5 + 3 = _____

e −2 − 1 = _____

f −5 − 4 = _____

5 Order the following from **smallest to largest**:

−2, 0, 5, −3, −10, 2, 10, −7

_____

6 Circle the **larger** number: −5, −2

7 Complete the **number sequence**:

6, 2, −2, _____, _____, _____

8 **Complete**: 5 − 4 = _____

9 Draw a **number line** and add the following:

-3, 0, $-1\frac{1}{2}$, 0.5, 4, $2\frac{1}{4}$

Addition review

1 Complete:

a   50 + 60 = _____

b   90 + 30 = _____

c   40 + 80 = _____

d   700 + 300 = _____

e   400 + 500 = _____

f   700 + 800 = _____

2 Complete:

a   129 + 66 = _____

b   347 + 47 = _____

c   876 + 37 = _____

d   247 + 38 = _____

e   164 + 29 = _____

f   293 + 58 = _____

3 Give an **estimate** for each of the following by first rounding each number to the **nearest hundred**:

a   425 + 369 _____

b   497 + 268 _____

c   876 + 281 _____

d   979 + 319 _____

e   1379 + 486 _____

f   2365 + 898 _____

4 Complete:

a   4 8 7   b   1 1 7 6
    + 9 2 5   +   2 4 7

c   4 1 5 8   d   8 4 3 6
   + 4 9 2 5   + 5 2 1 9

e   4 2 6 8   f   5 2 8 1
   + 3 4 9 6   + 2 9 8 6

5 Complete: 4000 + 7000 = _____

6 Complete: 187 + 298 = _____

7 Give an **estimate** by first rounding each number to the **nearest hundred**:

4263 + 107 _____

8 Complete: 2 1 4 7
            + 8 7 3 6

9 Two country towns were merged together to form one. If the two towns had populations of 27 846 and 39 468, what was the **total** population of the new town?

_____

Adding to 999 999

1 Complete:

a   4 6 0   b   1 4 7   c   9 7 6
    3 2 0   8 2 0   3 4 2
  + 9 8 0   + 4 7 6   + 8 9 7

d   1 2 4 8   e   4 9 7 8   f   7 8 5 6
  + 3 6 8 7   + 8 5 6 0   + 9 2 7 8

2 Complete:

a $46 275   b $49 325   c $561 101
  + $12 386   + $80 652   + $299 980

d $86 456   e $759 704   f $124 980
  + $12 386   + $ 25 629   + $893 276

3 Give the **missing numbers** to complete the additions:

a   3 5 ☐ 6 4
   +   4 8 ☐ 5
    ☐☐ 4 0 ☐

b   6 3 2 ☐☐☐
  + 2 0 1 2 6 4
   8 ☐☐ 2 5 0

c   1 0 7 ☐ 3
   + ☐ 6 ☐ 1 ☐ 7
   5 ☐ 3 1 1 9

d   4 6 ☐ 3 2 ☐
   + 4 ☐ 2 ☐☐ 6
   9 0 0 6 2

e   3 2 ☐ 1 8 ☐
   + ☐ 6 2 ☐ 7 3
   7 ☐ 1 9 ☐ 7

f   ☐ 2 ☐ 8 ☐ 4
   + 2 ☐ 6 4 3 ☐
   8 8 4 ☐ 9 1

4 Solve:

a   Over 3 years, Albert saved $4621, $3283 and $2146. How much did Albert save **altogether**? _____

b   On a cattle station, one paddock had 46 291 cattle and the other 39 472. How many cattle **altogether**? _____

c   For a collect-a-cap competition, Year K – 2 collected 1249 caps, Year 3 – 4 1462 caps and Year 5 – 6 1739 caps. What was the **total** number of caps? _____

d   During the school holidays, the Smiths travelled 925 km in the first week and 1476 km in the second. How far did the Smiths travel **altogether**? _____

e   A house's first storey is 285 cm high, the second 329 cm. What is the **total** height of the house? _____

f   There were 476 sheets of paper in one pile, 521 in a second and 479 in a third. What was the **total** number of pieces of paper? _____

5 Complete: 7 8 9
           2 4 8
        + 8 5 2

6 Complete: $214 386
        + $728 642

7 Give the **missing numbers** to complete:

   4 ☐ 3 7 8 ☐
  + ☐ 3 6 ☐ 4 8
   9 9 ☐ 6 ☐ 2

8 On a farm, there were 3 crates of avocados, 12 498 in one crate, 16 749 in a second and 24 925 in a third. What was the **total** number of avocados? _____

9 Complete: 942 100 + 38 617 + 12 496 + 10 748 _____

Adding large numbers

1 Complete:
```
a    462 381      b    849 106      c    249 861
     942 117           283 427           248 105
   + 107 437         + 346 110         + 624 177


d    432 105      e    406 109      f    805 216
     869 117           841 086            34 975
   + 348 052         +  92 471         +  98 647
```

2 Find:
```
a    140 421      b   4 281 021     c     486 325
      99 325           468 391            361 185
   +  68 429         + 1 486 342       + 1 428 593


d  3 846 000      e  11 000 000     f    840 000
   4 281 000          4 960 000        4 217 000
 + 3 401 000        + 1 423 000       + 8 673 000
```

3 Find the **total** of:
a $426 831.50 and $217 856.93 _____
b $1 024 309.25 and $4 629 326.54 _____
c $5 029 859.98 and $6 254 321.40 _____
d $1 500 450.10 and $900 428.50 _____
e $4 362 107.50 and $5 428 456.59 _____
f $9 752 321.05 and $2 489 652.25 _____

4 Complete:
```
a  grams       b  centimetres    c  tonnes
    2 468           4 980            46 832
    3 179           6 243            10 976
 + 48 561        + 10 479         + 27 486


d  litres      e  kilometres     f  hectares
   2478            12 479           461 079
   3956            15 862           213 461
 + 9875          + 10 972         + 874 982
```

5 Complete:
```
     925 486
     106 432
   + 119 751
```

6 Find:
```
   1 428 326
 + 9 864 102
```

7 Find the **total** of:
$1 073 426.90 and $2 487 112.45 _____

8 Complete:
```
   4263
   1079
 + 1148
```

9 Jorge bought a new car for $29 990 but added air conditioning for $1755, a CD player for $875 and a sun roof for $2465. What was the **total** cost of the car?

Subtraction review

1 Complete:
```
a    465       b    890       c    462
   -  38          -  56          -  88


d    436       e    248       f    756
   - 175          - 109          - 237
```

2 Find:
```
a   6109       b   3501       c   4096
  - 1487         - 2617         - 3825


d   4862       e   5497       f   2471
  - 1975         - 3859         - 1865
```

3 Fill in the **missing boxes**:
```
a   5 6 1 7     b   5 1 □ 4     c   9 5 □ 1
  - 4 □ 1 □       - 3 □ 2 7       - □ □ 7 2
    1 3 □ 4         □ 0 3 □         6 8 6 □


d   8 7 □ 3     e   8 □ 7 0     f   8 □ 0 □
  - □ 4 0 □       -   7 □ 3       - □ 0 □ 4
    6 □ 5 5         □ 8 4 □         1 1 9 6
```

4 Find the **difference** between:
a   4706 and 2305 _____
b   8975 and 1723 _____
c   7506 and 1986 _____
d   5630 and 146 _____
e   7400 and 6558 _____
f   3248 and 967 _____

5 Complete:
```
     793
   - 246
```

6 Find:
```
    4018
  - 1463
```

7 Fill in the **missing boxes**:
```
     4 0 □ 6
   - □ □ 2 □
     2 6 9 1
```

8 Find the **difference** between 3217 and 1094.

9 If an item was bought for $2385 and sold for $3192, what was the **profit** made on the item?

Mental strategies for subtraction

1 **Find**:
  a 270 – 160 = _____
  b 370 – 80 = _____
  c 450 – 260 = _____
  d 540 – 360 = _____
  e 630 – 470 = _____
  f 790 – 650 = _____

2 Find the **difference** between:
  a 475 and 328 _____
  b 252 and 214 _____
  c 344 and 486 _____
  d 284 and 464 _____
  e 719 and 527 _____
  f 825 and 377 _____

3 **Complete**:

  a   6000   b   8000
      –   486   –   798

  c   3000   d   4000
      –   109   –   527

  e   9000   f   5000
      –   895   –   211

4 **Complete**:
  a   75 – 39 = _____
  b 157 – 28 = _____
  c 196 – 49 = _____
  d 187 – 58 = _____
  e 156 – 77 = _____
  f   93 – 49 = _____

5 **Find**: 470 – 180 = _____

6 Find the **difference** between 575 and 329: _____

7 **Complete**:   7000
                    –   627

8 **Complete**:
  292 – 48 = _____

9 Jordan has a collection of 256 football cards, but he sold 79 of them. How many cards did he **have left**?
  _____

Rounding numbers

1 Round each of the following to the **nearest ten**:
  a 47 _____   b 63 _____
  c 98 _____   d 114 _____
  e 256 _____   f 486 _____

2 Round each of the following to the **nearest hundred**:
  a 106 _____   b 398 _____
  c 860 _____   d 1268 _____
  e 4986 _____   f 4507 _____

3 Round each of the following to the **nearest thousand**:
  a 986 _____   b 1 046 _____
  c 2 793 _____   d 17 600 _____
  e 29 826 _____   f 126 108 _____

4 Estimate an answer to each of the following by first rounding each number to the **nearest thousand**:

	Question	Rounded	Estimate
a	5778 + 3697		
b	2866 + 3105		
c	1249 + 2958		
d	35 977 + 6104		
e	55 394 + 5106		
f	9999 + 27 108		

5 Round 732 to the **nearest ten**. _____

6 Round 52 817 to the **nearest hundred**. _____

7 Round 135 463 to the **nearest thousand**. _____

8 Estimate the answer, by first rounding each number to the **nearest thousand**.

Question	Rounded	Estimate
4687 + 3721		

9 k is used to represent 1000 in **large numbers**. For example, 7000 = 7 k. Write each of the following using k as an abbreviation:
  a 9000 _____   b 14 000 _____
  c 21 000 _____   d 51 000 _____
  e 37 000 _____   f 85 000 _____

Subtraction to 999 999

1 Complete:

a	b	c
46 321	52 187	46 379
− 9 860	− 7 950	− 8 660

d	e	f
86 000	39 870	22 100
− 51 360	− 14 600	− 17 850

2 **Estimate** the answer to each question by rounding each number to the **nearest thousand**.

a	b	c
46 785	83 472	92 110
− 21 391	− 67 957	− 42 689

d	e	f
66 852	59 850	43 281
− 41 461	− 17 082	− 10 925

3 Complete:

a kilograms	b metres	c litres
875 926	491 253	555 998
− 321 520	− 124 685	− 432 565

d tonnes	e hectares	f centimetres
147 973	421 046	875 869
− 98 699	− 274 819	− 423 590

4 Find the **difference** between:

a 924 685 and 143 847 _____

b 120 801 and 462 398 _____

c 502 196 and 475 230 _____

d 421 114 and 673 895 _____

e 794 503 and 306 040 _____

f 526 807 and 304 752 _____

5 Complete:
17 849
− 9 211

6 **Estimate** the answer by rounding each number to the **nearest thousand**.
63 851
− 39 574

7 Complete:
846 217 mm
− 783 504 mm

8 Find the **difference** between 810 432 and 268 009.

9 Write a **word problem** that is a subtraction question and gives the answer 221 635.

Subtracting large numbers

1 Complete:

a	b	c
1 683 000	7 624 000	5 280 000
− 429 000	− 938 000	− 1 752 000

d	e	f
4 630 000	8 049 000	1 946 000
− 2 741 000	− 3 520 000	− 897 000

2 Complete:

a	b	c
$4 527 930	$3 684 900	$1 104 365
− $ 604 705	− $ 758 610	− $ 587 112

d	e	f
$6 894 170	$4 387 105	$11 059 528
− $2 431 856	− $2 416 801	− $ 9 237 000

3 The area of each state and territory (km^2) is given below.

Tas.	Vic.	ACT	NSW
67 897	227 516	2330	801 431
Qld	**SA**	**WA**	**NT**
1 727 200	984 381	2 525 500	1 356 176

Find the **difference** in area between:

a Tas. and Vic. _____ b NSW and SA _____

c WA and SA _____ d NT and ACT _____

e Qld and WA _____ e NSW and NT _____

4 Find:

a 672 589 kg **minus** 361 876 kg _____

b 120 479 L **subtract** 109 326 L _____

c 473 981 tonnes **less** 98 756 tonnes _____

d the difference **between** $879 352 and $1 462 108

_____

e 719 430 cm **less** 87 956 cm _____

f 1 426 398 g **take away** 721 085 g _____

5 Complete:
2 468 000
− 1 987 000

6 Complete:
$3 219 856
− $1 759 061

7 Find the **difference** in area between Vic. and NSW.

_____

8 Find 21 763 805 L **less** 9 428 119 L

_____

9 What is the **greatest difference** in area between two states or territories?

_____

Estimation

1 Estimate each of the additions by first rounding each number to the **nearest hundred**.

a
```
    46 215
 +  37 986
```
b
```
    17 580
 +  19 271
```
c
```
    24 831
 +  46 028
```

d
```
   142 853
 + 173 127
```
e
```
   429 050
 + 140 271
```
f
```
   873 056
 + 117 820
```

2 Estimate each of the subtractions by first rounding each number to the **nearest thousand**.

a
```
    42 107
 −  19 658
```
b
```
    25 963
 −   7 631
```
c
```
    47 285
 −  33 863
```

d
```
   129 427
 − 114 306
```
e
```
   168 301
 − 123 497
```
f
```
   850 176
 − 327 871
```

3 Estimate the answer by first rounding each amount to the **nearest dollar ($)**.

a $421.95 + $62.35 _____
b $121.75 + $156.85 _____
c $643.06 + $249.16 _____
d $479.15 − $135.66 _____
e $846.27 − $137.98 _____
f $649.29 − $377.88 _____

4 Estimate each of the additions by first rounding each number to the **nearest hundred**.

a
```
    4 2 6 7
 +  1 9 5 8
```
b
```
    7 3 5 6
 +  1 2 7 9
```
c
```
    8 7 9 1
 +  4 0 7 6
```

d
```
    4 8 8 0
 +  3 9 3 5
```
e
```
    6 2 1 7
 +  7 4 6 3
```
f
```
    9 5 8 7
 +    9 9 8
```

5 Estimate the addition by first rounding each number to the **nearest hundred**.
```
   721 098
 + 385 175
```

6 Estimate the subtraction by first rounding each number to the **nearest thousand**.
```
   478 321
 − 169 427
```

7 Estimate the answer by first rounding each amount to the **nearest dollar ($)**: $732.56 − $457.95

_____

8 Estimate the addition equation by first rounding each number to the **nearest hundred**:
```
    47 981
 +  23 501
```

9 Estimate the subtraction by first rounding each number to the **nearest thousand**:
```
   2 143 856
 − 1 794 301
```

Multiplication tables (1)

1 **Find**:
a 7 groups of 4 _____
b 3 groups of 9 _____
c 12 groups of 10 _____
d 8 groups of 5 _____
e 9 groups of 6 _____
f 2 groups of 2 _____

2 **Find**:
a $3 \times 8 =$ _____
b $12 \times 3 =$ _____
c $11 \times 7 =$ _____
d $4 \times 10 =$ _____
e $3 \times 6 =$ _____
f $7 \times 7 =$ _____

3 **Complete** the boxes:
a $7 \times \boxed{} = 21$
b $\boxed{} \times 10 = 90$
c $8 \times \boxed{} = 64$
d $2 \times \boxed{} = 14$
e $\boxed{} \times 5 = 20$
f $\boxed{} \times 4 = 48$

4 Find the total cost of:
a 10 hats at $9 each _____
b 4 drinks at $3 each _____
c 7 magazines at $12 each _____
d 3 bags of potatoes at $5 each _____
e 12 snacks at $2 each _____
f 4 movie tickets at $8 each _____

5 **Find** 9 groups of 12: _____

6 **Find** 11 x 11: _____

7 **Complete** the box: $7 \times \boxed{} = 63$

8 Find the **total cost** of 5 birthday cakes at $11 each.

_____

9 **Complete**:

×	4	7	9	11	12
6					

Multiplication tables (2)

1 Find the **product** of:

  a　10 and 10 _____

  b　7 and 6 _____

  c　9 and 4 _____

  d　2 and 5 _____

  e　0 and 8 _____

  f　11 and 3 _____

2 **True or false?**

  a　$6 \times 3 = 2 \times 9$ _____

  b　$5 \times 7 = 3 \times 10$ _____

  c　$7 \times 7 = 5 \times 10$ _____

  d　$12 \times 3 = 6 \times 6$ _____

  e　$10 \times 11 = 12 \times 10$ _____

  f　$5 \times 8 = 4 \times 10$ _____

3 **Complete:**

  a　$\begin{array}{r} 6 \\ \times\ 4 \\ \hline \end{array}$　　b　$\begin{array}{r} 10 \\ \times\ 6 \\ \hline \end{array}$　　c　$\begin{array}{r} 8 \\ \times\ 9 \\ \hline \end{array}$

  d　$\begin{array}{r} 3 \\ \times\ 7 \\ \hline \end{array}$　　e　$\begin{array}{r} 12 \\ \times\ 5 \\ \hline \end{array}$　　f　$\begin{array}{r} 0 \\ \times\ 4 \\ \hline \end{array}$

4 Find the **total** number of days in:

  a　6 weeks _____

  b　1 week _____

  c　10 weeks _____

  d　4 weeks _____

  e　12 weeks _____

  f　7 weeks _____

5 Find the **product** of 8 and 3: _____

6 **True or false?** $9 \times 8 = 12 \times 6$ _____

7 **Complete:** $\begin{array}{r} 11 \\ \times\ 4 \\ \hline \end{array}$

8 Find the **total** number of days in 9 weeks.

_____

9 **Complete** the multiplication circle:

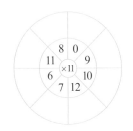

Multiplication review

1 Find:

  a　the **product** of 9 and 7 _____

  b　8 **groups of** 2 _____

  c　11 **times** 5 _____

  d　12 **multiplied** by 7 _____

  e　6 **lots of** 8 _____

  f　12 and 12 **multiplied** _____

2 **Find:**

  a　$\begin{array}{r} 12 \\ \times\ 8 \\ \hline \end{array}$　　b　$\begin{array}{r} 6 \\ \times\ 0 \\ \hline \end{array}$　　c　$\begin{array}{r} 4 \\ \times\ 7 \\ \hline \end{array}$

  d　$\begin{array}{r} 5 \\ \times\ 9 \\ \hline \end{array}$　　e　$\begin{array}{r} 7 \\ \times\ 5 \\ \hline \end{array}$　　f　$\begin{array}{r} 3 \\ \times\ 2 \\ \hline \end{array}$

3 **Complete** the boxes:

  a　$6 \times \boxed{} = \boxed{} = 12 \times 1$

  b　$9 \times \boxed{} = 72 = 6 \times \boxed{}$

  c　$\boxed{} \times 3 = \boxed{} = 6 \times 4$

  d　$6 \times 5 = \boxed{} = 3 \times \boxed{}$

  e　$2 \times 9 = \boxed{} = 6 \times \boxed{}$

  f　$5 \times \boxed{} = \boxed{} = 10 \times 2$

4 Find the **product** and answer in words:

  a　nine and three _____

  b　eight and six _____

  c　one and seven _____

  d　twelve and eleven _____

  e　twelve and nine _____

  f　zero and seven _____

5 Find 7 **times** 10. _____

6 **Find:** $\begin{array}{r} 12 \\ \times\ 9 \\ \hline \end{array}$

7 **Complete** the boxes:　$5 \times \boxed{} = \boxed{} = 25 \times 2$

8 Find the **product** of seven and eight. _____

9 Find the **total** number of animals if there were:

  5 paddocks with 12 cows in each _____

  2 paddocks with 3 horses in each _____

  2 sties with 2 pigs in each _____

  5 pens with 10 chickens in each _____

Multiplication of tens, hundreds and thousands (1)

1 Find:

a 4×2 tens = ☐ tens

b 9×3 tens = ☐ tens

c 6×7 hundreds = ☐ hundreds

d 5×5 hundreds = ☐ hundreds

e 8×4 thousands = ☐ thousands

f 7×8 thousands = ☐ thousands

2 Complete:

a   40 × 7   b   50 × 3   c   60 × 10

d   90 × 5   e   70 × 4   f   80 × 6

3 Complete:

a   200 × 7   b   400 × 4   c   900 × 2

d   800 × 5   e   600 × 9   f   500 × 7

4 Complete:

a   8000 × 4   b   4000 × 6   c   2000 × 3

d   3000 × 9   e   7000 × 2   f   6000 × 5

5 Find: 8×2 thousands = ☐ thousands

6 Complete: 30 × 9

7 Complete: 700 × 9

8 Complete: 9000 × 9

9 Each night Jenny used 700 L of water for a shower. **How much** water did she use in 1 week (7 days)?

Multiplication of tens, hundreds and thousands (2)

1 Complete:

a $10 \times 23 =$ ___   b $10 \times 14 =$ ___
    $20 \times 23 =$ ___ $20 \times 14 =$ ___
    $30 \times 23 =$ ___ $30 \times 14 =$ ___

c $10 \times 76 =$ ___   d $10 \times 34 =$ ___
    $20 \times 76 =$ ___ $20 \times 34 =$ ___
    $30 \times 76 =$ ___ $30 \times 34 =$ ___

e $10 \times 52 =$ ___   f $10 \times 17 =$ ___
    $20 \times 52 =$ ___ $20 \times 17 =$ ___
    $30 \times 52 =$ ___ $30 \times 17 =$ ___

2 Complete:

a $10 \times 20 =$ ___   b $10 \times 50 =$ ___
    $20 \times 20 =$ ___ $20 \times 50 =$ ___
    $30 \times 20 =$ ___ $30 \times 50 =$ ___

c $10 \times 90 =$ ___   d $10 \times 70 =$ ___
    $20 \times 90 =$ ___ $20 \times 70 =$ ___
    $30 \times 90 =$ ___ $30 \times 70 =$ ___

e $10 \times 40 =$ ___   f $10 \times 80 =$ ___
    $20 \times 40 =$ ___ $20 \times 80 =$ ___
    $30 \times 40 =$ ___ $30 \times 80 =$ ___

3 Complete:

a $60 \times 60 =$ ___   b $80 \times 50 =$ ___
c $90 \times 30 =$ ___   d $40 \times 70 =$ ___
e $90 \times 60 =$ ___   f $70 \times 20 =$ ___

4 Find the total number of:

a   4 lots of 300 books ___
b   pay for 7 days at $80 a day ___
c   30 groups of 20 students ___
d   40 stories of 90 words ___
e   50 packets of 30 biscuits ___
f   70 crates of 10 L of milk ___

5 Complete: $10 \times 26 =$ ___
           $20 \times 26 =$ ___
           $30 \times 26 =$ ___

6 Complete: $10 \times 30 =$ ___
           $20 \times 30 =$ ___
           $30 \times 30 =$ ___

7 Complete: $50 \times 50 =$ ___

8 Find the **total** number of 30 eggs in baskets of 40 Easter eggs.

9 The school shop ordered 20 boxes of snacks and there were 89 snacks in each box. If 15 snacks were sold from each box, how many **were left** in total?

Multiplication of tens, hundreds and thousands (3)

1 Complete:

a $300 \times 50 = $ _____   b $800 \times 20 = $ _____

c $40 \times 600 = $ _____   d $90 \times 500 = $ _____

e $30 \times 900 = $ _____   f $70 \times 400 = $ _____

2 Complete the **chart**:

×	10	100	1000
a 40			
b 70			
c 83			
d 29			
e 200			
f 167			

3 Complete:

a $\begin{array}{r} 120 \\ \times\ \ 30 \\ \hline \end{array}$ b $\begin{array}{r} 250 \\ \times\ \ 40 \\ \hline \end{array}$

c $\begin{array}{r} 110 \\ \times\ \ 20 \\ \hline \end{array}$ d $\begin{array}{r} 500 \\ \times\ \ 70 \\ \hline \end{array}$

e $\begin{array}{r} 110 \\ \times\ \ 80 \\ \hline \end{array}$ f $\begin{array}{r} 140 \\ \times\ \ 30 \\ \hline \end{array}$

4 Find the **product** of:

a 70 and 10 _____

b 800 and 100 _____

c 423 and 100 _____

d 126 and 1000 _____

e 47 and 1000 _____

f 93 and 100 _____

5 **Complete:** $60 \times 700 = $ _____

6 Complete the **chart**:

×	10	100	1000
123			

7 **Complete:** $\begin{array}{r} 120 \\ \times\ \ 70 \\ \hline \end{array}$

8 Find the **product** of 98 and 1000. _____

9 On average there are 519 students at each of 30 schools. Approximately how many students are there **altogether**?

_____

Multiplication

1 Complete:

a $\begin{array}{r} 14 \\ \times\ \ 6 \\ \hline \end{array}$ b $\begin{array}{r} 19 \\ \times\ \ 3 \\ \hline \end{array}$ c $\begin{array}{r} 42 \\ \times\ \ 9 \\ \hline \end{array}$

d $\begin{array}{r} 37 \\ \times\ \ 5 \\ \hline \end{array}$ e $\begin{array}{r} 63 \\ \times\ \ 7 \\ \hline \end{array}$ f $\begin{array}{r} 81 \\ \times\ \ 4 \\ \hline \end{array}$

2 Complete:

a $\begin{array}{r} 149 \\ \times\ \ 3 \\ \hline \end{array}$ b $\begin{array}{r} 258 \\ \times\ \ 4 \\ \hline \end{array}$ c $\begin{array}{r} 301 \\ \times\ \ 5 \\ \hline \end{array}$

d $\begin{array}{r} 825 \\ \times\ \ 6 \\ \hline \end{array}$ e $\begin{array}{r} 714 \\ \times\ \ 7 \\ \hline \end{array}$ f $\begin{array}{r} 552 \\ \times\ \ 8 \\ \hline \end{array}$

3 Find the **product** of:

a 4311 and 2 _____

b 2481 and 3 _____

c 8051 and 4 _____

d 1192 and 5 _____

e 5352 and 6 _____

f 1052 and 7 _____

4 **Find:**

a $\begin{array}{r} 4860 \\ \times\ \ 3 \\ \hline \end{array}$ b $\begin{array}{r} 9240 \\ \times\ \ 4 \\ \hline \end{array}$

c $\begin{array}{r} 1070 \\ \times\ \ 5 \\ \hline \end{array}$ d $\begin{array}{r} 20\ 300 \\ \times\ \ 6 \\ \hline \end{array}$

e $\begin{array}{r} 43\ 000 \\ \times\ \ 9 \\ \hline \end{array}$ f $\begin{array}{r} 18\ 000 \\ \times\ \ 2 \\ \hline \end{array}$

5 **Complete:** $\begin{array}{r} 17 \\ \times\ \ 8 \\ \hline \end{array}$

6 **Complete:** $\begin{array}{r} 685 \\ \times\ \ 4 \\ \hline \end{array}$

7 Find the **product** of 2104 and 7 _____

8 **Find:** $\begin{array}{r} 36\ 100 \\ \times\ \ 3 \\ \hline \end{array}$

9 a Find how many **seconds** in 1 hour. _____

b How many **seconds** in 6 hours? _____

c How many **seconds** in 10 hours? _____

Multiplication by 2-digit numbers

1 Estimate the answers to each of the following by rounding the first number to the **nearest ten**:

a   521
   $\times$ 4

b   258
   $\times$ 4

c   301
   $\times$ 5

d   825
   $\times$ 6

e   714
   $\times$ 7

f   552
   $\times$ 8

2 Find:

a $13 \times 61 = (10 \times 61) + (3 \times 61) = \boxed{}$

b $23 \times 47 = (20 \times 47) + (3 \times 47) = \boxed{}$

c $29 \times 58 = (20 \times 58) + (9 \times 58) = \boxed{}$

d $32 \times 76 = (\boxed{} \times 76) + (\boxed{} \times 76) = \boxed{}$

e $17 \times 63 = (\boxed{} \times 63) + (\boxed{} \times 63) = \boxed{}$

f $43 \times 85 = (\boxed{} \times 85) + (\boxed{} \times 85) = \boxed{}$

2 Complete:

a $27 \times 63 =$
   63   63
   $\times 20$ $\times$ 7
   $\boxed{} + \boxed{} = \boxed{}$

b $53 \times 87 =$
   87   87
   $\times 50$ $\times$ 3
   $\boxed{} + \boxed{} = \boxed{}$

c $37 \times 96 =$
   96   96
   $\times 30$ $\times$ 7
   $\boxed{} + \boxed{} = \boxed{}$

d $47 \times 26 =$
   26   26
   $\times 40$ $\times$ 7
   $\boxed{} + \boxed{} = \boxed{}$

e $22 \times 78 =$
   78   78
   $\times 20$ $\times$ 2
   $\boxed{} + \boxed{} = \boxed{}$

f $45 \times 53 =$
   53   53
   $\times 40$ $\times$ 5
   $\boxed{} + \boxed{} = \boxed{}$

4 **Calculate** each of the following:

a   425
   $\times$ 30

b   572
   $\times$ 60

c   835
   $\times$ 50

d   701
   $\times$ 33

e   259
   $\times$ 26

f   107
   $\times$ 47

5 By rounding to the **nearest ten**, estimate the answer to:
   861
   $\times$ 4

6 **Find:** $17 \times 26 = (\boxed{} \times 26) + (\boxed{} \times 26) = \boxed{}$

7 **Calculate:** $72 \times 75 =$
   75   75
   $\times 70$ $\times$ 2
   $\boxed{} + \boxed{} = \boxed{}$

8 **Complete:**
   231
   $\times$ 35

9 Find the answer to one thousand, one hundred and twenty-six **multiplied by** thirty-seven. _____

Extended multiplication (1)

1 Complete:

a $7 \times 60 =$ _____

b $9 \times 200 =$ _____

c $4 \times 800 =$ _____

d $30 \times 6 =$ _____

e $60 \setminus 500 =$ _____

f $50 \ v \ 30 =$ _____

2 Complete:

a $4 \times 30 =$ _____
   $40 \times 30 =$ _____
   $400 \times 30 =$ _____

b $9 \times 70 =$ _____
   $90 \times 70 =$ _____
   $900 \times 70 =$ _____

c $5 \times 80 =$ _____
   $50 \times 80 =$ _____
   $500 \times 80 =$ _____

d $70 \times 40 =$ _____
   $700 \times 40 =$ _____
   $7000 \times 40 =$ _____

e $60 \times 20 =$ _____
   $600 \times 20 =$ _____
   $6000 \times 20 =$ _____

f $80 \times 60 =$ _____
   $800 \times 60 =$ _____
   $8000 \times 60 =$ _____

3 Complete:

a   4126
   $\times$ 7

b   8359
   $\times$ 8

c   1027
   $\times$ 4

d   4623
   $\times$ 5

e   5350
   $\times$ 6

f   6636
   $\times$ 6

4 Complete:

a   43
   $\times 25$
     $(\ 5 \times 43)$
  $+ \ (20 \times 43)$

b   12
   $\times 48$
     $(\ 8 \times 73)$
  $+ \ (40 \times 73)$

c   96
   $\times 37$
     $(\ 7 \times 96)$
  $+ \ (30 \times 96)$

d   65
   $\times 53$
     $(\ 3 \times 65)$
  $+ \ (50 \times 65)$

e   59
   $\times 17$
     $(\ 7 \times 59)$
  $+ \ (10 \times 59)$

f   88
   $\times 66$
     $(\ 6 \times 88)$
  $+ \ (60 \times 88)$

5 **Complete:** $80 \times 40 =$ _____

6 **Complete:**
  $30 \times 50 =$ _____ $300 \times 50 =$ _____

7 **Complete:**
   4276
   $\times$ 5

8 **Complete:**
   86
   $\times 14$
     $(\ 4 \times 86)$
  $+ \ (10 \times 86)$

9 There were 24 eggs in each of 75 large egg cartons. How many eggs were there **altogether**? _____

Extended multiplication (2)

1 Complete:

a
```
    92
  ×17
   (☐×☐)
+  (☐×☐)
```

b
```
    73
  ×25
   (☐×☐)
+  (☐×☐)
```

c
```
    56
  ×49
   (☐×☐)
+  (☐×☐)
```

d
```
    28
  ×75
   (☐×☐)
+  (☐×☐)
```

e
```
    63
  ×82
   (☐×☐)
+  (☐×☐)
```

f
```
    37
  ×53
   (☐×☐)
+  (☐×☐)
```

2 **Complete** each of the following:

a
```
   96
× 12
```

b
```
   75
× 26
```

c
```
   81
× 14
```

d
```
   46
× 22
```

e
```
   63
× 24
```

f
```
   51
× 19
```

3 Find the **product** of:

a 28 and 36 _____
b 95 and 52 _____
c 16 and 42 _____
d 99 and 14 _____
e 83 and 25 _____
f 53 and 41 _____

4 **Calculate** how much each person saved if they saved:

a $36 a week for 22 weeks _____
b $57 a week for 19 weeks _____
c $85 a week for 12 weeks _____
d $40 a week for 17 weeks _____
e $38 a week for 25 weeks _____
f $43 a week for 18 weeks _____

5 Complete:
```
    45
  ×63
   (☐×☐)
+  (☐×☐)
```

6 Complete:
```
    84
  × 36
```

7 Find the **product** of 27 and 85. _____

8 **Calculate** how much Sonia saved, if she saved $39 a week for 13 weeks. _____

9 Each month Josh spent $32 in dry food and $5 in treats for his pet cats. **How much** did he spend on cat food each year?

_____

Extended multiplication (3)

1 Complete:

a
```
    48
×  17
```

b
```
    38
×  16
```

c
```
    97
×  43
```

d
```
   148
×   52
```

e
```
   678
×   69
```

f
```
   437
×   75
```

2 Find:

a 16 × 42 _____
b 33 × 59 _____
c 25 × 75 _____
d 92 × 46 _____
e 85 × 63 _____
f 47 × 68 _____

3 Insert the **missing numbers** in the correct calculation:
19, 27, 35, 32, 65, 26

a
```
     92
×   ☐
    184
+ 2760
   2944
```

b
```
     47
×   ☐
    235
+ 2820
   3055
```

c
```
     72
×   ☐
    432
+ 1440
   1872
```

d
```
     69
×   ☐
    483
+ 1380
   1863
```

e
```
     83
×   ☐
    415
+ 2490
   2905
```

f
```
     33
×   ☐
    297
+ 330
   627
```

4 Calculate the **total number** of fruit:

a 15 boxes, 98 bananas in each box _____
b 27 boxes, 83 avocados in each box _____
c 52 boxes, 56 oranges in each box _____
d 3 boxes, 66 apples in each box _____
e 42 boxes, 75 mandarins in each box _____
f 67 boxes, 19 pineapples in each box _____

5 Complete:
```
   142
×   23
```

6 **Find**: 73 × 21 = _____

7 Insert the correct **missing number** in the calculation:
43, 54, 53, 34, 32, 26
```
     57
×   ☐
    171
+ 2280
   2451
```

8 Calculate the **total number** of fruit in 26 boxes if there are 85 plums in each box. _____

9 It is approximately 575 km to drive from Mildura to Melbourne. There are 34 trucks leaving Mildura to drive to Melbourne. What is the **total distance** they cover?

_____

Extended multiplication (4)

1 **Complete**:

a	321	b	856	c	413
	× 45		× 27		× 37

d	212	e	179	f	522
	× 94		× 17		× 51

2 The school is buying new electronic equipment. The **total** of each set of purchases is:

a 14 $79 telephones _____

b 13 $156 fax machines _____

c 22 $446 printers _____

d 12 $375 scanners _____

e 27 $390 digital cameras _____

f 87 $2450 computers _____

3 **Find**:

a 38 x 6510 _____   b 26 x 6400 _____

c 29 x 2100 _____   d 42 x 3200 _____

e 56 x 3040 _____   f 19 x 9640 _____

4 **Complete** the inventory for the department:

	Item	No. of items	Cost of each item	Total cost
a	hats	98	$17	
b	glasses	56	$89	
c	T-shirts	110	$48	
d	singlets	126	$26	
e	thongs	85	$32	
f	shorts	92	$35	

5 **Complete**: 423 × 76

6 A school is buying 52 new $187 palm pilots. What is the **total** cost of the purchase? _____

7 **Find**: 27 x 3090 _____

8 **Complete**:

Item	No. of items	Cost of each item	Total cost
Shirts	43	$78	

9 In the insect enclosure at the animal park, the butterflies laid approximately 250 eggs of which 179 hatched. If this happens every second week for a year (26 weeks), how many butterfly eggs are hatched in **total** for a year?

Multiples, factors and divisibility

1 **Circle the numbers** that are:

a	divisible by 2	302	491	682	1105	6234	8255	95253
b	divisible by 3	173	735	828	1143	1276	7827	23412
c	divisible by 4	423	536	984	1364	1649	6385	26424
d	divisible by 5	105	621	898	1462	1700	9515	83966
e	divisible by 8	256	452	984	1076	1935	6456	73265
f	divisible by 9	198	356	899	1368	8753	9981	12420

2 **True or false**?

a 9 is a factor of 90 _____

b 7 is a factor of 26 _____

c 8 is a factor of 70 _____

d 11 is a factor of 132 _____

e 6 is a factor of 32 _____

f 4 is a factor of 28 _____

3 List all the **factors** of:

a 12 _____

b 18 _____

c 24 _____

d 30 _____

e 48 _____

f 60 _____

4 Write down the **first 8 multiples** of:

a 7 _____

b 6 _____

c 11 _____

d 12 _____

e 10 _____

f 8 _____

5 **Circle the numbers** that are divisible by 10:

321, 460, 703, 1011, 4200, 9090, 12 345

6 **True or false**?

12 is a factor of 84. _____

7 List all the **factors** of 100.

_____

8 Write down the **first 8 multiples** of 9.

_____

9 List all the **factors** of 5000.

_____

Multiplication strategies

1   **Answer** the following:

a $20 \times 9 =$ _____   b $40 \times 8 =$ _____

c $60 \times 7 =$ _____   d $400 \times 5 =$ _____

e $500 \times 3 =$ _____   f $800 \times 9 =$ _____

2   **Multiply by ten** and **then halve** to find the answer to:

a $16 \times 5 =$ _____   b $24 \times 5 =$ _____

c $36 \times 5 =$ _____   d $46 \times 5 =$ _____

e $38 \times 5 =$ _____   f $54 \times 5 =$ _____

3   Use **doubles** to find:

a $16 \times 4 =$ _____   b $18 \times 4 =$ _____

c $24 \times 4 =$ _____   d $22 \times 8 =$ _____

e $33 \times 8 =$ _____   f $47 \times 8 =$ _____

4   **Mentally** complete each of the following:

a $63 \times 4 =$ _____   b $45 \times 5 =$ _____

c $74 \times 5 =$ _____   d $126 \times 2 =$ _____

e $225 \times 3 =$ _____   f $363 \times 6 =$ _____

5   **Answer**: $600 \times 6 =$ _____

6   **Multiply by 10** and **then halve** to find the answer to:

$43 \times 5 =$ _____

7   Use **doubles** to find: $19 \times 8 =$ _____

8   **Mentally** complete: $263 \times 4 =$ _____

9   Use **doubles** to find:

a $18 \times 16 =$ _____

b $24 \times 16 =$ _____

c $33 \times 16 =$ _____

Estimating products

1   Round each first number to the **nearest ten** to make an **estimate**:

a 31×6 _____   b 49×7 _____

c 53×5 _____   d 103×9 _____

e 204×8 _____   f 298×4 _____

2   Find an **estimate** by first rounding each number to the **nearest ten**:

a 82×21 _____   b 47×29 _____

c 43×63 _____   d 38×19 _____

e 54×67 _____   f 31×72 _____

3   Round each first number to the **nearest ten** and each second number to the **nearest hundred** to find an **estimate** to:

a 76×436 _____   b 81×667 _____

c 24×549 _____   d 11×589 _____

e 43×621 _____   f 58×869 _____

4   **Estimate** the answer and then **check** with a calculator:

a 623×47 E _____ A _____

b 408×36 E _____ A _____

c 89×127 E _____ A _____

d 204×69 E _____ A _____

e 579×23 E _____ A _____

f 255×45 E _____ A _____

5   Round the first number to the **nearest ten** to make an **estimate**:

396×7 _____

6   Find an **estimate** by first rounding each number to the **nearest ten**:

68×34 _____

7   Round the first number to the **nearest ten** and the second number to the **nearest hundred** to find an **estimate** to:

62×389 _____

8   **Estimate** the answer to 653×39 _____ and then **check** with a calculator. _____

9   Each week for 23 weeks, Sally delivers 379 newspapers. Estimate the **total number** of newspapers Sally delivered.

_____

Division practice

1 **Complete** the division equations using the multiplication equations:

a $9 \times 8 = 72$

$72 \div 8 = \boxed{}$

$72 \div 9 = \boxed{}$

b $6 \times 5 = 30$

$30 \div 5 = \boxed{}$

$30 \div 6 = \boxed{}$

c $7 \times 4 = 28$

$28 \div 4 = \boxed{}$

$28 \div 7 = \boxed{}$

d $12 \times 8 = 96$

$96 \div 8 = \boxed{}$

$96 \div 12 = \boxed{}$

e $8 \times 6 = 48$

$48 \div 6 = \boxed{}$

$48 \div 8 = \boxed{}$

f $3 \times 12 = 36$

$36 \div 3 = \boxed{}$

$36 \div 12 = \boxed{}$

2 **Complete**:

a $81 \div 9 = \underline{}$

b $24 \div 3 = \underline{}$

c $10 \div 10 = \underline{}$

d $40 \div 5 = \underline{}$

e $49 \div 7 = \underline{}$

f $90 \div 9 = \underline{}$

3 **Complete**:

a $8 \times \boxed{} = 16$

b $3 \times \boxed{} = 27$

c $11 \times \boxed{} = 110$

d $12 \times \boxed{} = 144$

e $7 \times \boxed{} = 56$

f $6 \times \boxed{} = 54$

4 **Complete**:

a $2 \overline{)6\,4}$

b $6 \overline{)5\,4}$

c $8 \overline{)9\,6}$

d $3 \overline{)6\,9}$

e $4 \overline{)8\,8}$

f $9 \overline{)1\,0\,8}$

5 **Complete** the division equations using the multiplication equation: $6 \times 12 = 72$

$72 \div 6 = \boxed{}$ $72 \div 12 = \boxed{}$

6 **Complete**: $24 \div 2 = \underline{}$

7 **Complete**: $5 \times \boxed{} = 0$

8 **Complete**: $5 \overline{)5\,5}$

9 Josie has 164 pencils to put in 4 boxes evenly.
How many pencils are there in each box? _____

Division review

1 Find a **fair share** if these balls were shared among:

a 4 boys _____

b 6 girls _____

c 8 students _____

d 2 teachers _____

e 12 parents _____

f 3 grandparents _____

2 Find **one share and the remainder**, if the balls from question 1 were shared among:

a 5 boys _____

b 7 girls _____

c 9 parents _____

d 10 schools _____

e 20 teams _____

f 11 dogs _____

3 **Complete**:

a $180 \div 3 = \underline{}$

b $450 \div 5 = \underline{}$

c $240 \div 6 = \underline{}$

d $350 \div 7 = \underline{}$

e $400 \div 8 = \underline{}$

f $360 \div 9 = \underline{}$

4 **Complete** the table:

	Question	Quotient	Remainder
	$20 \div 3$	6	2
a	$30 \div 4$		
b	$51 \div 7$		
c	$38 \div 4$		
d	$40 \div 9$		
e	$55 \div 10$		
f	$63 \div 6$		

5 Find a **fair share** if the balls are shared among 3 people.

_____

6 For the balls in question 5, find **one share and the remainder** if the balls are shared among 5 policemen.

_____

7 **Complete**: $490 \div 7 = \underline{}$

8 **Complete**:

Question	Quotient	Remainder
$14 \div 6$		

9 **Complete** the table:

Question	Quotient	Remainder
$\boxed{} \div 6$	5	2
$\boxed{} \div 8$	1	6
$\boxed{} \div 3$	9	1
$\boxed{} \div 7$	8	4

Division with remainders

1 Complete:

a 52 ÷ 6 = _____

b 40 ÷ 3 = _____

c 70 ÷ 9 = _____

d 50 ÷ 11 = _____

e 80 ÷ 12 = _____

f 34 ÷ 4 = _____

2 Complete:

a $2\overline{)648}$ b $3\overline{)369}$ c $5\overline{)560}$

d $8\overline{)976}$ e $7\overline{)924}$ f $4\overline{)504}$

3 Complete:

a $10\overline{)722}$ b $10\overline{)655}$ c $5\overline{)547}$

d $8\overline{)2644}$ e $3\overline{)9026}$ f $9\overline{)2735}$

4 Find:

a Isabel had $465; this is 10 times as much as Katie. **How much** does Katie have? _____

b 497 eggs have to be placed into cartons of 6. **How many** cartons are needed? _____

c Each car needs 4 tyres. If there is a pile of 639 tyres, **how many** cars can be completed? _____

d Liam used 742 mL of milk to fill 7 glasses. **How much** milk was poured into each? _____

e I had a 985 cm length of string, which had to be cut into 5 equal pieces. What was the **length of each** piece? _____

f 4027 thumbtacks had to be put into 3 boxes equally. **How many** thumbtacks were there in each box?

_____

5 **Complete**: 67 ÷ 8 = _____

6 Complete:
$3\overline{)705}$

7 Complete:
$7\overline{)4065}$

8 8568 letters were divided equally into 8 mail bags. **How many** letters were there in each bag?

_____

9 Sara had 3 pieces of ribbon of length 48 cm, 52 cm and 64 cm. What was the **average length** of the ribbon?

_____

Division with remainders – fractions

1 **How much** would each person receive if 5 children shared?

a 5 pieces of fruit _____

b 6 pieces of fruit _____

c 10 pieces of fruit _____

d 7 pieces of fruit _____

e 12 pieces of fruit _____

f 23 pieces of fruit _____

2 Write each answer as a **mixed number**:

a $2\overline{)43}$ b $3\overline{)31}$ c $4\overline{)29}$

d $6\overline{)80}$ e $5\overline{)94}$ f $7\overline{)50}$

3 Write each answer as a **mixed number**:

a $6\overline{)902}$ b $4\overline{)503}$ c $7\overline{)629}$

d $8\overline{)594}$ e $9\overline{)256}$ f $5\overline{)433}$

4 Complete each of the equations writing the **remainders as a fraction**:

a $6\overline{)7265}$ b $8\overline{)9650}$ c $3\overline{)5471}$

d $7\overline{)9350}$ e $9\overline{)2468}$ f $4\overline{)5363}$

5 **How much** would each person receive if 5 children shared 16 pieces of fruit?

_____

6 Write the answer as a **mixed number**:

$8\overline{)75}$

7 Write the answer as a **mixed number**:

$3\overline{)247}$

8 Complete the equation writing the **remainder as a fraction**:

$5\overline{)5307}$

9 Complete each of the following writing the answer as a **fraction**:

a $10\overline{)7}$ b $4\overline{)1}$ c $7\overline{)5}$

Division with zeros in the answer

1. **Complete:**

   a   10) 390   b   10) 850   c   10) 400

   d   10) 671   e   10) 349   f   10) 850

2. **Complete:**

   a   3) 3135   b   5) 5055   c   6) 5472

   d   8) 9616   e   7) 4921   f   4) 8360

3. **Complete:**

   a   4) 2013   b   5) 7019   c   3) 1605

   d   9) 91 803   e   8) 70 615   f   6) 36 102

4. **Find:**

   a   4963 plants were planted in 7 rows. **How many** plants were there in each row? _____

   b   A band with 5 players earned $975. **How much** did each player receive? _____

   c   The same number of newspapers was placed in 8 piles. **How many** newspapers were there in each pile, if there were 1656 newspapers to begin with?

   _____

   d   714 students at university rode bikes. **How many** bikes were there in each of 7 racks, if they were all full? _____

   e   There were 4563 chocolates to place in box trays. **How many** box trays were needed if there were 9 chocolates in each tray? _____

   f   **How many** weeks is 8407 days? _____

5. **Complete:**

   10) 259

6. **Complete:**

   9) 9018

7. **Complete:**

   7) 2143

8. **How many** 6 cm lengths are there in 5004 cm? _____

9. Find the **missing number:**   10 304 r 3

       5) _____

Division with zeros in the divisor

1. **Complete:**

   a   10) 4301   b   10) 7438   c   10) 5060

   d   10) 8497   e   10) 6635   f   10) 9010

2. Write the number of **tens** in:

   a   4360 _____

   b   21 070 _____

   c   46 000 _____

   d   21 040 _____

   e   39 110 _____

   f   61 270 _____

3. **Complete:**

   a   10) 24 680   b   10) 71 020

   c   10) 87 630   d   10) 190 416

   e   10) 487 951   f   10) 847 315

4. Change each of the following to **centimetres:**

   a   9600 mm _____

   b   17 500 mm _____

   c   490 mm _____

   d   8710 mm _____

   e   38 420 mm _____

   f   1120 mm _____

5. **Complete:**

   10) 4371

6. Write the number of **tens** in 14 260 _____

7. **Complete:**

   10) 471 805

8. Change 39 100 mm to **centimetres:** _____

9. Ten plastic stars fit in one box. **How many** boxes are filled with 350 000 plastic stars?

   _____

See START UPS page 4

Division by numbers with zeros

1 Complete:

a. 10) 5760   b. 10) 2490   c. 10) 3100

d. 10) 23 000   e. 10) 46 900   f. 10) 48 700

2 Complete:

a. 100) 2100   b. 100) 3700

c. 100) 2900   d. 100) 48 000

e. 100) 52 000   f. 100) 39 000

3 Complete by **first dividing both numbers by 10**:

a. 50) 1050   b. 30) 3600

c. 40) 2800   d. 70) 42 000

e. 90) 10 710   f. 60) 1800

4 Complete:

a. 90) 3033   b. 70) 2485

c. 60) 2142   d. 80) 7632

e. 50) 4635   f. 40) 7288

5 Complete:

10) 4320

6 Complete:

100) 10700

7 Complete by **first dividing both numbers by 10**:

80) 2400

8 Complete:

30) 1014

9 Round each answer to the **nearest whole number**:

a. 40) 6175   b. 50) 8432

See START UPS page 4

Division of numbers larger than 999

1 Complete:

a. 6) 8628   b. 3) 1554   c. 5) 7215

d. 4) 1936   e. 8) 8496   f. 7) 7245

2 Complete:

a. 7) 63 159   b. 4) 12 648   c. 6) 35 691

d. 10) 42 681   e. 9) 71 463   f. 5) 42 183

3 Solve:

a. **How many** students were at camp, if $\frac{1}{4}$ of 2000 students were there?

b. 5648 L **divided** into 8 containers

c. 746 325 m^2 of land **divided** into 5 equal paddocks

d. 46 392 km **divided** into 4 equal sections

e. 1128 tonnes **loaded equally** onto 8 different boats

f. If 396 points were scored in 6 games, what was the **average number** of points per game?

4 Find the **missing numbers**:

a. 3) 1234   b. 6) 1021   c. 7) 631

d. 9) 802   e. 4) 2116   f. 8) 739

5 Complete:

9) 6399

6 Complete:

8) 46 321

7 $8935 was shared among 5 workers. **How much** did each one receive? _____

8 Find the **missing number**:

5) 1731

9 Find the **missing number**:

7) 2 4 1 3 r 5

Extended division

1 **Complete**:

a 12) 288
−   [ ] 2
−   [ ] 4

b 8) 1128
−   [ ] 1
−   [ ] 4
−   [ ] 1

c 11) 484
−   [ ] 4
−   [ ] 4

d 14) 168
−   [ ] 1
−   [ ] 2

e 22) 286
−   [ ] 1
−   [ ] 3

f 31) 403
−   [ ] 1
−   [ ] 3

2 Use the above method to **complete**:

a 6) 188   b 8) 142   c 13) 496

d 63) 756   e 27) 290   f 13) 625

3 **Find**:

a 299 ÷ 18 = _____   b 600 ÷ 12 = _____
c 496 ÷ 25 = _____   d 147 ÷ 13 = _____
e 735 ÷ 15 = _____   f 78 ÷ 14 = _____

4 Find the **missing numbers**:

a   10 r 5   b   46 r 2   c   21 r 8
   27)   14)   17)

d   24 r 1   e   79 r 3   f   216 r 3
   57)   12)   45)

5 **Complete**:   6) 498
                     − [ ] 8
                     − [ ] 3

6 Use the above method to **complete**:
                     11) 416

7 **Find** 362 ÷ 32 = _____

8 Find the missing numbers: 32 r 7
                              15)

9 **How many** cartons would 184 eggs fill if each carton holds one dozen eggs? _____

Averages (1)

1 Find the **average** of each pair of numbers:

a 4 and 6 _____
b 12 and 14 _____
c 0 and 100 _____
d 50 and 150 _____
e 125 and 200 _____
f 7 and 8 _____

2 Find the **average** of each group of numbers:

a 1, 7, 9, 3 _____
b 76, 14, 63, 22, 15 _____
c 11, 9, 12, 46, 53, 3 _____
d 921, 435, 407, 608, 110, 213 _____
e $4.15, $2.90, $3.25 _____
f $10, $11.75, $12.15, $2.10 _____

3 Find the **average speed** for each of the following:

a I travelled 500 km in 10 hours. [ ] km/h
b It took 6 hours to travel 5.4 kilometres. [ ] km/h
c The snail moved 9.6 cm in 4 minutes. [ ] cm/min
d We flew 1764 km in 7 hours. [ ] km/h
e The grasshopper travelled 5 m in 2 minutes. [ ] m/min
f The boat travelled 4800 km in 4 days. [ ] km/day

4 Here are the temperatures at 4:00 pm for a week.

Day	Mon.	Tues.	Wed.	Thurs.	Fri.	Sat.	Sun.
Temp °C	24	26	22	25	29	18	23

What is the average temperature at 4:00 pm for:

a Monday and Tuesday? _____
b Thursday and Friday? _____
c Tuesday, Wednesday and Thursday? _____
d the weekend? _____
e Monday to Friday? _____
f the entire week? _____

5 Find the **average** of 17 and 26: _____

6 Find the **average** of 19, 26, 41, 43, 31: _____

7 Find the **average speed** of a rock climber, climbing

60 metres in 30 minutes [ ] m/min

8 What is the **average temperature** of Friday, Saturday and Sunday for question 4? _____

9 **Find 3 numbers** that give an average of 27.

Averages (2)

1. Write the **answer as a decimal**:

   a. $8\overline{)308}$ b. $4\overline{)150}$ c. $4\overline{)37}$

   d. $5\overline{)248}$ e. $8\overline{)474}$ f. $5\overline{)396}$

2. Find the **average** of:

   a. 5, 9, 13, 9, 17, 7 _____

   b. 50, 111, 59, 93, 77 _____

   c. 7, 9, 13, 10, 9, 12, 10 _____

   d. 2, 40, 29, 15, 21, 19 _____

   e. 71, 63, 51, 29, 36 _____

   f. 38, 2, 25, 15, 20 _____

3. Find the **average score** for each of the hockey teams for the 6 game pre-season:

	Team	Score	Average
a	Numbers	0, 3, 4, 2, 1, 2	
b	Totals	6, 5, 2, 1, 3, 1	
c	Dividers	0, 2, 1, 3, 0, 0	
d	Multipliers	4, 6, 3, 7, 1, 3	
e	Adders	5, 7, 3, 9, 1, 2	
f	Subtracters	5, 6, 7, 8, 3, 3	

4. What is the **average**:

   a. temperature of 28°C, 32°C, 30°C and 35°C?

   _____

   b. number of marbles in jars of 112, 116 and 120?

   _____

   c. number of runs of 22, 36, 16, 29 and 56 runs?

   _____

   d. number of fruit in baskets of 7, 8, 19, 21 and 13?

   _____

   e. number of pencils in packets of 12, 10, 9, 8, 11 and 14?

   _____

   f. number of matches in boxes of 85, 72, 53, 107 and 92?

   _____

5. Write the **answer as a decimal**.

   $5\overline{)248}$

6. Find the **average** of 6, 9, 14, 36 and 15. _____

7. Find the **average score** for the hockey team for the six game pre-season tournament:

Team	Score	Average
Powers	4, 7, 3, 8, 5, 3	

8. What is the **average cost** of $9, $15, $26, $39 and $22?

   _____

9. The batting average of a cricketer for 8 matches is 60. Find the **missing score** from game 3:

Game	1	2	3	4	5	6	7	8
Score	82	62		47	48	100	54	70

Inverse operations and checking answers

1. Use addition to **check** the subtraction equations. Tick the boxes for those that are correct and write the answers for those that are incorrect:

   a. $176 - 93 = 83$ ☐

   b. $427 - 256 = 172$ ☐

   c. $302 - 175 = 127$ ☐

   d. $579 - 286 = 393$ ☐

   e. $2817 - 1439 = 1476$ ☐

   f. $1951 - 786 = 1165$ ☐

2. Use multiplication to **check** the division equations. Tick the boxes for those that are correct and write the answers for those that are incorrect:

   a. $200 \div 10 = 2$ ☐   b. $420 \div 60 = 7$ ☐

   c. $180 \div 60 = 90$ ☐   d. $100 \div 20 = 5$ ☐

   e. $132 \div 11 = 12$ ☐   f. $840 \div 70 = 12$ ☐

3. Use inverse operations to **check** the following statements. Answer true or false:

   a. $126 + 235$ is less than 360 _____

   b. 50×20 is greater than 900 _____

   c. $800 \div 15$ is less than 50 _____

   d. $1246 - 728$ is more than 500 _____

   e. 700×12 is less than 9000 _____

   f. $4000 \div 20$ is greater than 250 _____

4. **Match** the inverse equations:

   a. $6 \times * = 150$ A. $40 \times 2 = *$

   b. $40 \times * = 120$ B. $15 - 6 = *$

   c. $* - 25 = 9$ C. $* = 25 - 9$

   d. $\frac{1}{2}$ of $* = 40$ D. $150 \div 6 = *$

   e. $9 + * = 25$ E. $9 + 25 = *$

   f. $6 + * = 15$ F. $120 \div 40 = *$

5. Use addition to **check** the subtraction equation:

   $2176 - 385 = 1781$

6. Use multiplication to **check** the division equation:

   $6000 \div 500 = 12$

7. Use inverse operations to **check** the equation:

   $1462 + 927 = 2389$ (answer true or false) _____

8. **Match** the inverse equation:

   $12 = * \div 8$ $12 \times 8 = *$
                          $12 + 8 = *$
                          $12 - 8 = *$
                          $8 \div 12 = *$

9. Jodie started with a number of pet birds; she sold 5 of them, bought 4 others and then gave 3 away. She now has 12 birds. **How many** birds did Jodie have to start with? _____

Number lines and operations

① Complete the **number lines** to show each of the following:

a start at 10 and count by 7s

⟵――――――――――――――――――⟶

b start at 50 and count by 3s

⟵――――――――――――――――――⟶

c start at 113 and count by 5s

⟵――――――――――――――――――⟶

d start at 92 and count backwards by 6s

⟵――――――――――――――――――⟶

e start at 375 and count backwards by 9s

⟵――――――――――――――――――⟶

f start at 1000 and count backwards by 250s

⟵――――――――――――――――――⟶

② Use the **number lines** to find:

a $632 + 107 =$ ⟵――――――――――⟶

b $856 + 402 =$ ⟵――――――――――⟶

c $438 + 756 =$ ⟵――――――――――⟶

d $1079 + 987 =$ ⟵――――――――――⟶

e $1159 + 248 =$ ⟵――――――――――⟶

f $1469 + 1328 =$ ⟵――――――――――⟶

③ Use the **number lines** to find:

a $486 - 195 =$ ⟵――――――――――⟶

b $738 - 297 =$ ⟵――――――――――⟶

c $555 - 489 =$ ⟵――――――――――⟶

d $1428 - 739 =$ ⟵――――――――――⟶

e $1095 - 876 =$ ⟵――――――――――⟶

f $2416 - 1482 =$ ⟵――――――――――⟶

④ Use the **number lines** to find:

a $13 \times 6 =$ ⟵――――――――――⟶

b $22 \times 5 =$ ⟵――――――――――⟶

c $45 \times 5 =$ ⟵――――――――――⟶

d $135 \div 9 =$ ⟵――――――――――⟶

e $119 \div 7 =$ ⟵――――――――――⟶

f $156 \div 6 =$ ⟵――――――――――⟶

⑤ Draw a **number line** to show, start at 1126 and count by 8s.

⑥ Use the **number line** to find $4728 + 1059 =$

⟵――――――――――――――――――⟶

⑦ Use the **number line** to find $4305 - 2416 =$

⟵――――――――――――――――――⟶

⑧ Use the **number line** to find $35 \times 6 =$

⟵――――――――――――――――――⟶

⑨ a Draw a **number line** from 1 to 3, showing each quarter.

b Show the following **equations** on the number line:

i $3 - 2\frac{1}{4} =$

ii $2 \div \frac{1}{4} =$

iii $\frac{1}{2} \times 4 =$

iv $1\frac{3}{4} + \frac{1}{2} =$

Order of operations (1)

① Complete the **brackets first**:

a $(20 - 5) \times 10 =$ ―――――――

b $(7 + 5) \times 3 =$ ―――――――

c $6 \times (2 + 5) - 9 =$ ―――――――

d $(100 - 12 \times 3) \div 4 =$ ―――――――

e $(40 + 20) \div 5 + 15 =$ ―――――――

f $7 \times (5 + 6) =$ ―――――――

② **Work left to right**:

a $9 \times 8 \div 2 =$ ―――――――

b $11 \times 6 \div 2 =$ ―――――――

c $60 \div 10 \times 3 =$ ―――――――

d $200 \div 4 \div 5 =$ ―――――――

e $4 \times 8 \times 2 \div 8 =$ ―――――――

f $12 \times 4 \div 6 =$ ―――――――

③ Complete the **multiplication and division first**:

a $20 + 3 \times 5 =$ ―――――――

b $30 - 12 \div 4 + 14 =$ ―――――――

c $200 - 12 \times 12 =$ ―――――――

d $26 + 5 \times 7 + 19 =$ ―――――――

e $36 + 84 \div 4 - 50 =$ ―――――――

f $46 - 66 \div 3 =$ ―――――――

④ Complete the **brackets first**, then multiplication and division, and finally addition and subtraction:

a $(4 + 6) \times 9 - 38 =$ ―――――――

b $(10 - 7) \times 5 - 2 \times 6 =$ ―――――――

c $7 \times 4 + 50 \div 2 =$ ―――――――

d $47 + 10 \times (12 + 3) =$ ―――――――

e $(400 \div 10) \div (5 \times 4) =$ ―――――――

f $52 + (7 + 9) \div 4 =$ ―――――――

⑤ Complete the **brackets first**:

$50 - (6 \times 6) + 27 =$ ―――――――

⑥ Work left to right: $90 \times 3 \times 2 \div 4 =$ ―――――――

⑦ Complete the **multiplication and division first**:

$7 \times 9 + 100 \div 5 =$ ―――――――

⑧ Complete the **brackets first**, then the multiplication and division, and finally addition and subtraction:

$5 \times (7 + 6) + 7 =$ ―――――――

⑨ **Add brackets** to make the equation true:

$17 + 3 + 5 \times 4 = 16 - 7 + 8 \times 5$

Order of operations (2)

1. **Complete:**

   a $7 + 8 \times 3 =$ _____

   b $14 - 14 \div 14 =$ _____

   c $(14 \times 3) + (2 \times 9) =$ _____

   d $24 \div (10 - 6) =$ _____

   e $20 - 16 \div 4 =$ _____

   f $6 \times 2 \times 2 + 13 =$ _____

2. **Complete:**

   a $36 \div 9 \times 4 + 6 =$ _____

   b $(36 \div 9) \times (4 + 6) =$ _____

   c $36 \div (9 \times 4) + 6 =$ _____

   d $(32 - 4) \times (5 \times 10) + 22 =$ _____

   e $(32 - 4) \times 5 \times (10 + 22) =$ _____

   f $320 - 4 \times 5 \times 10 + 22 =$ _____

3. **Complete:**

   a $(15 \div 15 \times 2) + 9 =$ _____

   b $(5 \times 10 \times 0) + 3 \times 5 =$ _____

   c $100 + (7 \times 4) - 18 =$ _____

   d $36 \div 12 \times 3 + 6 =$ _____

   e $200 - 10 \times 5 \times 2 =$ _____

   f $100 - (5 \times 2 \times 3) =$ _____

4. **Complete:**

   a $62 \div 2 + 12 \div 12 =$ _____

   b $92 \times 2 \times 7 \times 0 \times 4 =$ _____

   c $104 \times 3 \times 6 \times 0 \times 5 =$ _____

   d $4 \times 52 \div 10 =$ _____

   e $(40 + 36 + 95) \times 1 =$ _____

   f $(46 - 25 + 17) \times 10 =$ _____

5. **Complete:** $(120 - 25) \div 5 =$ _____

6. **Complete:** $320 - (4 \times 5) \times 10 + 22 =$ _____

7. **Complete:** $(7 \times 8) - (3 \times 6) + 10 =$ _____

8. **Complete:** $92 - 52 + 2 \times 0 =$ _____

9. **Complete** the following trail with 3 different numbers:

multiply by 2	add 8	subtract 10	add 5	subtract 8	add 5	divide by 2

   a **What** did you discover? _____

   b Do you know **why**? _____

Order of operations (3)

1. **Complete:**

   a $40 \div 4 - 6 =$ _____

   b $15 - 8 + 5 =$ _____

   c $6 \times 7 \times 10 =$ _____

   d $25 + 12 - 17 =$ _____

   e $10 - 6 - 4 =$ _____

   f $19 + 26 - 35 =$ _____

2. **Complete:**

   a $(9 \times 8) \div 2 =$ _____

   b $9 \times (8 \div 2) =$ _____

   c $9 \times 8 \div 2 =$ _____

   d $60 \div (4 + 11) =$ _____

   e $(60 \div 4) + 11 =$ _____

   f $60 \div 4 + 11 =$ _____

3. **Complete:**

   a $2 \times 5 + 6 \times 5 =$ _____

   b $(2 \times 5 + 6) \times 5 =$ _____

   c $2 \times (5 + 6) \times 5 =$ _____

   d $2 \times (5 + 6 \times 5) =$ _____

   e $(2 \times 5) + 6 \times 5 =$ _____

   f $(2 \times 5) + (6 \times 5) =$ _____

4. **Complete:**

   a $50 - 5 - 5 - 5 - 5 - 5 =$ _____

   b $50 - (5 + 5 + 5 + 5 + 5) =$ _____

   c $72 - 9 - 9 - 9 - 9 - 9 =$ _____

   d $72 - (9 + 9 + 9 + 9 + 9) =$ _____

   e $32 \div 2 \div 2 \div 2 \div 2 =$ _____

   f $32 \div (2 \times 2 \times 2 \times 2) =$ _____

5. **Complete:** $200 - 4 \times 6 + 12 =$ _____

6. **Complete:** $(200 \div 5) \times 10 =$ _____

   $200 \div (5 \times 10) =$ _____

7. **Complete:** $(9 \times 4) \div 4 + 1 =$ _____

   $9 \times (4 \div 4) + 1 =$ _____

8. **Complete:** $30 - 3 - 3 - 3 - 3 - 3 =$ _____

   $30 - (3 + 3 + 3 + 3 + 3) =$ _____

9. With the four numbers 10, 9, 5 and 6, write two **different** equations.

   _____

   _____

Order of operations with decimals and fractions

1 Complete the **brackets first**:

a $(5 + 2) \times \frac{1}{2} =$ _____

b $\frac{1}{4} \times (7 + 5) =$ _____

c $2 \times 6 \div (12 - 2) =$ _____

d $(4.3 + 2.7) \times 3 =$ _____

e $(1.9 + 0.1) \div 2 =$ _____

f $0.5 \times (6 + 12) - 3 =$ _____

2 **Work left to right**:

a $44 \times 2 \div 8 =$ _____

b $2 \times 4 \div 2 =$ _____

c $2.8 \div 4 \times 2 =$ _____

d $3.6 \div 6 \times 2 =$ _____

e $4.2 \times 4 \div 2 =$ _____

f $5.5 \times 7 \div 5 =$ _____

3 Do **multiplication and division before** addition and subtraction:

a $3.2 \times 5 + 6.1 \times 2 =$ _____

b $60 + 9.3 \times 4 + 12.3 =$ _____

c $14.4 \div 12 + 3.8 =$ _____

d $20 - 8.1 \div 3 + 4.6 =$ _____

e $2 \times 6.2 + 5.5 \div 5 =$ _____

f $100 \div 0.5 - 50 \times 2.5 =$ _____

4 Complete the **brackets first**, then multiplication and division, and finally addition and subtraction:

a $(\frac{3}{9} + \frac{2}{3}) \times 7 =$ _____

b $(\frac{1}{2} \times 6) \div (\frac{1}{4} \times 20) =$ _____

c $\frac{1}{8} \times (16 + 8) =$ _____

d $4 - (\frac{2}{10} + \frac{3}{10}) + 1\frac{1}{2} =$ _____

e $(8 + 3) \div 4 =$ _____

f $(9\frac{3}{5} - \frac{3}{5}) \times 5 =$ _____

5 Complete the **brackets first**: $(2 + 3) \times \frac{1}{5} =$ _____

6 **Work left to right**: $7.5 \times 2 \div 3 =$ _____

7 Do **multiplication and division before** addition and subtraction:

$40 - 4 \times 9.3 + 7.3 =$ _____

8 Complete the **brackets first**, then multiplication and division, and finally addition and subtraction:

$4 - (\frac{3}{4} + \frac{1}{4}) \times 2 =$ _____

9 Place in the **brackets** to make the number sentence true:

$0.4 + 0.3 \times 12 - 0.2 - 1.0 = 7.2$

Number patterns (2)

1 Complete the following **tables**:

a

1st No.	64	60	56	52	48
2nd No.	32			26	

b

1st No.	7	8	9	10	11
2nd No.	56				80

c

1st No.	70	63	56	49	42
2nd No.		9			6

d

1st No.	60	54	48	42	36
2nd No.		9			6

e

1st No.	1	2	3	4	5
2nd No.	$\frac{1}{2}$				$2\frac{1}{2}$

f

1st No.	0.5	0.6	0.7	0.8	0.9
2nd No.	5				9

2 Write the **rule** for each of the tables in question 1:

a _____ b _____

c _____ d _____

e _____ f _____

3 Write what the **next term** would be for each of the tables in question 1:

a _____ b _____

c _____ d _____

e _____ f _____

4 Write what the **10th term** would be for each of the tables in question 1:

a _____ b _____

c _____ d _____

e _____ f _____

5 Complete the **table**:

1st No.	9	19	29	39	49
2nd No.	26			56	

6 Write the **rule** for the table in question 5: _____

7 Write what the **next term** would be for the table in question 5: _____

8 Write what the **10th term** would be for question 5:

_____

9 Construct a **table** for the relationship between the number of triangles and the number of sides on the triangles. Do to four triangles.

For example: 1 triangle has 3 sides
2 triangles have 6 sides

Number patterns (3)

1 Continue each of the following **number patterns**:

  a   2, 3, 5, 8, _____, _____, _____

  b   1, 4, 9, 16, _____, _____, _____

  c   2, 2.5, 3.5, 5, _____, _____, _____

  d   101, 82, 65, 50, _____, _____, _____

  e   2, 5, 11, 20 _____, _____, _____, _____

  f   4, 32, 16, 128 _____, _____, _____, _____

2 Write a **rule** for each of the number patterns in question 1:

  a _____ b _____

  c _____ d _____

  e _____ f _____

3 **Complete** each of the number patterns:

a
1st No.	3	6	9	12	15	18
2nd No.	4	7	10			

b
1st No.	10	11	12	13	14	15
2nd No.	8	9	10			

c
1st No.	5	7	9	11	13	15
2nd No.	50	70	90			

d
1st No.	4	5	6	7	8	9
2nd No.	16	20	24			

e
1st No.	100	99	98	97	96	95
2nd No.	84	83	82			

f
1st No.	60	55	50	45	40	35
2nd No.	75	70	65			

4 Find the value of the **missing number** for each of the number patterns respectively in question 3:

a
1st No.	
2nd No.	101

b
1st No.	
2nd No.	46

c
1st No.	
2nd No.	240

d
1st No.	
2nd No.	400

e
1st No.	
2nd No.	0

f
1st No.	
2nd No.	25

5 Continue the **number pattern**:

$\frac{1}{4}, \frac{1}{2}, \frac{3}{4}, 1$, _____, _____, _____

6 Write a **rule** for the number pattern in question 5.

_____

7 Complete the **number pattern**:

1st No.	7	6	9	12	10	15
2nd No.	35	30	45			

8 Find the **missing number** of the number pattern in question 7:

1st No.	
2nd No.	500

9 Apply the rule to **complete the pattern**: $2 \times \square + 5 = \triangle$

$\square$	2	4	6	8	10	12	14
$\triangle$							

Mixed operations

1 Complete:

  a $725 - 346 + 107 =$ _____

  b $\frac{3}{4} + \frac{5}{4} - 2 =$ _____

  c $436 - 109 + 241 + 6 =$ _____

  d $(405 + 107) - (99 + 32) =$ _____

  e $0.9 + 1.1 + 4.3 - 2.9 =$ _____

  f $8246 + 1097 - 5559 =$ _____

2 Complete:

  a $(9 \times 2) \div 3 =$ _____

  b $(100 \div 2) \times 14 =$ _____

  c $(10 \times 10) \div (4 \times 5) =$ _____

  d $(50 \div 5) \times (2 \times 5) =$ _____

  e $4 \times 6 \times 7 \times 0 =$ _____

  f $90 \div 9 \times (7 \times 8) =$ _____

3 Complete:

  a $(4 \times 4) \div (2 + 6) =$ _____

  b $(107 - 98) \div 3 =$ _____

  c $(102 + 47) - 100 \div 2 =$ _____

  d $\frac{1}{2} \times 50 + 32 =$ _____

  e $(4.2 \times 3) + (4.8 \div 6) =$ _____

  f $(146 + 23) \div 13 =$ _____

4 **Complete** by finding the **value** of each letter/symbol:

  a M is 10 more than the product of 7, 3 and 2 _____

  b $\triangle$ is the sum of 16, 17 and 18, divided by 3 _____

  c   If I add 11 and 9, divide by 4 and multiply by 7, my answer is _____

  d   When I take 3×7 from the difference of 100 and 4, my answer is V _____

  e T is the answer to 11 multiplied by 12, divided by 2, then 4 added. _____

  f   The difference of 8×7, and 12 multiplied by 6, the result is equal to * _____

5 **Complete**: $71 + 96 - 45 =$ _____

6 **Complete**: $(4 \times 10) \div (5 \times 1) =$ _____

7 **Complete**: $(9 + 3) \times (15 - 3) =$ _____

8 **Complete**: 60 multiplied by 3 with 120 subtracted gives the answer of D. _____

9 **Find**: 9.8 divided by 2, 0.1 added and the result divided by 8 gives *.

   * = _____

Zero in operations

1 **Complete**:

a $4 \times 16 \times 3 \times 0 =$ _____   b $1000 \times 7 \times 0 =$ _____

c $(4 + 9 + 7) \times 0 =$ _____   d $(46 - 9) \times 0 =$ _____

e $(42 \div 7) \times (5 - 5) =$ _____

f $(9 - 9) \times (100 \div 5) =$ _____

2 **Complete**:

a
```
   428 199
   360 400
 + 901 000
```

b
```
   247 100
   836 900
 + 100 000
```

c
```
  4 750 000
  2 180 000
+ 4 603 000
```

d
```
   450 000
 - 263 000
```

e
```
   876 000
 -  98 500
```

f
```
  64 000 000
 - 2 750 000
```

3 **Complete**:

a
```
  410 270
×       3
```

b
```
  694 200
×       7
```

c
```
  8 391 000
×         8
```

d $4 \overline{)107\ 400}$ e $5 \overline{)7\ 632\ 000}$ f $10 \overline{)3\ 623\ 000}$

4 Complete the **missing boxes**:

a
```
    1 0 □ 7 6 □
  + 3 2 8 □ □ 7
  ─────────────
    □ □ 0 0 9 7
```

b
```
    4 7 1 □ 9 □ 4
  - 1 □ 6 4 □ 8 □
  ───────────────
    □ 0 4 8 3 1 0
```

c
```
      1 □ □ □ 8 0
  5 ) □ 9 3 4 □ □
```

d
```
        5 0 7
      ×   4 2
  ───────────
      1 □ □ 4
  + □ □ □ 8 □
  ───────────
    □ □ □ □ □
```

e
```
      □ 0 7
    ×   4 □
  ─────────
    2 1 4 9
  + 1 2 □ □ □
  ───────────
    □ □ □ □ □
```

f
```
        8 0 □
      ×   6 3
  ───────────
      □ □ 2 4
  + □ □ □ □ □
  ───────────
    □ □ □ □ □
```

5 **Complete**: $(90 \div 9) \times 0 =$ _____

6 **Complete**:
```
   416 700
   293 800
 + 460 000
```

7 **Complete**:

$5 \overline{)9\ 824\ 000}$

8 Complete the **missing boxes**:
```
    1 0 7 □ 8 □
  - □ □ □ 4 □ 0
  ─────────────
    6 9 0 2 0
```

9 A company makes 946 000 packets of salt and vinegar chips every month. **How many** packets of salt and vinegar chips are made in one year? _____

Equations

1 **Solve** each of the following equations:

a $M - 9 = 42$ _____   b $95 \div 5 = W$ _____

c $10 \times 10 = V^2$ _____   d $D - 3.2 = 6$ _____

e $50 + K = 76$ _____   f $9 \times X = 100 - 37$ _____

2 **Solve** each of the following:

a $\frac{1}{2} \times 40 + 1 = B$ _____

b $C = (5 \times 10) + (18 \div 3)$ _____

c $E = 36 \div (3 \times 2)$ _____

d $T = (49 \div 7) + 20$ _____

e $(3 \times 15) - (2 \times 5) = Z$ _____

f $(11 \times 11) \div (12 \times 12) = Y$ _____

3 **Solve** each of the following:

a $81 \div N = 27$ _____

b $30 - 5 = 17 + N$ _____

c $8.5 + P = 10$ _____

d $\frac{1}{4} \times R = 40$ _____

e $20 - S = 16.3$ _____

f $\frac{1}{6} + F = \frac{1}{2}$ _____

4 **Write an equation and solve** each of the following:

a 5 friends went to the movies. If the total cost of the tickets was $42.50, how much did each ticket cost?

_____

b Arthur had some apples, 4 bananas and 6 plums. If he had 13 pieces of fruit, how many apples did he have?

_____

c The chocolates were divided into 4 rows of 3 for each tray. If there are 60 chocolates, how many trays are needed?

_____

d The cost of the football was $25.50 plus a booking fee. If the total cost was $27.25, how much was the booking fee? _____

e The square had side lengths of 6 cm. What was the area of the square? _____

f In the garden, there are 5 rows of 7 tomato plants and 6 rows of lettuce plants. If there are 71 plants altogether, how many plants are in each row of lettuce?

_____

5 **Solve**: $Q + 9.8 = 12.7$ _____

6 **Solve**: $N = (6 \times 4) \div (8 \div 2)$ _____

7 **Solve**: $\frac{7}{10} + E = 1\frac{3}{10}$ _____

8 It rained a total of 6.3 cm over the weekend. If it rained 2.9 cm on Saturday, **write an equation and solve** to find Sunday's rainfall.

_____

9 I take a number, divide by the sum of seven and three, add fifty and subtract seven. If I end up at the number equal to nine multiplied by five, **what number** did I begin with?

_____

Binary numbers

1 Complete the **table**:

		2^4 (16)	2^3 (8)	2^2 (4)	2^1 (2)	2^0 (1)
a	5					
b	26					
c	17					
d	9					
e	11					
f	21					

2 Write each of the following numbers in **binary notation**:

a 3 _____
b 6 _____
c 10 _____
d 16 _____
e 15 _____
f 19 _____

3 Write each of the following binary numbers as **digits**:

a 111 _____
b 1001 _____
c 1110 _____
d 1100 _____
e 10 101 _____
f 11 101 _____

4 Write each of the following binary numbers as **digits and solve**:

a 111 + 101 = _____
b 1001 ÷ 11 = _____
c 10 101 − 1011 = _____
d 11 111 − 1101 = _____
e 1000 × 100 = _____
f 101 + 1010 = _____

5 Complete the **table**:

	2^4 (16)	2^3 (8)	2^2 (4)	2^1 (2)	2^0 (1)
2					

6 Write 23 in **binary notation**. _____

7 Write 11 000 as a **digit**. _____

8 Write 1100 ÷ 11 as **digits and solve** the equation.

_____

9 Leonardo Fibonacci discovered the following pattern. Complete the **next five terms**:

1, 1, 2, 3, 5, 8, 13, _____, _____, _____, _____, _____

Operations with money

1 Round each of the following to the **nearest 5 cents**:

a $4.73 _____
b $2.99 _____
c $81.67 _____
d $100.02 _____
e $3.44 _____
f $1010.89 _____

2 Find the **total cost** of:

a
$9.65
$2.35
+ $1.07

b
$6.75
$2.98
+ $4.55

c
$8.55
$6.32
+ $1.99

d
$4.20
− $3.98

e
$85.91
− $76.45

f
$112.62
− $ 98.85

3 Find:

a
$6.40
× 5

b
$9.29
× 7

c
$4.35
× 9

d
3) $8.55

e
5) $12.75

f
4) $9.56

4 Find the **change** from $14.50 if Jane spent:

a $9.85 _____
b $3.95 _____
c $4.20 _____
d $8.47 _____
e $12.79 _____
f $10.65 _____

5 Round $7.82 to the **nearest 5 cents**. _____

6 Find the **total cost** of:
$16.25
$ 9.47
+ $26.38

7 Find:
$7.65
× 3

8 Find the **change** from $14.50 if Jase spent $13.82.

_____

9 Find the **total cost** of 3 kg apples, 4 kg bananas and 2 kg oranges if: _____

Oranges	Bananas	Apples
$2.45/kg	$4.99/kg	$3.25/kg

Equations with numbers and words

1 Find the **value** of each letter:

a $d + d + d + d = 120$ _____

b $Y + 6 = 20$ _____

c $s \times s \times s = 27$ _____

d $T + T = 50$ _____

e $\frac{1}{4}$ of $W = 12$ _____

f $m^2 = 81$ _____

2 Write an **equation and solve**:

a multiply 5 by 100 and subtract six times seven

_____

b divide 49 by 7 and then add the product of eight and two

_____

c add 15 to nine, multiply by three and then divide by eight

_____

d to 11.9 add 6 before subtracting 9.3

_____

e square 5 and multiply by the product of 4 and 1

_____

f halve 22 and multiply by 12, and then add eight

_____

3 Find the **answers**:

a $(5 \times 3) + (7 \times 11) =$ _____

b $(10 \times 6) \div (5 \div 1) =$ _____

c $3 \times (1.5 + 2.6) =$ _____

d $49 \times 10 - (8 \times 12) =$ _____

e $15 \times 6 + 39 =$ _____

f $(100 - 70) \times 4 =$ _____

4 Complete the **table**:

Δ	2.3	6	7.8	9.05
□	1.7	4.2	d	6.11
Δ + □	a	c	11.3	15.16
Δ − □	b	1.8	e	f

5 Find the **value** of the letter p in:

$p - (15 \times 2) = 64$ _____

6 Write an **equation and solve**:

multiply 9 by 7 and subtract the product of 8 and 3

_____

7 Find the **answer**:

$7 + (3 \times 11) - 26 =$ _____

8 Complete the **table**:

Δ	4.6
□	1.07
Δ + □	a
Δ − □	b

9 **Match** the correct equation to the diagram:

A $24 - 3 \times 4 =$

B $9 \times 2 - 7 =$

C $2.5 \times 4 =$

D $7.3 + 3.7 =$

Substituting values

1 Write **true or false** for each of the given answers:

a $(8 \times \Delta) + 4 = 20$
$\Delta = 2$ _____

b $17 + (3 \times \Delta) = 34$
$\Delta = 5$ _____

c $(9 \div \Delta) \times 3 = 27$
$\Delta = 1$ _____

d $41 - (6 \times \Delta) = 18$
$\Delta = 4$ _____

e $(4 + \Delta) \times 2 = 40$
$\Delta = 18$ _____

f $41 - (6 \times \Delta) = 18$
$\Delta = 5$ _____

2 Find the **missing numbers** in each question:

a $\boxed{} - 42 = 35$

b $\boxed{} + 311 = 500$

c $4 \times \boxed{} = 64$

d $\boxed{} \div 3 = 60$

e $(5 \times \boxed{}) + 29 = 59$

f $(\boxed{} \div 5) + 10 = 20$

3 Find the **missing numbers** in each of the following:

a
$$\begin{array}{r} 607 \\ + \boxed{} \\ \hline 1389 \end{array}$$

b
$$\begin{array}{r} 4326 \\ - \boxed{} \\ \hline 3537 \end{array}$$

c
$$\begin{array}{r} 461 \\ + \boxed{} \\ \hline 3227 \end{array}$$

d
$$5\overline{)\boxed{1562}}$$

e
$$\begin{array}{r} 956 \\ + \boxed{} \\ \hline 1734 \end{array}$$

f
$$\begin{array}{r} 263\,900 \\ - \boxed{} \\ \hline 117\,400 \end{array}$$

4 **Find the number** if I:

a double it, then add 6. The answer is 50. _____

b multiply by 7, then subtract 15. The answer is 62. _____

c add 100, then divide by 5. The answer is 40. _____

d subtract 13, then multiply by 3. The answer is 237. _____

e halve it, then subtract 57. The answer is 50. _____

f divide it by 3, add 47. The answer is 69. _____

5 Write **true or false** for: $(7 + \Delta) \times 4 = 28$
$\Delta = 1$ _____

6 Find the **missing number** in: $(\boxed{} + 42) \div 2 = 45$

7 Find the **missing number**:
$$\begin{array}{r} 1234 \\ \times \boxed{} \\ \hline 9872 \end{array}$$

8 **Find the number** if I multiply it by itself, then add 9. The answer is 90. _____

9 **Find all the different pairs** of whole numbers which will make the number sentence true: $46 - 28 = \boxed{} \times \Delta$

_____

Number sentences (1)

1 Write **true or false** for each of the following:

a If $\Delta - 42 = 19$, then $\Delta = 61$ _____

b If $\Delta \times 3 + 4 = 24$, then $\Delta = 7$ _____

c If $100 \div \Delta + 5 = 30$, then $\Delta = 4$ _____

d If $4 \times \Delta + 1 = 2$, then $\Delta = \frac{1}{2}$ _____

e If $5 + (\Delta \times 2) = 38$, then $\Delta = 17$ _____

f If $20 - (5 \times \Delta) = 5$, then $\Delta = 3$ _____

2 Find the **value** of each of the missing numbers:

a $\boxed{} - 26 = 42$ b $\boxed{} \times 9 = 108$

c $\boxed{} \div 5 = 11$ d $84 \div \boxed{} = 21$

e $63 + \boxed{} = 147$ f $9 \times \boxed{} = 270$

3 Find the **value** of each of the missing numbers:

a $9 \times \boxed{} = 60 + 3$ b $24 \div 3 = 2 \times \boxed{}$

c $49 - \boxed{} = 5 \times 6$ d $56 + 12 = 80 - \boxed{}$

e $19 - \boxed{} = 18 \times 1$ f $400 \div 20 = 7 + \boxed{}$

4 **Check** if each of the following is correct:

a James bought 15 kg of cement at $9 per bag. He spent $145 in total. _____

b Yuko had 195 stamps in her collection, but after she gave 67 away she only had 128 left. _____

c Ajit divided 92 bottles into 4 crates. There were 24 bottles in each crate. _____

d Anthony shared 51 playing cards between 3 people. Each person had 17 cards. _____

e 84 treats were shared among 6 dogs. Each dog received 14 treats. _____

f There were 412 letters for delivery. By lunch time 256 had been delivered. 146 letters still needed to be delivered. _____

5 Write **true or false**: $(5 \times \Delta) \times 2 = 90$, then $\Delta = 9$ _____

6 Find the **value** of the missing number:

$47 - \boxed{} = 12$

7 Find the **value** of the missing number:

$12 \times \boxed{} = 100 - 4$

8 **Check** if the statement is correct:

The pet shop owner sold 79 of 146 goldfish. This left 65 goldfish. _____

9 **What is my number?**

If you divide me by 25 and multiply by 20, the answer is 80. _____

Number sentences (2)

1 Write **true or false** for each of the following statements:

a $476 + \Delta = 500$ $\Delta = 24$ _____

b $150 \div \Delta = 25$ $\Delta = 8$ _____

c $\Delta \times 3 = 4.5$ $\Delta = 1.5$ _____

d $\Delta - 246 = 375$ $\Delta = 621$ _____

e $20 - \Delta = 18.2$ $\Delta = 2.8$ _____

f $1\,096 + \Delta = 2\,045$ $\Delta = 959$ _____

2 Find the **value of** * in each of the following:

a $* \div 3 = 1.1$ _____   b $* - \frac{3}{4} = \frac{3}{4}$

c $14 + * = 16.2$ _____   d $* - 6 = \frac{3}{8}$

e $9 \times * = 9.9$ _____   f $6 + * = 11.7$

3 **Write an expression** if * is the missing number:

a 12 less than the number _____

b one third of the number _____

c the square of the number _____

d 9 times the number _____

e 76 more than the number _____

f the sum of 11 and the number _____

4 **Construct a number sentence** for each of the problems and **solve**:

a the product of 8 and a number is 24

_____

b the square of a number is 100

_____

c the sum of a number and 6 is 14

_____

d the difference between a number and 21 is 35

_____

e the quotient of a number and 4 is 12

_____

f a number is decreased by 17 to give 45

_____

5 Write **true or false** for: $9 \times \Delta = 9$, $\Delta = 1$ _____

6 Find the **value of** * in: $6 \times * = 3$ _____

7 **Write an expression** if * is the missing number:

40 less than the number. _____

8 **Construct a number sentence** for the statement and **solve**: a number is increased by 72 to give 95.

_____

9 **Create your own number sentences** by placing a number in each box:

a $\boxed{} - \boxed{} = \boxed{} \times \boxed{}$

b $\boxed{} + \boxed{} = \boxed{} - \boxed{} \div \boxed{}$

Number sentences (3)

1 Find the **missing number** for each of the following:

a　$7 \times \boxed{} = 84$

b　$\boxed{} + 215 = 639$

c　$190 - \boxed{} = 74$

d　$200 \div \boxed{} = 5$

e　$46 \times \boxed{} = 23$

f　$9 \times \boxed{} = 810$

2 Write **true or false** for each of the following:

a　$(2 \times \Delta) + 10 = 18$,　　　$\Delta = 4$ _____

b　$(20 - \Delta) \times 3 = 12$,　　　$\Delta = 14$ _____

c　$(\Delta \times 6) - 11 = 49$,　　　$\Delta = 9$ _____

d　$(10 \div \Delta) \times 7 = 14$,　　　$\Delta = 5$ _____

e　$(48 - \Delta) + 2 = 20$,　　　$\Delta = 30$ _____

f　$(90 + \Delta) \times \frac{1}{2} = 20$,　　　$\Delta = 10$ _____

3 **Construct a number sentence and solve** it for each of the following:

a　a number is increased by 10, then multiplied by 6 to equal 600 _____

b　a number is decreased by 5, then divided by 10 to equal 50 _____

c　a number is divided by 11, then 6 is added to give 15 _____

d　a number is multiplied by 7, then 40 is added to give 96 _____

e　a number is squared, then 9 is added to give 90 _____

f　102 less than a number, divided by 4 gives 24 _____

4 Find the **missing numbers**:

a　$38 + 17 = 55 \div \boxed{}$　　　b　$3 \times 9 = 19 + \boxed{}$

c　$49 \div 7 = 7 \times \boxed{}$　　　d　$5 \times \boxed{} = 26 + 14$

e　$11 - \boxed{} = 21 \div 3$　　　f　$39 + \boxed{} = 106 - 35$

5 Find the **missing number** for: $\boxed{} - 602 = 225$

6 Write true or false for: $(4 \times \boxed{}) - 17 = 27$, $\boxed{} = 11$

_____

7 **Construct a number sentence and solve** it for:

67 is added to a number, then it is divided by 4 to give 40 _____

8 Find the **missing number** in: $49 - \boxed{} = 4 \times 7$

9 Find the **missing numbers**:

a　$4.5 + \boxed{} = 13.6$　　　b　$3.9 \div \boxed{} = 1.3$

c　$1.2 \times \boxed{} = 4.8$　　　d　$\boxed{} - 6.3 = 2.9$

Square and cube numbers

1 **Complete**:

a　$9 \times 9 =$ _____

b　$20 \times 20 =$ _____

c　$14 \times 14 =$ _____

d　$3 \times 3 \times 3 =$ _____

e　$10 \times 10 \times 10 =$ _____

f　$4 \times 4 \times 4 =$ _____

2 **Complete**:

a　$8^2 =$ _____

b　$6^3 =$ _____

c　$7^2 =$ _____

d　$5^3 =$ _____

e　$12^2 =$ _____

f　$20^3 =$ _____

3 Complete the **table**:

Number	a 1	b 2	c 3	d 4	e 5	f 6
Squared						
Cubed						

4 **Complete**:

a　$4^2 + 3^2 =$ _____

b　$2^2 - 1^2 =$ _____

c　$9^2 - 5^2 =$ _____

d　$4^2 + 5^2 =$ _____

e　$12^2 - 8^2 =$ _____

f　$7^2 + 1^2 + 3^2 =$ _____

5 **Complete**: $6 \times 6 \times 6 =$ _____

6 **Complete**: $30^2 =$ _____

7 Complete the **table**:

Number	7
Squared	
Cubed	

8 **Find**: $11^2 - (4^2 + 2^2) =$ _____

9 **Complete** the following to **discover the pattern**:

a　$2^2 - 1^2 =$ _____

b　$3^2 - 2^2 =$ _____

c　$4^2 - 3^2 =$ _____

d　$5^2 - 4^2 =$ _____

e　$6^2 - 5^2 =$ _____

f　$7^2 - 6^2 =$ _____

pattern: _____

Working with numbers

1 Use **< or > or =** to make the number statements true:

a 12 000 100 ☐ 1 210 200

b 20 000 000 + 15 000 ☐ 20 000 + 15 000 000

c 9 637 210 ☐ 9 367 219

d 750 000 ☐ 75 000 × 100

e 10 000 × 100 ☐ 1 000 000

f 23 000 461 ☐ 2 397 246

2 Write the whole number:

a **immediately after** 46 201 499 _____

b 1000 **greater than** 46 789 208 _____

c 5 **more than** 21 698 _____

d **immediately before** 400 000 _____

e 10 000 **less than** 245 306 200 _____

f 1 000 000 **more than** 26 486 295 _____

3 A small four-wheel drive has a service every 10 000 km. **Record the odometer readings** for when the next two services are required for each of the different coloured four-wheel drives:

a yellow: 11 428 _____ and _____

b red: 4986 _____ and _____

c green: 21 489 _____ and _____

d blue: 46 725 _____ and _____

e black: 60 921 _____ and _____

f white: 90 675 _____ and _____

4 Complete the next line of the **tree diagram** for each of the following:

a   400   b   1000   c   256
    200 × 2   250 × 4   8 × 32
    ☐☐☐☐   ☐☐☐☐   ☐☐☐☐

d   96   e   450   f   1400
    6 × 16   18 × 25   50 × 28
    ☐☐☐☐   ☐☐☐☐   ☐☐☐☐

5 Use **< or > or =** to make the number statement true:

50 000 + 1 000 000 + 4000 ☐ 1 000 000 + 40 000 + 5000

6 Write the number **immediately before** 29 000 000

_____

7 **Write the odometer readings** for the next two services for the beige four-wheel drive:

100 052 _____ and _____

8 Complete the next line of the **tree diagram**:   81 000
                                                      900 × 90
                                                      ☐☐☐☐

9 In the number 4 683 250.07, which digit:

a has the **greatest value**? _____

b **will change** when 1 million is added? _____

c means $\frac{7}{100}$? _____

Change of units

1 Change each of the following lengths to **metres**:

a 96 cm _____

b 20 km _____

c 5000 cm _____

d 10 000 mm _____

e 6.12 km _____

f 980 mm _____

2 Change each of the following weights to **kilograms**:

a 4000 g _____

b 90 g _____

c 4 tonnes _____

d 7.2 tonnes _____

e 2967 g _____

f 0.8 tonnes _____

3 Change each of the following times to **minutes**:

a 6 hours _____

b 420 s _____

c $3\frac{1}{4}$ days _____

d 24 hours _____

e 5400 s _____

f 5 days _____

4 Complete each number statement with **<, > or =**:

a 460 min ☐ 20 000 s   b 600 cm ☐ 0.6 km

c 0.3 tonnes ☐ 360 kg   d 4500 mL ☐ 5 L

e 2 days ☐ 3000 min   f 0.9 L ☐ 950 mL

5 Change the length 4600 mm to **metres**. _____

6 Change the weight 650 g to **kilograms**. _____

7 Change the time 1500 s to **minutes**. _____

8 Complete with **<, > or =**

4 tonnes ☐ 46 000 kg

9 **Circle any combination of the weights** to balance the scales:

1 kg	200 g	400 g
200 g	50 g	100 g
5 kg	5 g	1 tonne

Negative numbers

1 Place each set of numbers in **ascending order**:

a 3, –3, 1, –5, 0, –2, –1, 4, 6

_____

b –10, I, –5, 0, 2, 5, –3, –1, 6

_____

c 2, 4, 0, –2, –4, –6, 6

_____

d –1, –3, 5, 0, 3, –5, 1, 7

_____

e –20, 10, 20, –30, –15, –10, 0, 5

_____

f 19, 18, 14, 13, 0, –10, 15, –15, –13, –6

_____

2 On June 30th the temperature was 5°C. What would the **temperature** be on July 1st if it was:

a 4 degrees warmer? _____

b 5 degrees cooler? _____

c 2 degrees colder? _____

d 10 degrees warmer? _____

e 7 degrees colder? _____

f 11 degrees colder? _____

3 Adam had $25 in his bank account. What would his **bank balance** be if he wrote a cheque for:

a $20? _____ b $17? _____ c $25? _____

d $30? _____ e $49? _____ f $82? _____

4 Display the following equations on the **number lines**:

a $7 + 3 - 6 - 7 - 2 =$ <————————>

b $10 - 5 - 2 - 4 + 6 =$ <————————>

c $0 - 3 + 2 + 9 - 1 =$ <————————>

d $-4 + 2 - 6 + 7 - 1 =$ <————————>

e $-2 + 2 - 3 - 4 + 1 =$ <————————>

f $5 - 3 + 2 - 6 - 5 =$ <————————>

5 Place the set of numbers in **ascending order**:

25, –21, –23, 20, 0, 10, –14, –11

_____

6 On June 30th the temperature was 5°C. What would the **temperature** be on July 1st if it was 9 degrees colder?

_____

7 Adam had $25 in his bank account. What would his **bank balance** be if he wrote a cheque for $53?

_____

8 Display $-5 + 7 - 2 + 3 + 0 =$ on the **number line**:

<————————————————>

9 **Solve** the number sentences:

a $-10 + 10 - 7 + 7 + 3 =$ _____

b $0 - 2 + 5 + 6 =$ _____

c $-2 + 3 - 8 - 2 + 1 =$ _____

d $5 - 2 - 6 + 4 + 1 =$ _____

Prime and composite numbers

1 Identify which of the following are **prime** (p) and which are **composite** (c) numbers:

a 91 _____ b 63 _____ c 13 _____

d 71 _____ e 58 _____ f 83 _____

2 Circle the numbers in the grid which are **divisible** by the given divisor:

	Divisor						
a	2	16	38	91	156	344	1029
b	3	21	54	80	122	225	1471
c	4	40	88	102	164	490	1562
d	5	60	76	95	120	581	1247
e	6	72	90	110	149	684	1436
f	7	77	105	149	196	485	1260

3 Find **two prime numbers** which add to give:

a 78 _____

b 24 _____

c 100 _____

d 60 _____

e 30 _____

f 90 _____

4 Write all of the **composite numbers** between:

a 5 and 15 _____

b 17 and 24 _____

c 50 and 60 _____

d 80 and 100 _____

e 115 and 125 _____

f 150 and 160 _____

5 Identify if 93 is a **prime** (p) or a **composite** (c) number.

_____

6 Circle the numbers on the grid which are **divisible** by:

Divisor						
8	56	68	106	248	1480	1560

7 Find **two prime numbers** which add to give 19.

_____

8 Write all the **composite numbers** between 190 and 210.

_____

_____

9 List all the **prime numbers** less than 50.

_____

_____

Fractions

1 **What part** of each of the following shapes has been shaded?

a _____   b _____   c _____

d _____   e _____   f _____

2 **What part** of each shape in question 1 has not been shaded?

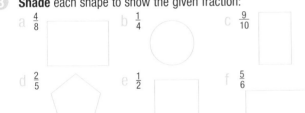

a _____   b _____   c _____

d _____   e _____   f _____

3 **Shade** each shape to show the given fraction:

a $\frac{4}{8}$ b $\frac{1}{4}$ c $\frac{9}{10}$

d $\frac{2}{5}$ e $\frac{1}{2}$ f $\frac{5}{6}$

4 **What part** of each group has been shaded?

a   b   c

_____   _____   _____

d   e   f

_____   _____   _____

5 **What part** of ⬠ is shaded? _____

6 **What part** of ⬠ is not shaded? _____

7 **Shade** ◯ to show $\frac{2}{3}$.

8 **What part** of ▦ has been shaded? _____

9 If $\frac{3}{4}$ of a set of pencils are broken, and there are 24 pencils in a set, **how many** pencils are not broken?

_____

Calculator – division

1 Use the array to **find** the fractions of 24.

a $\frac{1}{4}$ of 24 _____   b $\frac{1}{6}$ of 24 _____

c $\frac{1}{8}$ of 24 _____   d $\frac{1}{3}$ of 24 _____

e $\frac{1}{12}$ of 24 _____   f $\frac{1}{2}$ of 24 _____

2 **Find** and shade the fraction of each group:

a   b   c

$\frac{1}{3}$ of 6 = _____ $\frac{1}{4}$ of 12 = _____ $\frac{1}{5}$ of 10 = _____

d   e   f

$\frac{1}{2}$ of 8 = _____ $\frac{1}{6}$ of 18 = _____ $\frac{1}{4}$ of 20 = _____

3 **Find** the fraction of each group:

a $\frac{1}{5}$ of 55 = _____   b $\frac{1}{4}$ of 48 = _____

c $\frac{1}{10}$ of 110 = _____   d $\frac{1}{3}$ of 60 = _____

e $\frac{1}{8}$ of 32 = _____   f $\frac{1}{6}$ of 36 = _____

4 **Solve**:

a Abdullah had 10 postcards and sent $\frac{1}{2}$. How many postcards did he send? _____

b Amy had 42 bears. She gave $\frac{1}{6}$ away. How many bears did she have left? _____

c George had 90 marbles but lost $\frac{1}{10}$ of them through a hole in the bag. How many did he lose? _____

d The car yard had 120 cars. $\frac{1}{6}$ were sold. How many cars were sold? _____

e Di has 64 CD-ROMs but $\frac{1}{8}$ were used. How many were blank? _____

f Molly had a packet of 20 stamps. She used $\frac{1}{5}$ of them. How many stamps did she have left? _____

5 Use the array in question 1 to **find** $\frac{1}{24}$ of 24.

6 **Find** and shade $\frac{1}{4}$ of 16. _____

7 **Find** $\frac{1}{2}$ of 48. _____

8 There were 30 balls that could be used at lunchtime. If $\frac{1}{5}$ had been borrowed, **how many** were left?

_____

9 **Find**:

a $\frac{1}{3}$ of 180 _____   b $\frac{1}{4}$ of 400 _____

c $\frac{1}{6}$ of 240 _____   d $\frac{1}{5}$ of 125 _____

Fraction of a group (2)

1 **Find** the fractions of:

a $\frac{1}{2}$ of 8 = _____   b $\frac{3}{4}$ of 100 = _____

c $\frac{2}{5}$ of 20 = _____   d $\frac{3}{8}$ of 32 = _____

e $\frac{3}{5}$ of 80 = _____   f $\frac{3}{4}$ of 8 = _____

2 Find the **number** of balls for each fraction:

a $\frac{1}{3}$ = _____   b $\frac{1}{4}$ = _____

c $\frac{1}{2}$ = _____   d $\frac{1}{6}$ = _____

e $\frac{3}{4}$ = _____   f $\frac{4}{6}$ = _____

3 **Solve**:

a Ann had 50 fan letters and she replied to $\frac{4}{5}$ of them. How many did she still have to reply to? _____

b Ramjan recorded 20 songs, but only $\frac{2}{5}$ of them were used on the album. How many songs weren't used?

_____

c There were 24 DVDs in a TV series set. Daniel had collected $\frac{5}{8}$ of them. How many more DVDs did he need for the set? _____

d Antoine had 130 emails. She replied to $\frac{7}{10}$ of them. How many did she reply to? _____

e A concert special on TV went for $\frac{7}{12}$ of an hour. How many minutes did it go for? _____

f A mobile phone ring lasts for $\frac{3}{5}$ of 25 seconds. How many seconds does the phone ring? _____

4 **Draw a diagram** for each of the following and solve:

a $\frac{3}{5}$ of 15

b $\frac{5}{12}$ of 36

c $\frac{4}{10}$ of 40

d $\frac{2}{3}$ of 18

e $\frac{3}{4}$ of 24

f $\frac{4}{9}$ of 90

5 **Find** $\frac{2}{3}$ of 9. _____

6 Find the **number** of $\frac{2}{3}$ of the balls in question 2. _____

7 **Solve**: Jacinta won $\frac{2}{5}$ of $50. How much did she win?

_____

8 **Draw a diagram** to show $\frac{7}{8}$ of 16 and solve.

9 On the test, Mark said 4 of 90 was 74. **Was he right?** Explain. _____

Equivalent fractions (1)

1 Complete to make each of the following **equivalent fractions**:

a $\frac{1\,(\times 2)}{4\,(\times 2)}=\frac{\square}{\square}$ b $\frac{1\,(\times 2)}{3\,(\times 2)}=\frac{\square}{\square}$

c $\frac{5\,(\times 2)}{6\,(\times 2)}=\frac{\square}{\square}$ d $\frac{1\,(\times 2)}{2\,(\times 2)}=\frac{\square}{\square}$

e $\frac{2\,(\times 2)}{3\,(\times 2)}=\frac{\square}{\square}$ f $\frac{3\,(\times 2)}{10\,(\times 2)}=\frac{\square}{\square}$

2 Complete the **equivalent fractions** for:

a $\frac{1}{2}=\frac{\square}{8}$ b $\frac{2}{4}=\frac{\square}{8}$ c $\frac{2}{5}=\frac{\square}{10}$

d $\frac{1}{2}=\frac{\square}{4}$ e $\frac{2}{3}=\frac{\square}{6}$ f $\frac{2}{3}=\frac{\square}{9}$

3 Complete each of the following to make **equivalent**:

a $\frac{1}{3}=\frac{4}{\square}$ b $\frac{2}{5}=\frac{4}{\square}$ c $\frac{2}{5}=\frac{10}{\square}$

d $\frac{1}{2}=\frac{4}{\square}$ e $\frac{2}{3}=\frac{6}{\square}$ f $\frac{3}{5}=\frac{9}{\square}$

4 Write **true or false** for each of the following:

a $\frac{2}{8}=\frac{1}{4}$ _____

b $\frac{8}{10}=\frac{4}{5}$ _____

c $\frac{5}{8}=\frac{10}{12}$ _____

d $\frac{2}{3}>\frac{3}{4}$ _____

e $\frac{5}{8}<\frac{3}{4}$ _____

f $\frac{1}{4}<\frac{6}{12}$ _____

5 Complete to make the **equivalent fraction**:

$$\frac{5\,(\times 2)}{8\,(\times 2)}=\frac{\square}{\square}$$

6 Complete the **equivalent fraction** for:

$$\frac{3}{4}=\frac{\square}{12}$$

7 Complete to make **equivalent**: $\frac{4}{5}=\frac{8}{\square}$

8 Write **true or false** for: $\frac{2}{3}>\frac{4}{9}$

9 Find the **equivalent fractions** for $\frac{5}{10}$ and $\frac{3}{8}$ and circle the **larger fraction**.

Equivalent fractions (2)

1 Complete each of the **equivalent fractions**:

a $\dfrac{3}{4}\dfrac{(\times\,2)}{(\times\,2)}=\dfrac{\square}{\square}$ 　　　b $\dfrac{1}{2}\dfrac{(\times\,4)}{(\times\,4)}=\dfrac{\square}{\square}$

c $\dfrac{1}{4}\dfrac{(\times\,3)}{(\times\,3)}=\dfrac{\square}{\square}$ 　　　d $\dfrac{1}{10}\dfrac{(\times\,5)}{(\times\,5)}=\dfrac{\square}{\square}$

e $\dfrac{2}{5}\dfrac{(\times\,3)}{(\times\,3)}=\dfrac{\square}{\square}$ 　　　f $\dfrac{2}{3}\dfrac{(\times\,6)}{(\times\,6)}=\dfrac{\square}{\square}$

2 Multiply both the numerator and denominator by 3 to find the **equivalent fraction**:

a $\dfrac{1}{4}=$ 　　　b $\dfrac{1}{5}=$ 　　　c $\dfrac{2}{3}=$

d $\dfrac{4}{5}=$ 　　　e $\dfrac{3}{4}=$ 　　　f $\dfrac{5}{6}=$

3 **What number** has been used to multiply the numerator and the denominator in each of the following pairs of equivalent fractions?

a $\dfrac{1}{6}=\dfrac{2}{12}$ _____ 　b $\dfrac{1}{3}=\dfrac{4}{12}$ _____ 　c $\dfrac{1}{5}=\dfrac{2}{10}$ _____

d $\dfrac{3}{4}=\dfrac{6}{8}$ _____ 　e $\dfrac{1}{4}=\dfrac{3}{12}$ _____ 　f $\dfrac{2}{3}=\dfrac{4}{6}$ _____

4 **Continue** the equivalent fraction patterns:

a $\dfrac{1}{2}=\dfrac{\square}{4}=\dfrac{\square}{6}=\dfrac{\square}{8}$ 　　b $\dfrac{1}{4}=\dfrac{\square}{8}=\dfrac{\square}{12}=\dfrac{\square}{16}$

c $\dfrac{1}{3}=\dfrac{\square}{6}=\dfrac{\square}{9}=\dfrac{\square}{12}$ 　　d $\dfrac{1}{5}=\dfrac{\square}{10}=\dfrac{\square}{15}=\dfrac{\square}{20}$

e $\dfrac{1}{6}=\dfrac{\square}{12}=\dfrac{\square}{18}=\dfrac{\square}{24}$ 　　f $\dfrac{1}{8}=\dfrac{\square}{16}=\dfrac{\square}{24}=\dfrac{\square}{32}$

5 Complete the **equivalent fraction**: $\dfrac{3}{8}\dfrac{(\times\,2)}{(\times\,2)}=\dfrac{\square}{\square}$

6 Multiply both the numerator and denominator by 3 to find the **equivalent fraction** of: $\dfrac{5}{8}$ _____

7 **What number** has been used to multiply the numerator and denominator? $\dfrac{5}{6}=\dfrac{10}{12}$ _____

8 **Continue** the equivalent fraction pattern:

$\dfrac{1}{10}=\dfrac{\square}{20}=\dfrac{\square}{30}=\dfrac{\square}{40}$

9 Write as many different **equivalent fractions** as you can for $\dfrac{3}{12}$.

Equivalent fractions (3)

1 Complete the **equivalent fractions**:

a $\dfrac{2}{3}\dfrac{(\times\,4)}{(\times\,4)}=\dfrac{\square}{\square}$ 　　　b $\dfrac{5}{6}\dfrac{(\times\,2)}{(\times\,2)}=\dfrac{\square}{\square}$

c $\dfrac{1}{3}\dfrac{(\times\,5)}{(\times\,5)}=\dfrac{\square}{\square}$ 　　　d $\dfrac{1}{6}\dfrac{(\times\,10)}{(\times\,10)}=\dfrac{\square}{\square}$

e $\dfrac{3}{4}\dfrac{(\times\,3)}{(\times\,3)}=\dfrac{\square}{\square}$ 　　　f $\dfrac{4}{5}\dfrac{(\times\,6)}{(\times\,6)}=\dfrac{\square}{\square}$

2 Complete the **equivalent fractions**:

a $\dfrac{2}{4}\dfrac{(\div\,2)}{(\div\,2)}=\dfrac{\square}{\square}$ 　　　b $\dfrac{5}{10}\dfrac{(\div\,5)}{(\div\,5)}=\dfrac{\square}{\square}$

c $\dfrac{6}{8}\dfrac{(\div\,2)}{(\div\,2)}=\dfrac{\square}{\square}$ 　　　d $\dfrac{9}{15}\dfrac{(\div\,3)}{(\div\,3)}=\dfrac{\square}{\square}$

e $\dfrac{10}{15}\dfrac{(\div\,10)}{(\div\,5)}=\dfrac{\square}{\square}$ 　　　f $\dfrac{12}{24}\dfrac{(\div\,6)}{(\div\,6)}=\dfrac{\square}{\square}$

3 Complete with **< or > or =** to make the statements true:

a $\dfrac{1}{4}\,\square\,\dfrac{3}{8}$ 　　b $\dfrac{1}{8}\,\square\,\dfrac{1}{10}$ 　　c $\dfrac{3}{5}\,\square\,\dfrac{3}{4}$

d $\dfrac{1}{5}\,\square\,\dfrac{1}{4}$ 　　e $\dfrac{3}{4}\,\square\,\dfrac{6}{8}$ 　　f $\dfrac{4}{6}\,\square\,\dfrac{6}{9}$

4 Reduce each of the fractions to their **simplest form**:

a $\dfrac{20}{30}=$ 　　b $\dfrac{8}{12}=$ 　　c $\dfrac{4}{16}=$

d $\dfrac{15}{20}=$ 　　e $\dfrac{6}{8}=$ 　　f $\dfrac{3}{24}=$

5 Complete the **equivalent fraction**:

$\dfrac{2}{3}\dfrac{(\times\,8)}{(\times\,8)}=\dfrac{\square}{\square}$

6 Complete the **equivalent fraction**:

$\dfrac{10}{12}\dfrac{(\div\,2)}{(\div\,2)}=\dfrac{\square}{\square}$

7 Complete with **< or > or =** to make the statement true:
$\dfrac{16}{24}\,\square\,\dfrac{2}{3}$

8 Reduce $\dfrac{50}{60}$ to its **simplest form**.

9 Taz earns \$60 a month in pocket money. Calculate the **fraction of \$60** he spends on each item, and then reduce it to its **simplest form**:

Item	Amount	Fraction	Simplest form
movies	\$12		
food/drink	\$15		
bus fares	\$9		
books	\$10		
go-karts	\$14		

Improper fractions and mixed numbers

1 Write an **improper fraction and a mixed number** for the shaded part of each diagram:

a 　　　　　 ____ , ____

b 　　　　　 ____ , ____

c 　　　　　 ____ , ____

d 　　　　　 ____ , ____

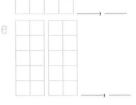
e 　　　　　 ____ , ____

f 　　　　　 ____ , ____

2 Write the **mixed number** for:

a $\frac{9}{5}$ ____　　　b $\frac{8}{3}$ ____　　　c $\frac{5}{2}$ ____

d $\frac{8}{5}$ ____　　　e $\frac{4}{3}$ ____　　　f $\frac{10}{6}$ ____

3 Write the **improper fraction** for:

a $2\frac{1}{2}$ ____　　　b $1\frac{2}{5}$ ____　　　c $2\frac{1}{3}$ ____

d $4\frac{3}{5}$ ____　　　e $2\frac{5}{8}$ ____　　　f $4\frac{2}{5}$ ____

4 Write the **mixed number** for:

a $\frac{15}{8}$ ____　　　b $\frac{21}{10}$ ____　　　c $\frac{11}{3}$ ____

d $\frac{17}{10}$ ____　　　e $\frac{15}{6}$ ____　　　f $\frac{19}{5}$ ____

5 Write an **improper fraction and a mixed number** for the shaded part of the diagram:

____ , ____

6 Write the **mixed number** for $\frac{6}{4}$ ____

7 Write the **improper fraction** for $4\frac{2}{3}$ ____

8 Write the **mixed number** for $\frac{26}{10}$ ____

9 Order the fractions from **smallest to largest**, writing them in the same format first:

$2\frac{3}{4}$, $\frac{16}{4}$, $\frac{1}{4}$, $\frac{14}{4}$, 3, $\frac{10}{4}$

Using fractions

1 Write **true or false** for each of the following:

a $\frac{4}{3} < \frac{5}{6}$ ____　　　b $\frac{11}{12} < \frac{5}{6}$ ____

c $\frac{3}{6} < \frac{2}{3}$ ____　　　d $\frac{7}{10} > \frac{3}{5}$ ____

e $\frac{9}{10} > \frac{4}{5}$ ____　　　f $\frac{5}{6} > \frac{2}{3}$ ____

2 Complete the **additions**:

a $\frac{2}{5} + \frac{1}{10} =$ 　　　　b $\frac{3}{4} + \frac{3}{8} =$

$\frac{\square}{10} + \frac{\square}{10} =$ ____　　$\frac{\square}{8} + \frac{\square}{8} =$ ____

c $\frac{1}{2} + \frac{3}{10} =$ 　　　d $\frac{7}{10} + \frac{2}{3} =$

e $\frac{3}{5} + \frac{3}{10} =$ 　　　f $\frac{1}{4} + \frac{5}{8} =$

3 Complete the **subtractions**:

a $\frac{5}{6} - \frac{1}{3} =$ 　　　　b $\frac{7}{10} - \frac{2}{5} =$

$\frac{\square}{6} - \frac{\square}{6} =$ ____　　$\frac{\square}{10} - \frac{\square}{10} =$ ____

c $\frac{7}{8} - \frac{1}{2} =$ 　　　d $\frac{6}{12} - \frac{1}{3} =$

e $\frac{3}{4} - \frac{1}{2} =$ 　　　f $\frac{1}{2} - \frac{1}{10} =$

4 Complete the **multiplications**:

a $2 \times \frac{3}{5} =$ 　　b $4 \times \frac{1}{3} =$ 　　c $2 \times \frac{5}{12} =$

d $3 \times \frac{6}{10} =$ 　　e $5 \times \frac{3}{4} =$ 　　f $4 \times \frac{3}{8} =$

5 Write **true or false** for: $\frac{7}{8} < \frac{3}{4}$ ____

6 **Complete:** $\frac{3}{5} + \frac{1}{2} =$

7 **Complete:** $\frac{9}{12} - \frac{2}{6} =$

8 **Complete:** $3 \times \frac{2}{5} =$

9 Order the following sets of fractions from **smallest to largest**:

one sixth, $\frac{4}{3}$, two and one third, $\frac{2}{6}$, two thirds, 1

Excel Start Up Maths Year 6
☞ Answers on page 13

Fraction addition

1 **Complete** (simplify if possible):

a $\frac{7}{12} + \frac{3}{12} =$ _____   b $\frac{2}{9} + \frac{4}{9} =$ _____   c $\frac{5}{8} + \frac{1}{8} =$ _____

d $\frac{1}{4} + \frac{1}{4} =$ _____   e $\frac{2}{5} + \frac{1}{5} =$ _____   f $\frac{3}{10} + \frac{5}{10} =$ _____

2 **Add** the following fractions using the number line:

```
|----------|----------|---------->
0         10          2
          10
```

a $\frac{8}{10} + \frac{5}{10} =$ _____   b $\frac{6}{10} + \frac{9}{10} =$ _____

c $\frac{11}{10} + \frac{6}{10} =$ _____   d $\frac{5}{10} + \frac{7}{10} =$ _____

e $\frac{8}{10} + \frac{7}{10} =$ _____   f $\frac{14}{10} + \frac{5}{10} =$ _____

3 **Add** the fraction and then convert the answers to a **mixed number**:

a $\frac{3}{5} + \frac{4}{5} =$ b $\frac{7}{8} + \frac{7}{8} =$

c $\frac{3}{4} + \frac{3}{4} =$ d $\frac{6}{10} + \frac{7}{10} + \frac{4}{10} =$

e $\frac{3}{4} + \frac{3}{4} + \frac{1}{4} =$ f $\frac{3}{5} + \frac{4}{5} + \frac{4}{5} =$

4 Rewrite the fractions with **common denominators** before **adding**:

a $\frac{1}{4} + \frac{7}{12} =$ b $\frac{1}{2} + \frac{3}{10} =$

c $\frac{1}{6} + \frac{2}{3} =$ d $\frac{3}{10} + \frac{4}{5} =$

e $\frac{1}{6} + \frac{2}{3} =$ f $\frac{1}{3} + \frac{2}{9} =$

5 **Complete** (simplifying if possible): $\frac{3}{8} + \frac{3}{8} =$

6 **Add** the fractions using the number line of question 2:
$\frac{9}{10} + \frac{4}{10} =$

7 **Add** and then convert the answer to a **mixed number**:
$\frac{5}{6} + \frac{4}{6} =$

8 Rewrite the fractions with a **common denominator** before **adding**:
$\frac{1}{8} + \frac{3}{4} =$

9 To follow the recipe, Li has to add $\frac{1}{4}$ of a cup of 3 different flours and $\frac{1}{2}$ a cup of sugar. **How much** flour and sugar does Li add? _____

Fraction subtraction

1 Reduce the fractions to the **simplest form**:

a $\frac{20}{30}$ _____   b $\frac{8}{12}$ _____   c $\frac{6}{8}$ _____

d $\frac{14}{16}$ _____   e $\frac{2}{10}$ _____   f $\frac{8}{24}$ _____

2 Complete the **subtractions**:

a $\frac{8}{10} - \frac{5}{10} =$ _____   b $\frac{11}{12} - \frac{9}{12} =$ _____

c $\frac{3}{8} - \frac{1}{8} =$ _____   d $\frac{5}{6} - \frac{4}{6} =$ _____

e $\frac{3}{4} - \frac{1}{4} =$ _____   f $\frac{7}{9} - \frac{4}{9} =$ _____

3 Complete the **subtractions** by rewriting the fractions with **common denominators** first:

a $\frac{9}{10} - \frac{2}{5} =$ b $\frac{7}{8} - \frac{1}{4} =$

c $\frac{5}{6} - \frac{2}{3} =$ d $\frac{4}{5} - \frac{1}{10} =$

e $\frac{1}{6} - \frac{2}{3} =$ f $\frac{5}{6} - \frac{3}{12} =$

4 Find the **difference** between:

a $\frac{6}{10}$ and $\frac{2}{5}$ _____

b $\frac{7}{12}$ and $\frac{3}{6}$ _____

c $\frac{4}{9}$ and $\frac{2}{3}$ _____

d $\frac{8}{10}$ and $\frac{2}{5}$ _____

e $\frac{1}{4}$ and $\frac{3}{8}$ _____

f $\frac{1}{2}$ and $\frac{4}{6}$ _____

5 Reduce the fraction $\frac{90}{100}$ to its **simplest form**. _____

6 Complete the **subtraction**:
$\frac{4}{5} - \frac{1}{5} =$

7 Complete the **subtraction** by rewriting the fractions with **common denominators** first:
$\frac{5}{8} - \frac{1}{2} =$

8 Find the **difference** between: $\frac{7}{8}$ and $\frac{3}{4}$

9 There were 7 slices out of 10 of the birthday cake left. If 3 people each took 1 slice and 1 person took $\frac{1}{5}$, what fraction of the cake **was left**? _____

Fraction addition and subtraction

1 Write the **improper fraction** for:

   a $1\frac{6}{10}$ _____   b $2\frac{1}{4}$ _____

   c $3\frac{2}{3}$ _____   d $4\frac{5}{8}$ _____

   e $7\frac{1}{2}$ _____   f $2\frac{4}{5}$ _____

2 Write the **mixed number** for:

   a $\frac{4}{3}$ _____   b $\frac{7}{5}$ _____

   c $\frac{21}{10}$ _____   d $\frac{8}{4}$ _____

   e $\frac{17}{8}$ _____   f $\frac{14}{6}$ _____

3 **Add** the following fractions:

   a $\frac{1}{4} + \frac{1}{2} =$ _____   b $\frac{2}{3} + \frac{4}{6} =$ _____

   c $\frac{3}{8} + \frac{1}{4} =$ _____   d $\frac{7}{10} + \frac{2}{5} =$ _____

   e $\frac{1}{9} + \frac{2}{3} =$ _____   f $\frac{1}{3} + \frac{5}{12} =$ _____

4 **Subtract** the following fractions:

   a $\frac{5}{8} - \frac{1}{4} =$ _____   b $\frac{9}{10} - \frac{4}{5} =$ _____

   c $\frac{5}{6} - \frac{2}{3} =$ _____   d $\frac{11}{12} - \frac{3}{4} =$ _____

   e $\frac{4}{5} - \frac{1}{2} =$ _____   f $\frac{7}{9} - \frac{2}{3} =$ _____

5 Write the **improper fraction** for: $8\frac{1}{5}$

6 Write the **mixed number** for: $\frac{12}{5}$

7 **Add**: $\frac{6}{10} + \frac{2}{5} =$ _____

8 **Subtract**: $\frac{7}{8} - \frac{1}{2} =$

9 Lisa has $\frac{3}{4}$ of an apple and $\frac{5}{8}$ of an orange. What was the **total amount** that Lisa had of the two pieces of fruit?

_____

Fraction multiplication (1)

1 Write the **mixed number** for each of the following:

   a $\frac{12}{5}$ _____   b $\frac{11}{3}$ _____

   c $\frac{7}{6}$ _____   d $\frac{15}{10}$ _____

   e $\frac{9}{4}$ _____   f $\frac{20}{8}$ _____

2 Write the **improper fraction** for each of the following:

   a $1\frac{2}{6}$ _____   b $3\frac{3}{4}$ _____

   c $5\frac{2}{3}$ _____   d $3\frac{5}{8}$ _____

   e $6\frac{7}{10}$ _____   f $3\frac{2}{5}$ _____

3 Use repeated addition to **complete** the table:

	Question	Repeated addition	Fraction	Simplified fraction
a	$2 \times \frac{3}{4}$	$\frac{3}{4} + \frac{3}{4}$		
b	$3 \times \frac{1}{4}$			
c	$4 \times \frac{2}{3}$			
d	$3 \times \frac{3}{5}$			
e	$2 \times \frac{6}{8}$			
f	$4 \times \frac{2}{10}$			

4 **Multiply**, using repeated addition. Write the answers as **mixed numbers**.

   a $\frac{1}{4} \times 5 =$ b $\frac{1}{6} \times 8 =$

   c $\frac{1}{2} \times 9 =$ d $\frac{1}{5} \times 3 =$

   e $\frac{1}{8} \times 10 =$ f $\frac{1}{3} \times 5 =$

5 Write the **mixed number** for: $\frac{21}{5}$

6 Write the **improper fraction** for: $3\frac{2}{5}$ _____

7 **Complete** the table:

Question	Repeated addition	Fraction	Simplest form
$5 \times \frac{2}{5}$			

8 **Multiply**, using repeated addition. Write the answer as a **mixed number**:

$\frac{1}{10} \times 15 =$

9 Nine children were given $\frac{1}{4}$ metre of a streamer. How many metres of streamer in **total** were used?

_____

Fraction multiplication (2)

1 **Simplify** each of the following:

a $\frac{2}{16}$ b $\frac{10}{15}$

c $\frac{12}{40}$ d $\frac{5}{20}$

e $\frac{9}{12}$ f $\frac{30}{100}$

2 **Complete** the table:

	Question	Repeated addition	Fraction	Mixed number
a	$3 \times \frac{2}{5}$			
b	$3 \times \frac{5}{8}$			
c	$2 \times \frac{2}{3}$			
d	$2 \times \frac{7}{10}$			
e	$8 \times \frac{1}{6}$			
f	$10 \times \frac{3}{4}$			

3 Complete the following **multiplications**:

a $3 \times \frac{3}{8} =$ b $2 \times \frac{3}{10} =$

c $5 \times \frac{2}{5} =$ d $4 \times \frac{2}{3} =$

e $6 \times \frac{3}{4} =$ f $9 \times \frac{5}{6} =$

4 **Find**:

a 6 lots of $\frac{2}{3}$ of a bag of apples

b 5 lots of $\frac{3}{8}$ of a cake

c 4 lots of $\frac{2}{5}$ of a bag of sweets

d 8 lots of $\frac{1}{6}$ of a bar of chocolate

e 9 lots of $\frac{1}{2}$ of a pineapple

f 12 lots of $\frac{3}{10}$ of a box of pencils

5 **Simplify**: $\frac{7}{21}$

6 **Complete** the table:

Question	Repeated addition	Fraction	Mixed number
$6 \times \frac{3}{8}$			

7 **Complete**: $7 \times \frac{3}{4} =$

8 **Find** 15 lots of $\frac{5}{6}$ of an egg carton.

9 Which is the **larger**?
$6 \times \frac{3}{4}$ or $3\frac{1}{2} + 1\frac{3}{4}$

Fraction multiplication (3)

1 Use **repeated addition** to complete:

a $4 \times \frac{2}{5} =$ b $4 \times \frac{3}{10} =$

c $3 \times \frac{1}{2} =$ d $5 \times \frac{3}{4} =$

e $6 \times \frac{5}{6} =$ f $5 \times \frac{2}{3} =$

2 Complete the **multiplications**:

a $4 \times \frac{2}{5} =$ b $4 \times \frac{2}{3} =$

c $6 \times \frac{1}{4} =$ d $5 \times \frac{1}{2} =$

e $9 \times \frac{3}{5} =$ f $7 \times \frac{6}{10} =$

3 **Complete** the following:

a $\frac{2}{3} \times \frac{1}{4} =$ b $\frac{2}{9} \times \frac{5}{6} =$

c $\frac{5}{8} \times \frac{2}{5} =$ d $\frac{6}{8} \times \frac{1}{4} =$

e $\frac{3}{5} \times \frac{3}{4} =$ f $\frac{4}{10} \times \frac{2}{3} =$

4 **Find**:

a $7 \times \frac{1}{4}$ of an hour _____

b $5 \times \frac{1}{10}$ of my money _____

c $4 \times \frac{1}{3}$ of a year _____

d $5 \times \frac{1}{6}$ of a metre _____

e $11 \times \frac{5}{6}$ of a kilogram _____

f $9 \times \frac{2}{5}$ of a day _____

5 Use **repeated addition** to complete:
$4 \times \frac{1}{3} =$

6 **Complete**: $7 \times \frac{3}{8} =$

7 **Complete**: $\frac{9}{10} \times \frac{1}{2} =$

8 **Find** $6 \times \frac{7}{8}$ of an apple.

9 **Find**:

a $\frac{1}{5} \times 60 - 4 =$

b $20 - \frac{1}{10} \times 20 =$

c $\frac{1}{3} \times 27 + 9 =$

d $14 + \frac{1}{4} \times 16 =$

Fraction multiplication (4)

1 Find the **missing numbers**:

a $\dfrac{\square}{2} = 4\dfrac{1}{2}$　　b $\dfrac{\square}{5} = 6\dfrac{2}{5}$　　c $\dfrac{\square}{4} = 1\dfrac{1}{4}$

d $3\dfrac{5}{6} = \dfrac{\square}{6}$　　e $2\dfrac{5}{8} = \dfrac{\square}{8}$　　f $7\dfrac{3}{10} = \dfrac{\square}{10}$

2 **Find**:

a $\dfrac{1}{5}$ of 40 =　　　　b $\dfrac{1}{6}$ of 72 =

c $\dfrac{1}{7}$ of 49 =　　　　d $\dfrac{1}{3}$ of 36 =

e $\dfrac{1}{4}$ of 32 =　　　　f $\dfrac{1}{10}$ of 200 =

3
a Anton ate $\dfrac{1}{4}$ of the pizza which cost $24. **What value** did he eat? _____

b Chris spent $\dfrac{1}{5}$ of his $200 salary on food. **How much** did he spend? _____

c Connie used $\dfrac{1}{3}$ of a piece of wood 4.5 m long. **What length** did she use? _____

d Albert poured $\dfrac{1}{10}$ of 900 mL of water into a measuring jug. **How much** did he use? _____

e The water tank holds 6000 L. If $\dfrac{1}{2}$ had been used over summer, **how much** was left? _____

f In a carton of 24 eggs, $\dfrac{1}{8}$ of them had been broken. **How many** eggs had been broken? _____

4 **Complete**:

a $\dfrac{2}{3} \times \dfrac{6}{8} =$　　　　b $\dfrac{1}{5} \times \dfrac{5}{6} =$

c $\dfrac{3}{8} \times \dfrac{7}{10} =$　　　　d $\dfrac{1}{9} \times \dfrac{1}{3} =$

e $\dfrac{3}{5} \times \dfrac{3}{5} =$　　　　f $\dfrac{3}{4} \times \dfrac{1}{6} =$

5 Find the **missing number**:

$\dfrac{\square}{3} = 4\dfrac{2}{3}$

6 **Find** $\dfrac{1}{8}$ of 56. _____

7 Of the 50 minute lesson, $\dfrac{1}{5}$ of it had been spent building towers. **How many** minutes had been spent building towers? _____

8 **Complete**: $\dfrac{2}{3} \times \dfrac{2}{3} =$

9 Lachie spent $\dfrac{1}{2}$ of his money on DVDs and $\dfrac{1}{4}$ on the movies, leaving $30. **How much money** did he spend on DVDs? _____

Decimal place value – thousandths

1 Draw each number on its abacus.

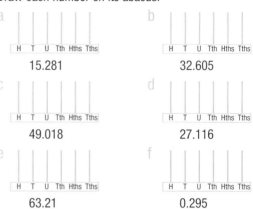

a 15.281　　b 32.605

c 49.018　　d 27.116

e 63.21　　f 0.295

2 Write the **numerals** for each of the following:

a nine and six tenths _____

b nine and twenty-seven hundredths _____

c nineteen and fourteen thousandths _____

d ninety and fifty-two thousandths _____

e ninety and two thousandths _____

f nineteen and twenty hundredths _____

3 What is the **value** of the 7 in each of the following?

a 5.37 _____　　b 9.207 _____

c 7.015 _____　　d 17.916 _____

e 2.075 _____　　f 3.74 _____

4 Write the **decimal** for each of the following:

a $\dfrac{22}{100}$ _____　　b $\dfrac{19}{100}$ _____

c $\dfrac{4}{10}$ _____　　d $\dfrac{236}{1000}$ _____

e $\dfrac{4}{100}$ _____　　f $\dfrac{143}{1000}$ _____

5 Draw 26.150 on the **abacus**:

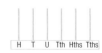

6 Write nine hundred and one and twenty-one thousandths as a **numeral**: _____

7 What is the **value** of the 7 in 2.417? _____

8 Write the **decimal** for: $\dfrac{6}{1000}$ _____

9 Write the **decimal** indicated by the arrow on the number line: _____

3.260　　　　　　　　　　　　　3.270

Decimal addition

1 Complete:

| a | 3.21
+ 4.63 | b | 9.70
+ 2.46 | c | 5.82
+ 7.95 |

| d | 3.486
+ 7.219 | e | 4.372
+ 2.765 | f | 9.810
+ 6.243 |

2 Complete:

| a | 8.40
2.16
+ 3.85 | b | 7.98
2.10
+ 4.83 | c | 3.79
2.40
+ 8.70 |

| d | 6.142
3.08
+ 9.2 | e | 46.215
1.98
+ 17.246 | f | 21.05
19.173
+ 5.62 |

3 Find the **cost** of:

 $83.95 $15.35 $8.95 $98.15

$49.50 $67.55

a a CD and a game _____

b 2 comics and a skateboard _____

c a T-shirt and a pair of shoes _____

d 4 CDs _____

e a comic and 2 games _____

f 2 T-shirts and a skateboard _____

4 Find:

| a | $16.25
$ 4.98
+ $21.55 | b | $ 17.29
$125.45
+ $ 32.00 | c | $ 21.75
$146.52
+ $125.95 |

| d | $58.62
$39.80
+ $27.45 | e | $326.45
$ 19.65
$ 21.30
+ $ 3.57 | f | $212.45
$ 86.65
$110.50
+ $142.95 |

5 Complete: 2.285
+ 9.816

6 Complete: 2.745
3.06
+ 19.45

7 Find the **total cost** of one of each of the items in question 3. _____

8 Find: $16.25
$32.45
+ $76.92

9 **Write a problem** that matches the number sentence and **solve it**:   4.29 km + 3.60 km + 15 km

_____

_____

Decimal subtraction

1 Complete:

a 1.0 − 0.8 = _____

b 2.0 − 0.9 = _____

c 1.16 − 0.14 = _____

d 2.45 − 0.32 = _____

e 5.7 − 2.4 = _____

f 7.5 − 2.63 = _____

2 Complete:

| a | 2.47
− 1.83 | b | 6.95
− 2.18 | c | 42.83
− 21.95 |

| d | 4.768
− 2.193 | e | 3.061
− 0.539 | f | 5.876
− 2.417 |

3 Find the **difference** between:

a $25.63 and $19.48 _____

b $176.25 and $90.72 _____

c $430.90 and $275.17 _____

d $402.40 and $165.82 _____

e $176.50 and $95 _____

f $210 and $173.47 _____

4 Complete:

| a | 96.5
− 38.72 | b | 2.63
− 1.7 | c | 14.2
− 9.605 |

| d | 21.43
− 16.756 | e | 11.00
− 2.43 | f | 102.3
− 98.651 |

5 Complete: 6.7 − 2.41 =

6 Complete: 19.217
− 13.846

7 Find the **difference** between $125 and $39.75:

_____

8 Complete: 16.30
− 12.49

9 Johnny bought 6.75 m of wire for his school project. After he was finished, there was 2.83 m left. **How much wire did Johnny use?** _____

Decimal multiplication

1 **Complete**:

a $\begin{array}{r} 4.61 \\ \times 3 \\ \hline \end{array}$ b $\begin{array}{r} 7.98 \\ \times 2 \\ \hline \end{array}$ c $\begin{array}{r} 2.44 \\ \times 8 \\ \hline \end{array}$

d $\begin{array}{r} 1.537 \\ \times 3 \\ \hline \end{array}$ e $\begin{array}{r} 6.215 \\ \times 2 \\ \hline \end{array}$ f $\begin{array}{r} 19.214 \\ \times 8 \\ \hline \end{array}$

2 Find the **cost** of:

$2.75 $4.26
$2.05 $4.10
$4.39

a 3 loaves of bread _____

b 5 packets of biscuits _____

c 6 litres of milk _____

d 2 jars of jam and 1 packet of cheese _____

e 2 loaves of bread and 1 packet of cheese _____

f 1 litre of milk, 2 packets of biscuits and 2 jars of jam

_____

3 **Find**:

a $\begin{array}{r} \$6.95 \\ \times 6 \\ \hline \end{array}$ b $\begin{array}{r} \$7.27 \\ \times 3 \\ \hline \end{array}$ c $\begin{array}{r} \$51.65 \\ \times 2 \\ \hline \end{array}$

d $\begin{array}{r} \$11.45 \\ \times 8 \\ \hline \end{array}$ e $\begin{array}{r} \$133.59 \\ \times 9 \\ \hline \end{array}$ f $\begin{array}{r} \$321.65 \\ \times 4 \\ \hline \end{array}$

4 What is the **total length** of:

a 6 lengths of 1.26 m of wood? _____

b 3 lengths of 1.75 m of ribbon? _____

c 9 lengths of 8.25 m of tape? _____

d 5 lengths of 15.29 m of hose? _____

e 7 lengths of 37.85 m of string? _____

f 4 lengths of 12.63 m of steel? _____

5 Complete: $\begin{array}{r} 19.26 \\ \times 9 \\ \hline \end{array}$

6 Referring to question 2, find the **total cost** of 3 loaves of bread, 2 packets of cheese and 1 jar of jam. _____

7 Find: $\begin{array}{r} \$14.56 \\ \times 7 \\ \hline \end{array}$

8 What is the **total length** of 8 lengths of 10.63 m of carpet? _____

9 Which of the following represents the **best value** for money?

2 L of milk for $2.50 or 600 mL for $1.60? _____

Decimal division

1 **Complete**:

a $2\overline{)6.86}$ b $3\overline{)12.93}$

c $4\overline{)16.2}$ d $7\overline{)64.47}$

e $6\overline{)18.384}$ f $8\overline{)34.728}$

2 **Complete**:

a $2\overline{)16.2}$ b $3\overline{)16.2}$

c $4\overline{)16.5}$ d $5\overline{)16.2}$

e $6\overline{)16.2}$ f $7\overline{)16.2}$

3 Write the **cost per book** if each set cost:

a $92.75 for 10 books _____

b $42.68 for 8 books _____

c $22.50 for 2 books _____

d $24.48 for 4 books _____

e $84.77 for 7 books _____

f $21.69 for 3 books _____

4 **Find**:

a the cost of 1 bar of soap if 5 cost $6.15 _____

b the cost of 1 toilet roll if 8 cost $6.98 _____

c the cost of 1 packet of chips if 3 cost $2.00 _____

d the cost of 1 packet of sweets if 4 cost $3.00 _____

e the cost of 1 juice pack if 6 cost $4.65 _____

f the cost of 1 can of drink if 12 cost $3.96 _____

5 **Complete**: $9\overline{)45.36}$

6 **Complete**: $8\overline{)16.2}$

7 Write the cost **per book** if a set cost $65.35 for 5 books.

_____

8 Find the **cost of 1 packet** of soup if 4 cost $3.12.

_____

9 Is the answer to the **division equation** correct? If not, find the correct answer.

$\begin{array}{r} 14.48 \\ 8\overline{)99.92} \end{array}$ _____

Multiplication and division of decimals (1)

1 **Find** each of the following:

  a $0.436 \times 10 = $ _____

  b $2.176 \times 10 = $ _____

  c $6.173 \times 10 = $ _____

  d $0.9 \times 10 = $ _____

  e $46.35 \times 10 = $ _____

  f $0.071 \times 10 = $ _____

2 **Find** each of the following:

  a $6.31 \times 100 = $ _____

  b $0.472 \times 100 = $ _____

  c $81.79 \times 100 = $ _____

  d $6.421 \times 1000 = $ _____

  e $110.421 \times 1000 = $ _____

  f $26.5 \times 1000 = $ _____

3 **Find** each of the following:

  a $0.452 \div 10 = $ _____

  b $6.71 \div 10 = $ _____

  c $12.96 \div 10 = $ _____

  d $130.21 \div 10 = $ _____

  e $421.639 \div 10 = $ _____

  f $214.853 \div 10 = $ _____

4 **Find** each of the following:

  a $0.421 \div 100 = $ _____

  b $697.3 \div 100 = $ _____

  c $4.91 \div 100 = $ _____

  d $321.01 \div 1000 = $ _____

  e $1049.85 \div 1000 = $ _____

  f $24.691 \div 1000 = $ _____

5 **Find** $21.63 \times 10 = $ _____

6 **Find** $49.285 \times 100 = $ _____

7 **Find** $745.21 \div 10 = $ _____

8 **Find** $6931.20 \div 1000 = $ _____

9 **Complete** the table:

× 1000	× 100	× 10	Number	÷ 10	÷ 100
			46.831		
			924.101		
			4.631		
			10.481		
			110.216		
			30.05		

Multiplication and division of decimals (2)

1 **Complete** the following **equations**:

  a $14 \times 6 \div 100 = $ _____

  b $23 \times 7 \div 100 = $ _____

  c $42 \times 4 \div 100 = $ _____

  d $58 \times 1 \div 1000 = $ _____

  e $22 \times 3 \div 1000 = $ _____

  f $42 \times 2 \div 1000 = $ _____

2 **Complete** the following **multiplications** with the aid of a **calculator**:

  a $1.4 \times 0.6 = $ _____

  b $2.3 \times 0.7 = $ _____

  c $4.2 \times 0.4 = $ _____

  d $5.8 \times 0.01 = $ _____

  e $2.2 \times 0.03 = $ _____

  f $4.2 \times 0.02 = $ _____

3 **Complete** the following **divisions** with the aid of a **calculator**:

  a $498 \div 70 = $ _____

  b $217 \div 30 = $ _____

  c $986 \div 80 = $ _____

  d $3487 \div 700 = $ _____

  e $2469 \div 600 = $ _____

  f $1165 \div 300 = $ _____

4 **Complete** the following **divisions** with the aid of a **calculator**:

  a $49.8 \div 7 = $ _____

  b $21.7 \div 3 = $ _____

  c $98.6 \div 8 = $ _____

  d $34.87 \div 7 = $ _____

  e $24.69 \div 6 = $ _____

  f $11.65 \div 3 = $ _____

5 **Complete** the **equation**:

$34 \times 3 \div 100 = $ _____

6 **Complete** the **multiplication** equation:

$3.4 \times 0.3 = $ _____

7 **Complete** the **division** equation: $4987 \div 400 = $ _____

8 **Complete** the **division** equation: $49.87 \div 4 = $ _____

9 **Explain** why the answers to the following equations are the same:

$24 \times 2 \div 100 = $ _____

$2.4 \times 0.2 = $ _____

Fractions and decimals

① Write the **decimals** for each of the following fractions:

  a $\frac{63}{100}$ = _____   b $\frac{246}{1000}$ = _____

  c $\frac{8}{10}$ = _____   d $\frac{9}{100}$ = _____

  e $\frac{42}{1000}$ = _____   f $\frac{6}{10}$ = _____

② Write the **fraction** for each of the following decimals:

  a 0.2 =   b 0.85 =   c 0.326 =

  d 0.04 =   e 0.406 =   f 0.001 =

③ Find each of the **decimals** for the following fractions:

  a $\frac{1}{5}$ = _____   b $\frac{1}{20}$ = _____

  c $\frac{3}{4}$ = _____   d $\frac{1}{8}$ = _____

  e $\frac{3}{5}$ = _____   f $\frac{3}{8}$ = _____

④ **Complete** the table:

		Fraction of 100	Decimal
a			
b			
c			
d			
e			
f			

⑤ Write the **decimal** for: $\frac{56}{100}$ _____

⑥ Write the **fraction** for: 0.123

⑦ Find the **decimal** for: $\frac{7}{20}$ _____

⑧ **Complete** the table:

	Fraction of 100	Decimal

⑨ **Shade** the hundreds square to show $\frac{6}{10}$:

Rounding decimals

① Round each of the following decimals to **one decimal place**:

  a 6.23 _____   b 4.69 _____

  c 1.08 _____   d 143.461 _____

  e 28.012 _____   f 17.965 _____

② Round each of the following decimals to **two decimal places**:

  a 6.493 _____   b 8.021 _____

  c 7.395 _____   d 211.0873 _____

  e 42.1197 _____   f 879.6382 _____

③ Round each of the following to the **nearest whole number** and **estimate** the answer:

  a 10.045 + 2.673 + 105.95 _____

  b 2.216 + 3.63 + 19.04 _____

  c 902.5 + 18.699 + 15.02 _____

  d 7.041 + 8.92 + 3.856 _____

  e 421.02 + 1.03 + 4.71 _____

  f 12.58 + 2.6 + 19.058 _____

④ Do each of these calculations and then round each of the answers to **one decimal place**:

  a
$$\begin{array}{r} 0.463 \\ 7.21 \\ + \ 9.805 \\ \hline \end{array}$$
  b
$$\begin{array}{r} 16.248 \\ 1.119 \\ + \ 32.6 \\ \hline \end{array}$$

  c
$$\begin{array}{r} 42.809 \\ 10.7 \\ + \ 46.37 \\ \hline \end{array}$$
  d
$$\begin{array}{r} 241.82 \\ - \ 97.63 \\ \hline \end{array}$$

  e
$$\begin{array}{r} 827.106 \\ - \ 413.942 \\ \hline \end{array}$$
  f
$$\begin{array}{r} 780.29 \\ - \ 356.025 \\ \hline \end{array}$$

⑤ Round 17.063 to **one decimal place**. _____

⑥ Round 96.215 to **two decimal places.** _____

⑦ Round to the **nearest whole number** and **estimate** the answer to: 46.83 + 21.85 + 8.029

_____

⑧ Do the addition and then round the answer to **one decimal place**:
$$\begin{array}{r} 92.36 \\ - \ 48.715 \\ \hline \end{array}$$

⑨ Elsie wanted to see if she had enough money. Round each amount to the **nearest dollar** to estimate the **total cost**:

Orange juice	$4.48
Bread	$2.95
Milk	$3.56
Butter	$3.27
Jam	$3.79

Percentages (1)

1 Express the following decimals as **percentages**:

a 0.2 _____   b 0.9 _____   c 0.6 _____

d 0.81 _____   e 0.36 _____   f 0.02 _____

2 Express each of the following as **decimals**:

a 47% _____   b 63% _____   c 98% _____

d 4% _____   e 7% _____   f 125% _____

3 **Complete** the table:

	Fraction	Decimal	Percentage
a	$\frac{3}{10}$		
b	$\frac{9}{10}$		
c	$\frac{41}{100}$		
d	$\frac{73}{100}$		
e	$\frac{27}{100}$		
f	$\frac{14}{100}$		

4 Circle the **largest amount** in each group:

a $\frac{6}{10}$, 0.59, 61%

b 26%, $\frac{25}{100}$, 0.24

c 0.4, 39%, $\frac{41}{100}$

d 0.89, 90%, $\frac{75}{100}$

e 50%, 0.45, $\frac{49}{100}$

f $\frac{75}{100}$, 0.77, 72%

5 Express 0.07 as a **percentage**. _____

6 Express 163% as a **decimal**. _____

7 **Complete** the table:

Fraction	Decimal	Percentage
$\frac{22}{100}$		

8 Circle the **largest amount** of: $\frac{16}{100}$, 15%, 0.17

9 Write each of the following fractions as a **percentage**:

a $\frac{1}{5}$ _____   b $\frac{3}{4}$ _____   c $2\frac{1}{2}$ _____

Percentages (2)

1 Find the **percentage** of each quantity:

a 10% of 60 = _____   b 90% of 100 = _____

c 25% of 40 = _____   d 50% of 70 = _____

e 20% of 80 = _____   f 30% of 90 = _____

2 Find the **percentage** of each amount:

a 10% of $20 _____   b 20% of $50 _____

c 25% of $48 _____   d 50% of $64 _____

e 30% of $60 _____   f 10% of $80 _____

3 Draw lines to **match** the percentages and fractions:

a $\frac{1}{2}$ 10%

b $\frac{1}{4}$ 5%

c $\frac{1}{20}$ 75%

d $\frac{1}{5}$ 20%

e $\frac{3}{4}$ 50%

f $\frac{1}{10}$ 25%

4 Find the **discount** on:

a $300 camera with 10% discount _____

b $95 skateboard with 10% discount _____

c $80 computer game with 25% discount _____

d $60 DVD box set with 20% discount _____

e $120 rollerblades with 25% discount _____

f $150 printer with 30% discount _____

5 **Find** 10% of 70. _____

6 **Find** 20% of $66. _____

7 **Match** the percentages and fractions:

a $\frac{1}{4}$ 100%

b 1   30%

c $\frac{3}{10}$ 40%

8 Find the discount on a $200 television with a 20% discount. _____

9 Using a **calculator**, find:

a 25% of 360 _____

b 30% of 320 _____

c 20% of 28 _____

d 15% of 25 _____

Percentages (3)

1 **Shade** each of the following shapes the given percentage and state the **answers**:

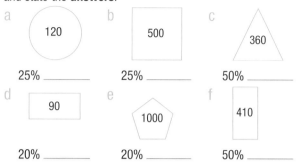

a (circle) 120   25% _____

b (square) 500   25% _____

c (triangle) 360   50% _____

d (rectangle) 90   20% _____

e (pentagon) 1000   20% _____

f (rectangle) 410   50% _____

2 Find the **percentage** of each amount:

a 10% of $25 _____   b 50% of $17 _____

c 25% of $36 _____   d 20% of $55 _____

e 10% of $19 _____   f 50% of $153 _____

3 Find the **percentage** of each quantity:

a 10% of 80 pigs _____

b 20% of 45 goats _____

c 25% of 100 cats _____

d 50% of 36 chickens _____

e 100% of 7 horses _____

f 10% of 110 birds _____

4 **Complete** the table:

	a	b	c	d	e	f
Price	$20	$50	$30	$80	$900	$120
% off	10	50	20	25	5	20
Discount						
Discount price						

5 Shade 20% of the circle and state the **answer**:

(circle) 150   _____

6 **Find** 25% of $480: _____

7 **Find** 50% of 260 cows: _____

8 **Complete** the table:

Price	$20
% off	10
Discount	
Discount price	

9 If a box of pencils cost $16 after a discount of 20%, what was the **original price** of the pencils? _____

Fractions, decimals and percentages

1 Express each of the following as **percentages**:

a 0.2 _____
b 0.9 _____
c 0.01 _____
d 0.12 _____
e 0.56 _____
f 1.3 _____

2 Express each of the following percentages as **decimals**:

a 7% _____
b 3% _____
c 40% _____
d 59% _____
e 63% _____
f 121% _____

3 Express each of the following fractions as **percentages**:

a $\frac{4}{10}$ _____
b $\frac{8}{10}$ _____
c $\frac{8}{100}$ _____
d $\frac{90}{100}$ _____
e $\frac{47}{100}$ _____
f $\frac{136}{100}$ _____

4 Circle the **largest value** in each group:

a $\frac{89}{100}$, 0.85, 87%

b 0.33, $\frac{3}{10}$, 34%

c $\frac{5}{100}$, 0.5, 15%

d 98%, 0.99, $\frac{100}{100}$

e 1.21, $\frac{120}{100}$, 123%

f 7.6, 750%, $\frac{759}{100}$

5 Express 1.26 as a **percentage**.

6 Express 246% as a **decimal**.

7 Express $\frac{229}{100}$ as a **percentage**.

8 Circle the **largest value** of: 421%, 4.23, $\frac{420}{100}$

9 Express each percentage as a **fraction in its simplest form**:

a 20%   b 16%
c 140%   d 290%

Money in shopping

① List the **smallest number** of notes and coins needed to make the following amounts:

a $3.75 ____　　b $11.80 ____　　c $27.15 ____

d $43.95 ____　　e $87.70 ____　　f $126.45 ____

② **How much change** would be received from $40 after spending the following?

a $23.40 ____　　b $17.85 ____

c $34.15 ____　　d $11.90 ____

e $7.05 ____　　f $26.80 ____

③ **Find**:

a If 1 tube of toothpaste costs $1.75, how much do 4 tubes cost? ____

b If 3 cans cost $4.85, how much are 12 cans? ____

c What was the total cost of 2 loaves of bread @ $2.95 each, 1 tub of margarine $1.75 and 1 jar of jam $4.15?

____

d Could Albert buy 2 magazines at $8.95 each and 2 chocolate bars at $1.20 each for $20? ____

e Which box of cereal is better value for money? A: 1.5 kg for $4.85 or B: 2.75 kg for $8.50 ____

f If Joe bought 3 bottles of drink for $4.35, how much change did he receive from $20? ____

④ Find the **total** of each amount and round to the **nearest 5 cents**.

a
```
   $2.35
   $1.07
   $4.98
 + $6.62
```

b
```
   $11.25
   $ 6.37
   $ 4.21
 + $ 3.02
```

c
```
   $5.88
   $6.29
   $3.45
 + $1.06
```

d
```
   $4.77
   $2.98
   $1.06
 + $3.48
```

e
```
   $4.96
   $1.07
   $4.26
 + $3.98
```

f
```
   $4.44
   $2.06
   $1.99
 + $4.68
```

⑤ List the **smallest number** of notes and coins needed to make $75.90 ____

⑥ **How much change** would be received from $40 after spending $19.60? ____

⑦ If 1 bag of potatoes costs $2.55, what would be the **total cost** of 7 bags of potatoes? ____

⑧ Find the **total** and round to the **nearest 5 cents**.
```
   $6.36
   $1.19
   $7.52
 + $1.29
```

⑨ Which is **better value**?

5 oranges for $1.00 or a bag of oranges at $2.55 which has 15 oranges in it?

Money in banking

①

Date	Details	Debit	Credit	Balance
1/1	Brought forward			1529.55
2/1	Deposit		500.00	1529.55
4/1	Home loan	347.26		1682.29
9/1	Cheque	92.76		1589.53
10/1	Deposit		200.00	1789.53
11/1	Cash withdrawal	100.00		1689.53

a **How much** was the account at the start of the month?

____

b **How much** was the account on 5/1? ____

c What was the **total** of all the deposits (credits)?

____

d **What amount** was deducted for the home loan?

____

e **How much** cash was withdrawn? ____

f What was the **total amount** of cheques written?

____

② For the above account, find the **final balance** after:

a salary deposit $350 on 13/1 ____

b 2 different cheques written on 14/1 for $52 and $68.30 ____

c cash withdrawal of $200 on 21/1 ____

d interest paid $13.25 on 24/1 ____

e deposit of $426 on 25/1 ____

f government payment $16.85 on 26/1 ____

③ **Complete** the table:

	A$1 =	$28 souvenir =
a	C$0.83	
b	NZ$1.12	
c	€0.60	
d	£0.42	
e	S$0.93	
f	HK$4.20	

④ Using the information from question 3, write **true or false**.

a A$1 < NZ$1 ____　　b £1 > €1 ____

c HK$1 > A$1 ____　　d S$1 < HK$1 ____

e C$1 < €1 ____　　f S$1 < NZ$1 ____

⑤ **How much money** was withdrawn from the account between 1 and 10 January in question 1? ____

⑥ What was the **final balance** of the account in question 2?

____

⑦ **Complete** the table:

A$1	$28 souvenir
Bht22.16	

⑧ Write **true or false**: Bht1 > HK$1 ____

⑨ If A$1 = €0.60

a **How much** would A$2500 be worth in Europe?

____

b If I earned €3000, how much Australian money would I have? ____

Symmetry

1 How many **lines of symmetry** do each of the following have?

  a   b   c

  d   e   f

2 Draw all the **lines of symmetry** for each of the following:

  a   b   c

  d   e   f

3 Complete each of the following shapes by using the **lines of symmetry**:

  a   b   c

  d   e   f

4 Mark all of the shapes that have **rotational symmetry**:

  a   b   c

  d   e   f

5 How many **lines of symmetry** does 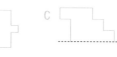 have? _____

6 Draw all the **lines of symmetry** for:

7 Complete the shape using the **line of symmetry**:

8 Does have **rotational symmetry**?

9 **Complete** the picture:

Rotational symmetry

1 Do each of the following shapes have rotational symmetry?

  a   b   c

  d   e   f

2 What is the **order of rotational symmetry** of each of the following?

  a   b   c

  d   e   f

3 Do each of the following have **rotational symmetry**?

  a    b   c

  d   e   f

4 **Draw** the following shapes, after each has been **rotated** 90° clockwise about the marked point:

  a   b   c

  d   e   f

5 Indicate if has **rotational symmetry**. _____

6 What is the **order of rotational symmetry** of:

_____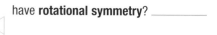

7 Does have **rotational symmetry**? _____

8 **Draw** the shape after it has been **rotated** 180° clockwise about the marked point:

9 Does the shape have **rotational symmetry**? _____ If so, what order?

UNIT 97   See START UPS page 9

Diagonals, parallel and perpendicular lines

1 Circle the **perpendicular lines**:

2 Write **true or false** for each of the following statements about the diagram:

a lines AD and CD are perpendicular _____

b lines AB and CD are perpendicular _____

c lines BC and AD are parallel _____

d lines AB and BC are at right angles _____

e line CD is a diagonal _____

f line AC is a diagonal _____

3 Draw the **diagonals** on each of the following shapes:

4 **Complete** the table:

	Shape	No. of sides	No. of diagonals
a	square		
b	rectangle		
c	pentagon		
d	hexagon		
e	heptagon		
f	octagon		

5 Are the lines _____ perpendicular? _____

6 Write **true or false** for the statement of the diagram in question 2: Lines BC and CD are parallel. _____

7 Draw the **diagonals** on:

8 **Complete** the table:

Shape	No. of sides	No. of diagonals
nonagon		

9 Of the numbers 0 to 10, which contain **perpendicular lines**? _____

UNIT 98   See START UPS page 10

Parallel, horizontal and vertical lines

1 Circle the **parallel lines**:

2 Label the following as **vertical, horizontal** or **neither**:

3 Answer **true or false** for each of the statements of the diagram:

a line AC is a diagonal _____

b line BC is horizontal _____

c lines AB and CD are parallel _____

d lines AC and BD are parallel _____

e lines AD and AB are perpendicular _____

f lines AD and BC are horizontal _____

4 Circle the following letters which have **parallel lines**:

5 Are _____ parallel? _____

6 Label the following line as **vertical, horizontal** or **neither**.

_____

7 Answer **true or false** for the statement about the diagram in question 3. Line AD and AC are vertical.

_____

8 Does the letter W have **parallel lines**? _____

9 Draw diagrams of the following regular shapes to find which contain **parallel lines**:

a pentagon   b hexagon

Angles

1. Read each angle to the **nearest degree** and write its size in degrees.

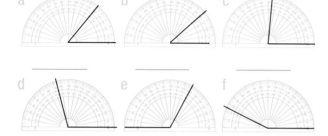

2. Measure to the **nearest degree** each of the following:

3. Indicate which of the following angles are **acute**:

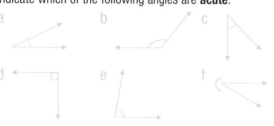

4. Indicate which of the following angles are **obtuse**:

5. Read the angle to the **nearest degree** and write its size in degrees.

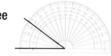

6. Measure to the **nearest degree**: _____

7. Is _____ **acute**? _____

8. Is _____ **obtuse**? _____

9. **Measure** with a protractor to find the smallest angle between the hands.

Reading angles (1)

1. Indicate which of the following are **reflex angles**:

2. Indicate which of the following are **straight angles**:

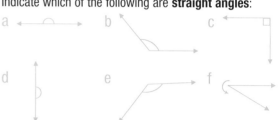

3. **Estimate the size** of each of the following angles:

4. Use a protractor to **measure** each of the following angles and then name each angle:

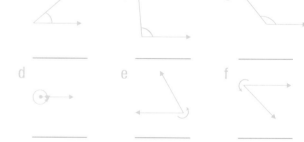

5. Is _____ a **reflex angle**? _____

6. Is _____ a **straight angle**? _____

7. **Estimate the size** of: _____

8. Use a protractor to **measure and name**: _____

9. **Measure** with a protractor each of the angles of a pentagon. What did you discover?

_____

Reading angles (2)

1 **Estimate the size** of each angle before **measuring** it accurately with a protractor:

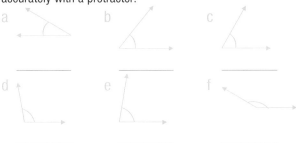

a   b   c

d   e   f

2 Find the **size of each reflex angle** by measuring the smaller angle first:

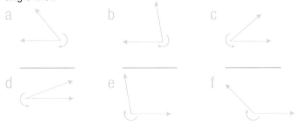

a   b   c

d   e   f

3 Name each of the following **angle types**:

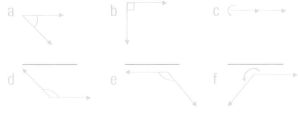

a   b   c

d   e   f

4 **Measure** each of the reflex angles:

a   b   c

d   e   f

5 **Estimate the size** of the angle before **measuring** it accurately with a protractor:

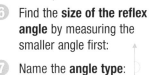

6 Find the **size of the reflex angle** by measuring the smaller angle first:

7 Name the **angle type**:

8 **Measure** the reflex angle:

9 Write the **angle** shown on the 360° protractor:

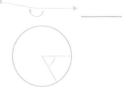

Drawing angles

1 **Draw** each of the following angles:

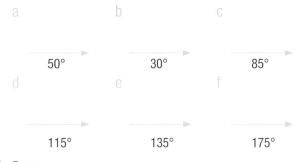

a   b   c

    50°   30°   85°

d   e   f

    115°   135°   175°

2 **Draw**:

a   an acute angle   b   an obtuse angle

c   a straight angle   d   a revolution

e   a reflex angle < 270°   f   a reflex angle > 270°

3 On a piece of paper, **draw an angle** of:

a   15°   b   145°   c   75°

d   100°   e   60°   f   45°

4 On a piece of paper, **draw the reflex angles**:

a   310°   b   275°   c   190°

d   280°   e   345°   f   210°

5 **Draw**:

     70°

6 **Draw** an **acute angle** < 45°.

7 **Draw** a **95°** angle.

8 **Draw** a **325°** reflex angle.

9 Using a protractor, draw a **regular pentagon** accurately.

Angle facts

1 In each question a to f the angles make a **straight angle**. Find the size of each **missing angle**:

 a 51° b 141° c 110°

 d 77° e 45° f 89°

2 In each question a to f the angles together measure 60°. Find the value of each **missing adjacent angle**:

 a 19° b 40° c 50°

 d 20° e 47° f 12°

3 Find the **missing angles** in each of the following triangles:

 a 30° 60° b 60° 60° 20° c 130°

 d 30° 100° e 70° 70° f 90° 45°

4 Find the value of each of the **missing angles**:

 a b 100° c 125°

d 30° e 50° f 40°

5 The angles together make a **straight angle**. Find the **missing angle**: _____ 125°

6 If the angles together measure 60°, find the value of the **missing adjacent angle**: _____ 48°

7 Find the **missing angle**: _____ 10° 50°

8 Find the value of the **missing angle**, g. _____ g 105°

9 Find the size of the **missing angle**: _____  140° 40° 40°

3D objects

1 **Match** the name to each object: triangular prism, rectangular prism, triangular pyramid, cube, pentagonal prism, hexagonal pyramid

 a b c

 d e f

2 Name each of the following **solids**:

a b c

d e f

3 **Match** each of the cross-sections with the solids listed above in question 1:

a b c

d e f

4 Complete the **table**:

	Object	Faces	Edges	Vertices
a	cube			
b	rectangular prism			
c	triangular prism			
d	hexagonal prism			
e	square pyramid			
f	triangular pyramid			

5 **Match** the name to the object: rectangular prism square pyramid cube

6 Name the **solid**: _____

7 **Match** the cross-section with the object: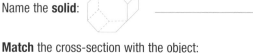

8 Complete the **table**:

Object	Faces	Edges	Vertices
rectangular pyramid			

9 **What am I**? I have 5 vertices, 5 faces and 8 edges. I am made from 4 equilateral triangles and a square.

_____

Drawing 3D objects

1. List the **shapes** that make up a:

   a rectangular prism _____

   b square pyramid _____

   c cube _____

   d rectangular pyramid _____

   e triangular prism _____

   f hexagonal prism _____

2. Place dotted lines in each of the following to provide the hidden detail:

3. Look at each of the following objects and **practice drawing** them:

4. Name the **3D objects** that are constructed from:

   a 2 octagons and 8 rectangles _____

   b 4 triangles _____

   c 1 rectangle and 4 triangles _____

   d 1 rectangle and 2 circles _____

   e 2 squares and 4 rectangles _____

   f 1 hexagon and 6 triangles _____

5. List the **shapes** that make up a pentagonal prism.

   _____

6. Draw in **dotted lines** to show the hidden detail:

7. Look at the rectangular prism and **practice drawing** it.

8. Name the **3D object** that is constructed from 2 triangles and 3 rectangles. _____

9. Name a **solid** that has:

   a less than 8 faces _____

   b an even number of vertices _____

Properties and views of 3D objects

1. **Complete** the table:

   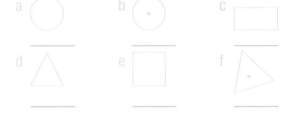

a	Name			
b	No. of surfaces			
c	No. of edges			
d	No. of vertices			
e	No. of curved surfaces			
f	Front view			

2. Which of the shapes in question 1 could have a **view** of:

   a ◯   b ⊙   c ▭

   _____   _____   _____

   d △   e □   f ◁

   _____   _____   _____

3. Write the **name of the container** used in each stack:

   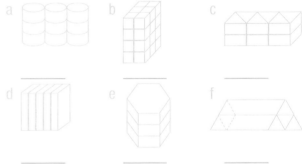

   a _____   b _____   c _____

   d _____   e _____   f _____

4. Write **how many containers** have been placed in each of the stacks in question 3:

   a _____   b _____   c _____

   d _____   e _____   f _____

5. **Complete** the table:

Top view				

6. Which of the shapes in question 1 has the **view**:

   △

7. Write the **name of the container** used in the stack.

8. Write **how many containers** have been placed in the stack of question 7. _____

9. a How many **corners** does a tetrahedron have? _____

   b Do tetrahedrons **stack** well? _____

Cylinders, spheres and cones

1 Name each of the following objects:

a   b   c

_____ _____ _____

d   e   f

_____ _____ _____

2 **Complete** the table:

		Cone	Cylinder	Sphere	Cube
a	Side view				
b	No. of edges				
c	No. of surfaces				
d	No. of corners				
e	No. of curved surfaces				
f	Does it roll?				

3 Of the **objects** in question 1:

a   Which object **rolls** the best? _____

b   How does a cone **roll**? _____

c   How does a cylinder **roll**? _____

d   Which object has no **sides**? _____

e   Which object **meets at a point**? _____

f   Which object has only one surface which is curved? _____

4 **Sketch**:

a   a cone

b   a cylinder

c   a sphere

d   a cone on top of a cylinder

e   a cylinder with a sphere at each end

f   a sphere on top of a cone

5 **Name**:    _____

6 **Complete** the table:

	Cone	Cylinder	Sphere	Cube
Top view				

7 Of the objects in question 1, which has all points on the surface the **same distance** from the centre?

_____

8 **Sketch** 4 cylinders stacked in 2 rows of 2.

9 Is it easier to **stack** spheres, cones or cylinders? _____
Draw a diagram to illustrate your answer.

Parallelograms and rhombuses

1 **Match** the names and diagrams:

a   square
b   rhombus
c   circle
d   kite
e   rectangle
f   parallelogram

2 Circle the following which are **parallelograms**:

a   b   c

d   e   f

3 Circle the following which are **rhombuses**:

a   b   c

d   e   f

4 Complete each of the **parallelograms**:

a   b   c

d   e   f

5 **Match** the name to the shape:
parallelogram, rhombus, trapezium

6 Circle the following which are **parallelograms**:

7 Circle the following which are **rhombuses**:

8 Complete the **parallelogram**:

9 Draw a **tessellating pattern** using a rhombus:

Geometric patterns

1 Complete the following table:

Number of triangles	1	2	3	4	5	6	7
	△	△△					
Number of sides	3	a	b	c	d	e	f

2 **Complete** the following table:

Number of triangles	1	2	3	4	5	6	7
	⬠						
Number of sides	a	b	15	c	d	e	f

3 **Complete** the following table:

Number of triangles	1	2	3	4	5	6	7
	⬡						
Number of sides	a	b	c	d	40	e	f

4 Repeat the following **patterns**:

a △, □, ○, _____, _____, _____

b △, △, ○, ○, □, □, ____, ____, ____, ____, ____, ____

c △, □, ▽, _____, _____, _____

d ⌐, ⌐, ⌐, _____, _____, _____

e ◠, ▽, _____, _____, _____

f ◣, ▷, ◤, _____, _____, _____

5 Write the **rule** for question 1:

_____

6 Write the **rule** for question 2:

_____

7 Write the **rule** for question 3:

_____

8 Complete the **pattern**:

▱, □, ▱, _____, _____, _____

9 Write a **rule** for:

Circles

1 **Match** the picture with its label:

a centre
b radius
c diameter
d circumference
e arc
f sector

2 **Match** the label and description:

a	centre	circles with a common centre
b	semicircle	the perimeter of the circle
c	concentric circles	part of the circumference
d	circumference	the point in the middle
e	arc	half the inside of the circle
f	sector	an area bound by two radii and an arc

3 Measure the **diameter** of each of the following circles:

a   b   c

d   e   f

4 Measure the **radius** of each of the following circles:

a   b   c

d   e   f

5 **Match** the picture with its label:

a quadrant
b sector
c semicircle

6 **Match** the label and its description:

a semicircle   quarter of a circle
b quadrant   part of the circumference
c arc   half of a circle

7 Measure the **diameter** of the circle:

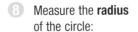
_____

8 Measure the **radius** of the circle: _____

9 **Copy this design** inside a circle, using the diameter to help you.

Nets and 3D objects

① **Complete** the following table:

	Shape	Diagram	No. of edges	No. of vertices	No. of surfaces
a	cube				
b	cylinder				
c	cone				
d	sphere				
e	triangular prism				
f	rectangular prism				

② Draw the **top view** of a:

a cube   b cylinder
c cone   d sphere
e triangular pyramid   f rectangular prism

③ Name the **3D object** the net makes:

a   b   c

d   e   f

④ Indicate which of the following nets makes up into an **open cube**:

a    b   c

d   e   f

⑤ **Complete** the table:

Shape	Diagram	No. of edges	No. of vertices	No. of surfaces
triangular pyramid				

⑥ Draw the **top view** of a triangular prism.

⑦ Name the **3D object** the net makes: _____

⑧ Indicate if 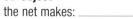 makes up into an open cube.

⑨ Draw the net of an **octagonal pyramid**.

Scale drawings

① If the scale for the following intervals is 1 cm : 2 km, what is the **length** represented by each?

a _____
b _____
c _____
d _____
e _____
f _____

② If the scale for the following intervals is 1:10, what is the **length** represented by each?

a _____
b _____
c _____
d _____
e _____
f _____

③ This ant has been drawn to a scale of 2 :1 (it is 2 times larger than in real life).

What does this ant measure (in millimetres)?

a length   b width   c length of head
_____   _____   _____

What does a real ant measure (in millimetres)?

d length   e max. body width   f length of head
_____   _____   _____

④ **Complete** the following table:

	Description	Length	Width	Scale	Scale length	Scale width
a	backyard	50 m	30 m	1 cm : 5 m		
b	sports ground	200 m	150 m	1 cm : 20 m		
c	swimming pool	25 m	10 m	1 cm : 5 m		
d	school ground	900 m	500 m	1 cm : 100 m		
e	park	7500 m	4500 m	1 cm : 500 m		
f	garage	7 m	6 m	1 cm : 1 m		

⑤ If the scale of the interval is 1 cm : 2 km, what is the **length** represented? _____
_____

⑥ If the scale of the interval is 1 : 10, what is the **length** represented? _____
_____

⑦ Using the ant in question 3, what is the **length** of a real ant's front leg? _____

⑧ **Complete** the table:

Description	Length	Width	Scale	Scale length	Scale width
courtyard	16 m	8 m	1 cm : 2 m		

⑨ **Redraw** the following triangle using a scale of 1: 1.5

Scale drawings and ratios

1. Label the **dimensions** of each of the polygons if the scale is 1 cm : 4 m (1 : 400).

a   b

c   d

e   f

2. If the scale is 1 : 10 for each of the shapes in question 1, what are their **dimensions**?

a _____
b _____
c _____
d _____
e _____
f _____

3. Each of the following pictures is drawn to the given scale. Find the **height** of each of the animals:

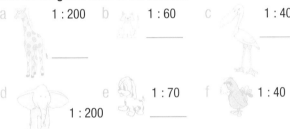

a   1 : 200   b   1 : 60   c   1 : 40

d   1 : 200   e   1 : 70   f   1 : 40

4. For the rectangle, calculate the **total number** of squares when the side lengths are made:

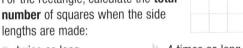

a twice as long _____   b 4 times as long _____
c 6 times as long _____   d 10 times as long _____
e 5 times as long _____   f 3 times as long _____

5. Label the **dimensions** of the diamond if the scale is 1 cm : 2 m (1 : 200).

6. If the scale is 1 : 10 for the diamond in question 5, what are its **dimensions**? _____

7. The possum is drawn to the given scale. Find the **height** of the possum: 1 : 40

_____

8. For the rectangle, what happens to the total number of squares when the side length is made $\frac{1}{2}$ as long?

9. A tree 1.2 m tall throws a shadow 480 cm long. What is the **ratio** of the tree's height to the shadow? _____

Tessellation and patterns

1. Which of the following shapes **tessellate**?

a   b   c

_____   _____   _____

d   e   f

_____   _____   _____

2. **Reflect** each of the following shapes in the dotted line:

a   b   c

d   e   f

3. **Translate** each of the following shapes to the right:

a   b   c

d   e   f

4. **Rotate** each of the following shapes clockwise through 90° about the dot:

a   b   c

d   e   f

5. Does ⟩   **tessellate**? _____

6. **Reflect** the shape in the dotted line:

7. **Translate** the shape to the right:

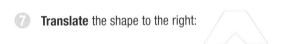

8. **Rotate** the shape clockwise through 90° about the dot:

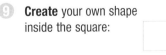

9. **Create** your own shape inside the square:

Draw it into the top left box and **rotate** the small box about the black dot to complete:

Compass directions

1 What is the **direction halfway between**:

a north and east? _____

b north and west? _____

c north and south? _____

d south and east? _____

e south and west? _____

f east and west? _____

2 If you are facing north, **what direction** is:

a to your left? _____   b to your right? _____

c behind you? _____   d in front of you? _____

e diagonally (45°) to your left? _____

f diagonally (45°) to your right? _____

3 Using the grid, **name the shape** that is:

a east of the star _____

b south of the rectangle _____

c north-east of the rectangle _____

d south-west of the oval _____

e north-west of the oval _____

f west of the diamond _____

4 Starting from the point X and using north as up, following each of the directions below, **describe where you end up**:

a go 20 cm N, then 15 cm W, then 30 cm S

_____

b go 10 cm E, then 8 cm S, then 8 cm W

_____

c go 15 cm W, then 20 cm N, then 20 cm E, then 10 cm S

_____

d go 12 cm S, then 5 cm E, then 6 cm N, then 5 cm W

_____

e go 14 cm N, then 12 cm S, then 5 cm W, then 9 cm E

_____

f go 35 cm E, 20 cm N, then 20 cm W, then 40 cm S

_____

5 What is the **direction halfway between** south and north?

_____

6 If you are facing north, **what direction** is diagonally (45°) behind you to the left? _____

7 Using the grid in question 3, **name the shape** that is north of the square. _____

8 Starting from the point X, and using north as up, **describe where you end up** after you go 20 cm N, then 15 cm E, then 45 cm S and finally 30 cm W.

9 **What angle** lies between the compass directions?

a south and west? _____

b north and east? _____

c east and west? _____

Maps (1)

1 Use the directions and distances to find each **destination**:

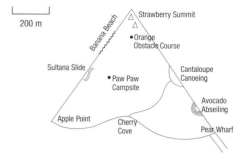

a start at Paw Paw campsite and travel north 200 m

_____

b then travel 200 m south-west _____

c then travel 200 m south, then 200 m west _____

d then travel east 400 m _____

e then travel north 400 m _____

f then travel north 100 m _____

2 Give the **direction** for each of the following:

a Avocado Abseiling to Apple Point _____

b Cherry Cove to Orange Obstacle Course _____

c Apple Point to Strawberry Summit _____

d Pear Wharf to Paw Paw Campsite _____

e Banana Beach to Cantaloupe Canoeing _____

f Sultana Slide to Cherry Cove _____

3 Estimate the **distance** between each of the locations:

a Avocado Abseiling to Apple Point _____

b Cherry Cove to Orange Obstacle Course _____

c Apple Point to Strawberry Summit _____

d Pear Wharf to Paw Paw Campsite _____

e Banana Beach to Cantaloupe Canoeing _____

f Sultana Slide to Cherry Cove _____

4 Give the **direction** of each of the following from Paw Paw Campsite:

a Apple Point _____   b Pear Wharf _____

c Banana Beach _____   d Sultana Slide _____

e Cherry Cove _____   f Avocado Abseiling _____

5 Find the **destination** when starting at Cherry Cove and travelling north-west for 300 m. _____

6 Give the **direction** from Orange Obstacle Course to Cantaloupe Canoeing. _____

7 Give the **distance** between Orange Obstacle Course and Cantaloupe Canoeing. _____

8 Give the **direction** of Strawberry Summit from Pear Wharf.

_____

9 a **Draw a path** on the map from Apple Point around the coast to Strawberry Summit.

b List the **directions** and **distances** travelled.

_____

Maps (2)

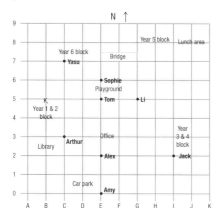

1 Give the **coordinates** of the position of the children marked on the map:

a Yasu _____

b Tom _____

c Arthur _____

d Amy _____

e Jack _____

f Li _____

2 Mark the following **coordinates** on the map:

a C2   b F3   c I8

d D6   e G7   f A6

3 Use the scale to calculate the **shortest distance** between the:

a Car park and the Office _____

b Office and the Year 3 & 4 block _____

c bridge at the top of the playground and the Year 6 block _____

d Year 5 and Year 6 block _____

e Library and the Office _____

f Year 6 block and the Car park _____

4 Use the direction to find each **location** from the Office:

a to the building north-west _____

b to the location south-west _____

c to the location 150 m north _____

d to the location 50 m north _____

e to the location 100 m west _____

f to the location 200 m north-east _____

5 Give the **coordinates** of the position of Sophie marked on the map. _____

6 Mark the **coordinate** E4 with a circle.

7 Use the scale to calculate the **shortest distance** between the Lunch area and the Office. _____

8 Find the **location** from the Office 50 m south.

_____

9 Draw and **describe the path** from the Car park to the Lunch area.

Maps (3)

1 Draw **vertical lines** and label them A – H. Use the marks that have been supplied.

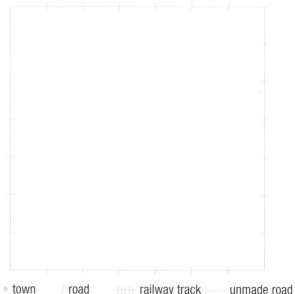

• town   / road   ┼┼┼┼ railway track ······ unmade road

2 Draw the **horizontal lines** and label them 0 – 7 to complete the coordinate grid.

2 Use the **coordinate points** to add the following towns on the map with a green cross:

a Green Town (B6)   b Blue Town (C2)

c Yellow Town (E4)   d Orange Town (F3)

e Red Town (G5)   f Purple Town (D1)

4 Complete the paths on the map by **drawing**:

a a road between Green Town and Red Town.

b a railway line between Blue Town and Purple Town.

c an unmade road between Yellow Town and Orange Town.

d a road between Blue Town and Red Town via Yellow Town.

e a railway line between Orange Town and Purple Town via Green Town.

f an unmade road between Red Town and Purple Town via Orange Town.

5 **Mark** north on the map.

6 **Add** a lake at G1.

7 Use the **coordinate points** to add Black Town to B2 with a dot.

8 **Draw a road** between Black Town and Green Town.

9 Give the **compass direction** from:

a Black Town to Green Town _____

b Orange Town to Purple Town _____

c Purple Town to Blue Town _____

Coordinates (1)

1 Name the American State that has the coordinates:

a J6   b G3   c C7

d L9   e M5   f G7

2 Give the **coordinates** for:

a Iowa _____   b Washington _____

c California _____   d Wisconsin _____

e Texas _____   f Georgia _____

3 Give the **direction** of:

a Utah from Arizona _____

b North Dakota from Montana _____

c Arkansas from Louisiana _____

d Ohio from Kentucky _____

e South Dakota from Oklahoma _____

f Colorado from Kansas _____

4 Give **what state** is:

a west of Idaho _____

b north of Illinois _____

c east of Louisana _____

d south of Kentucky _____

e west of Montana _____

f west of Georgia _____

5 **Name** the American state that has the coordinates H5.

_____

6 Give the **coordinates** for Mississippi. _____

7 Give the **direction** of Texas from Nevada.

_____

8 Give **what state** is south-east of Kansas.

_____

9 **List the states** that you would travel through if you left California and finished up in Louisiana.

_____

Coordinates (2)

1000 km

1 Name the **location** that has the coordinates:

a E5 _____   b C6 _____

c H2 _____   d G3 _____

e D1 _____   f G0 _____

2 Give the **coordinates** of:

a Golmud _____   b Yining _____

c Shanghai _____   d Harbin _____

e Taipei _____   f Beijing _____

3 Which **location** is immediately:

a west of Xining _____

b north of Zhengzhou _____

c south of Harbin _____

d east of Guiyang _____

e north-east of Kunming _____

f south-east of Urumqi _____

4 Give the **approximate direct distance** between the two locations to the nearest 1000 km:

	Location 1	Location 2	Distance between
a	Nanning	Guiyang	
b	Beijing	Shanghai	
c	Nanchang	Taipei	
d	Harbin	Beijing	
e	Karamay	Urumqi	
f	Lhasa	Golmud	

5 Name the **location** that has the coordinate C7.

_____

6 Give the **coordinates** of Lhasa.

7 Which **location** is immediately north-west of Changsha?

_____

8 Give the **approximate direct distance** between:

Location 1	Location 2	Distance between
Xi'an	Hong Kong	

9 Give a list of **coordinates** that could be used for the Yangtze River.

Analog time

1 Draw each of the following times on the **clock faces**:

a half past 9   b 4 o'clock   c 12 o'clock

d half past 7   e half past 11   f 8 o'clock

2 Draw each of the following times on the **clock faces**:

a quarter to 3   b quarter past 5   c quarter to 12

d quarter past 2   e quarter to 9   f quarter past 8

3 Write each of the following times in **words**:

a   b   c

d   e   f

4 Find the **difference** between half past 1 and the time shown:

a   b   c

d   e   f

5 Draw half past 2 on the **clock face**:

6 Draw quarter to 7 on the **clock face**:

7 Write in words. _____

8 Find the **difference** between half past 1 and ten to 5.

_____

9 Lunch time ends at 25 minutes past 1. If there is $1\frac{3}{4}$ hours left of school, **what time** will the bell ring to go home? _____

Digital time

1 Write each of the following in **digital time**:

a   b   c

d   e   f

2 For each of the following digital times, write **before midday or after midday**:

a   b   c

d   e   f

3 Use **am or pm** to write:

a 6:58 morning _____

b 7:10 evening _____

c 3:16 afternoon _____

d 2:11 morning _____

e 1:23 afternoon _____

f 1:06 morning _____

4 Find the **difference** between:

a 1:30 pm and 4:59 pm _____

b 7:48 am and 9:15 am _____

c 4:25 pm and 7:12 pm _____

d 4:47 pm and 10:19 pm _____

e 10:40 am and 2:37 pm _____

f 11:05 am and 5:52 pm _____

5 Write in digital time. _____

6 For 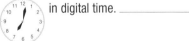, write **before midday or after**

midday. _____

7 Use **am or pm** to write 9:27 in the morning. _____

8 Find the **difference** between 9:03 am and 3:22 pm.

_____

9 Complete the clock faces to show a **difference** in time of 6 hours and 26 minutes.

Digital and analog time

1 Write each of the following times in **words**:

a

b

c

_____   _____   _____

d

e

f

_____   _____   _____

2 Draw each of the following times on the **clock faces**:

a 1:59 am   b 8:26 pm   c 6:44 am

d 5:09 pm   e 2:21 pm   f 4:40 am

3 Write each of the following as a **digital time**:

a

b

c

_____   _____   _____

d

e

f

_____   _____   _____

4 Write each of the following as a **digital time**:

a quarter to 1 _____

b 27 minutes past 4 _____

c 42 minutes past 9 _____

d 6 minutes to midday _____

e quarter past 6 _____

f 19 minutes to 5 _____

5 Write in words. _____

6 Draw 10:41 on the **clock face**:

7 Write in digital time. _____

8 Write 34 minutes past 10 as a **digital time**. _____

9 Complete with **< or >** to make the number sentence true:

22 minutes to 3 [ ] 2:35

24-hour time (1)

1 Use **24-hour time** to write:

a 1:12 am _____

b 9:03 am _____

c 5:52 am _____

d 6:47 pm _____

e 2:41 pm _____

f 11:23 pm _____

2 Use **am or pm** to write:

a 1437 _____

b 2348 _____

c 0729 _____

d 0304 _____

e 1915 _____

f 1322 _____

3 Write each of the following in **24-hour time**:

a AM 3:16   b PM 10:47   c PM 6:29

_____   _____   _____

d AM 4:53   e PM 7:02   f PM 8:36

_____   _____   _____

4 The following clocks show 24-hour time. Use **am or pm** to rewrite the times:

a 1025   b 2007   c 0138

_____   _____   _____

d 1659   e 0646   f 1217

_____   _____   _____

5 Use **24-hour time** to write 4:45 pm. _____

6 Use **am or pm** time to write 1126. _____

7 Write in **24-hour time**. _____

8 1823 shows 24-hour time. Use **am or pm** to rewrite the time. _____

9 The flight for Melbourne from Sydney leaves at 2016. **What time** is this in the evening? _____

24-hour time (2)

1 Use **am or pm** to write:

a 1953 _____

b 0649 _____

c 2316 _____

d 1624 _____

e 2231 _____

f 0105 _____

2 Use **24-hour time** to write each of the following:

a 11:26 pm _____

b 1:13 pm _____

c 7:12 am _____

d 4:48 am _____

e 5:59 pm _____

f 9:35 am _____

3 Use **24-hour time** to write each of the following:

a 29 past 11 evening _____

b 6 to 9 morning _____

c 17 past 3 morning _____

d 23 to 4 afternoon _____

e 14 to 8 evening _____

f 6 past 5 morning _____

4 Find the **difference** between:

a 4:27 am and 9:35 am _____

b 6:45 pm and 8:00 pm _____

c 10:26 am and 4:07 pm _____

d 8:25 am and 1:32 pm _____

e 0907 and 1345 _____

f 1629 and 1800 _____

5 Use **am or pm** to write 1752. _____

6 Use **24-hour time** to write 7:36 pm. _____

7 Use **24-hour time** to write 12 minutes past 6, morning.

_____

8 Find the **difference** between 1412 and 1605.

_____

9 Complete the table:

	Analog time	Digital time	24-hour time
16 minutes to 4 in the afternoon			

Stopwatches

1 Write each of the following **times in full**:

a 06:24:14 _____

b 13:36:40 _____

c 00:06:29 _____

d 01:43:05 _____

e 25:13:19 _____

f 47:12:63 _____

2 Circle the **faster (shorter) time** in each pair:

	Time 1	Time 2
a	00:09:64	00:09:60
b	03:26:71	03:30:85
c	11:42:19	11:40:42
d	35:25:40	34:37:56
e	44:18:98	44:20:29
f	26:25:40	26:35:10

3 Write the **difference** in time between:

a 07:40:71 and 07:40:65 _____

b 10: 05:26 and 10:05:37 _____

c 28:12:43 and 28:14:28 _____

d 17:26:19 and 17:35:22 _____

e 41:37:56 and 42:45:58 _____

f 03:59:42 and 04:00:56 _____

4 **Convert** each of the following time facts:

a $4\frac{1}{2}$ hours = _____ minutes

b 75 minutes = _____ seconds

c 360 seconds = _____ minutes

d 35 days = _____ weeks

e $2\frac{1}{2}$ days = _____ hours

f $4\frac{1}{2}$ years = _____ weeks

5 Write 26:09:47 **in full**.

6 Circle the **faster (shorter) time**:

Time 1	Time 2
10:06:19	10:47:45

7 Write the **difference** in time between 20:07:38 and 20:08:12 _____

8 **Convert**: 1 day = _____ minutes

9 **Complete** the table:

Days	Hours	Minutes	Seconds
$1\frac{1}{2}$			

Timelines

1 Mark the beginning of each of the tropical cyclones in the Australian region on the **timeline**:

a Phoebe: 31 August
b Raymond: 31 December
c Sally: 7 January
d Tim: 23 January
e Vivienne: 5 February
f Ingrid: 5 March

Aug. Sep. Oct. Nov. Dec. Jan. Feb. Mar. Apr.
      2004   2005

2 **How many days** were between the beginning of the tropical cyclones:

a Phoebe and Raymond? _____
b Sally and Tim? _____
c Vivienne and Ingrid? _____
d Phoebe and Sally? _____
e Raymond and Ingrid? _____
f Tim and Vivienne? _____

3 Many tropical cyclones last for a number of days. Mark the **duration** of each of the following cyclones on the timeline:

a Raymond: 31 December – 3 January
b Kerry: 3 – 15 January
c Sally: 7 – 10 January
d Tim: 23 – 26 January
e Harvey: 5 – 14 February
f Vivienne: 5 – 10 February

31   5   10   15   20   25   30   4   9   14   19   24   1   6   11   16

4 **Design** a **timeline** to show the following events in Cooper's life:

a went to the Commonwealth Games 2006
b born 1995
c represented school basketball team 2005
d started school 2000
e went to America 2003
f broke arm 2002

5 Add the tropical cyclone Willy: 9 to 10 March to the **timeline** of question 1.

6 **How many days** were there between the beginning of the topical cyclones Phoebe and Vivienne? _____

7 Tropical cyclone Will lasted 9 – 17 March. Mark this **duration** on the timeline of question 3.

8 **Add** 'sister born 1997' to Cooper's life timeline of question 4.

9 Investigate volcanoes and create a **timeline of eruptions**.

Timetables

Monday to Friday train timetable					
	am	am	pm	pm	pm
Galah	10:55	11:20	12:00	12:55	1:20
Cocky	11:00	11:25	12:05	1:00	1:25
Parrot	11:07	11:32	12:12	1:07	1:32
Budgie	11:17	11:42	12:22	1:17	1:42
Swan	11:26	11:51	12:31	1:26	1:51
Duck	11:30	11:55	12:35	1:30	1:55

1 Use **24-hour time** to write:

a 11:07 am _____
b 1:55 pm _____
c 12:22 pm _____
d 11:32 am _____
e 1:20 pm _____
f 1:00 pm _____

2 Use **am or pm** to write:

a 1055 _____
b 1200 _____
c 1320 _____
d 1351 _____
e 1126 _____
f 1307 _____

3 Use the timetable to find **what time** the train leaves:

a Budgie Station the first time _____
b Duck Station the last time _____
c Parrot Station in the morning _____
d Cocky Station in the morning _____
e Swan Station in the afternoon _____
f Galah Station in the afternoon _____

4

Sydney to Hobart flight timetable					
Sydney	0830	1130	1430	1530	1830
Hobart	1030	1330	1630	1730	2030

How many flights leave Sydney:

a before noon? _____
b after midday? _____

Give the arrival time (am or pm time) in Hobart for the following Sydney departure times:

c 1530 _____
d 0830 _____
e 1830 _____
f 1130 _____

5 Use **24-hour time** to write 12:12. _____

6 Use **am or pm** time to write 1325. _____

7 Use the timetable to find **what time** the train leaves Parrot Street in the afternoon. _____

8 On the timetable in question 4, how long is the flight?

_____

9 If the next train leaves Galah Station at 2:50 pm, **what time** does it arrive at Swan Station? _____

Time zones (1)

1 Write in **24-hour time**:

a 6:45 pm _____   b 2:55 pm _____

c 9:07 am _____   d 11:29 am _____

e 3:46 pm _____   f 1:49 am _____

2

Eastern Standard Time (EST)

Central Standard Time (CST) $\frac{1}{2}$ hour behind EST

Western Standard Time (WST) 2 hours behind EST

Complete the table to show the time in each time zone:

	WST	CST	EST
a	0245		
b		0915	
c			1120
d		1430	
e	1655		
f			2110

3 When it is 11:55 am in Melbourne, **give the time** in:

a Hobart _____   b Brisbane _____

c Adelaide _____   d Darwin _____

e Perth _____   f Sydney _____

4 If it is 10:30 am in Sydney, show the time on each of the following clocks for **daylight savings**:

a Darwin   b Melbourne   c Hobart

d Adelaide   e Perth   f Brisbane

5 Write 10:45 pm in **24-hour time**. _____

6 Complete the table:

	WST	CST	EST
		1905	

7 **Give the time** in Adelaide if it is 2:50 pm in Melbourne.

_____

8 Show the time in Adelaide if it is 11:10 am in Sydney during **daylight savings**:

9 If Craig's flight leaves Perth at 4:35 pm, **what time** does it arrive in Melbourne (non-daylight savings time) if the flight takes $3\frac{1}{2}$ hours? _____

Time zones (2)

1
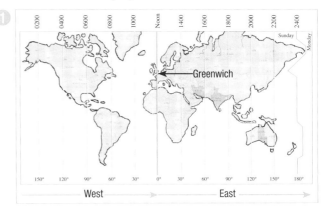

West   →   East

If it is noon at Greenwich, **what is the time** at the following longitudes?

a 30° west _____   b 60° east _____

c 120° east _____   d 90° west _____

e 150° west _____   f 90° east _____

2 If it is 7:00 pm at Greenwich, **what is the time** at the following longitudes?

a 30° east _____   b 90° west _____

c 120° west _____   d 60° west _____

e 150° east _____   f 90° east _____

3 If it is midnight in Hobart (150°E), **give the time** at:

a China 100°E _____   b Syria 40°E _____

c Greenland 40°W _____   d Alaska 160°W _____

e Iceland 20°W _____   f Poland 20°E _____

4 Find the **time at Greenwich** if it is noon at:

a Chad 20°E _____

b Cuba 80°W _____

c Argentina 60°W _____

d Indonesia 120°E _____

e India 80°E _____

f Ethiopia 40°E _____

5 If it is noon at Greenwich, **what is the time** at 60° west?

_____

6 If it is 7:00 pm at Greenwich, **what is the time** at 120° east? _____

7 If it is midnight in Hobart (150°E), **what time is it** at Mauritius 60°E? _____

8 Find the **time at Greenwich** if it is noon at Mongolia 100°E. _____

9 Using an atlas, find the countries that have the **same time zone** as Greenwich.

_____

Travelling speed

1 Give each of the following as an **average speed**.

a 100 km in 2 hours _____

b 50 km in 30 minutes _____

c 1500 km in 5 hours _____

d 270 km in 2 hours _____

e 100 m in 10 seconds _____

f 400 km in 2 minutes _____

2 Give the **distance** travelled in:

a 7 hours at 80 km/h. _____

b 5 hours at 110 km/h. _____

c 20 minutes at 200 m/min. _____

d 60 minutes at 2 m/min. _____

e 50 seconds at 10 m/s. _____

f $2\frac{1}{2}$ hours at 70 km/h. _____

3 Give the **time taken** to travel:

a 2 kilometres at 1 km/h. _____

b 200 metres at 5 m/s. _____

c 250 kilometres at 100 km/h. _____

d 650 metres at 15 m/s. _____

e 900 metres at 20 m/min. _____

f 35 kilometres at 70 km/h. _____

4 **Complete** the following table:

	Distance	Time	Av. speed
a	30 m	5 s	
b	100 m		50 m/s
c		10 s	20 m/s
d	1 km	10 min.	
e	100 km		50 km/h
f		3 h	80 km/h

5 What is the **average speed** of 80 kilometres in 2 hours?

_____

6 What **distance** is travelled in 90 seconds at 6 m/s?

_____

7 **How long** will it take to travel 375 kilometres at 75 km/h? _____

8 **Complete** the table:

Distance	Time	Av. speed
	3.5 h	200 m/h

9 A bus leaves at 6:15 am and arrives at its destination at 3:45 pm, 665 km away. What was the **average speed** of the bus? _____

Length in millimetres and centimetres

1 Use **decimal form** to write each of the following as centimetres:

a 39 mm _____   b 86 mm _____

c 91 mm _____   d 47 mm _____

e 23 mm _____   f 14 mm _____

2 Write each of the following in **millimetres**:

a 4.2 cm _____   b 8.9 cm _____

c 7.7 cm _____   d 1.2 cm _____

e 10.5 cm _____   f 13.6 cm _____

3 Order each of the following from **shortest to longest**:

a 19 cm, 200 mm, 21 cm, 19.8 cm

_____

b 46 mm, 4.2 cm, 5 cm, 51 mm

_____

c 87 mm, 8.3 cm, 8 cm, 86 mm

_____

d 400 mm, 46 cm, 0.5 m, 47.2 cm

_____

e 6.8 cm, 69 mm, 7 cm, 69.5 mm

_____

f 0.25 m, 290 mm, 26 cm, 27.3 cm

_____

4 Find the **total length** of each of the following:

a 21 cm and 240 mm _____

b 0.25 m and 48 cm _____

c 320 mm and 50 cm _____

d 90 cm and 1000 mm and 92.6 cm _____

e 420 mm and 38.6 cm and 20 cm _____

f 47.2 cm and 450 mm and 300 mm _____

5 Use **decimal** form to write 53 mm as centimetres.

_____

6 Write 27.3 cm in **millimetres**. _____

7 Order from **shortest to longest**:
2.6 m, 250 cm, 2100 mm, 270.8 cm

8 Find the **total length** of 81 cm and 560 mm and 900 mm.

_____

9 **How wide** is the living area if 12 tiles were needed to go across the room and each tile was 400 mm wide?

_____

Length in metres

1 Select the **most suitable unit** of measurement (mm, cm, m or km) for each of the following:

a the distance from your home to school _____

b the length of a pencil _____

c the width of a hair _____

d the length of a classroom _____

e the height of a drink bottle _____

f the distance between Canberra and Sydney _____

2 Use **decimal form** to write each of the following in **metres**:

a 3 m 26 cm _____

b 4 m 12 cm _____

c 8 m 91 cm _____

d 721 cm _____

e 847 cm _____

f 336 cm _____

3 How many **centimetres** are there in:

a 2 m? _____   b 7 m? _____

c 12 m? _____   d 4.69 m? _____

e 8.34 m? _____ f 5.76 m? _____

4 If a pool is 50 m long, indicate **how many laps** of the pool will be swum in each of the following:

a 200 m freestyle _____

b 400 m breaststroke _____

c 800 m backstroke _____

d 4 X 100 m relay _____

e 100 m butterfly _____

f 1500 m freestyle _____

5 Select the **most suitable unit** of measurement (mm, cm, m or km) for measuring the thickness of a piece of paper.

_____

6 Use **decimal form** to write 926 cm in metres.

_____

7 How many centimetres are there in 3.87 m? _____

8 If a pool is 25 m long, **how many laps** of the pool will be swum for the 400 m breaststroke? _____

9 **List 5 objects** that you can find that are approximately 1 metre long.

_____

Length in kilometres (1)

1 Write the number of **metres** in:

a 4 km _____

b 9 km _____

c 6 km _____

d 10 km _____

e 14 km _____

f 18 km _____

2 Convert the following to **kilometres**:

a 5000 m _____

b 3000 m _____

c 7000 m _____

d 11 000 m _____

e 16 000 m _____

f 20 000 m _____

3 Record each of the following in kilometres using **decimal notation**:

a 7436 m = _____

b 2163 m = _____

c 9105 m = _____

d 13 218 m = _____

e 16 243 m = _____

f 21 785 m = _____

4 Select the **most suitable unit** of measurement (mm, cm, m or km) to measure:

a the length of a basketball court _____

b the distance between Brisbane and Melbourne _____

c the thickness of a toothpick _____

d the length of a DVD box _____

e the width of New South Wales _____

f the distance around a sports ground _____

5 How many **metres** are there in 27 km? _____

6 How many **kilometres** are there in 13 000 m? _____

7 Record 2143 m in kilometres using **decimal notation**.

_____

8 Select the **most suitable unit** of measurement (mm, cm, m or km) to measure the length of the Sydney Harbour Bridge. _____

9 If a bus travelled at 78 km/h for 5 hours, **did it complete its journey** from Wagga Wagga to Mildura? The journey is approximately 600 km. _____

Length in kilometres (2)

1. Select the **most suitable unit** of measurement (cm, m or km) to measure:
   a the width of Bass Strait
   b the width of a road _____
   c the width of your book _____
   d the height of a basketball ring _____
   e the width of a computer screen _____
   f the distance between Sydney and London _____

2. Complete:

	metres	kilometres
a	3 720	
b	4 981	
c	6 342	
d	9 875	
e	14 264	
f	23 871	

3. Complete:

	kilometres	metres
a	2.31	
b	6.845	
c	2.8	
d	9.761	
e	12.31	
f	16.075	

4. Use the table to find the **distance** between:

Distances in kilometres	Adelaide	Alice Springs	Brisbane	Cairns	Canberra	Darwin
Adelaide		1320	1622	2779	970	2624
Alice Springs	1320		1966	1459	2258	1305
Brisbane	1622	1966		1391	951	3852
Cairns	2779	1459	1391		2210	1677
Canberra	970	2258	951	2210		3392
Darwin	2624	1305	3852	1677	3392	

   a Adelaide and Cairns _____
   b Brisbane and Cairns _____
   c Alice Springs and Darwin _____
   d Adelaide and Canberra _____
   e Canberra and Cairns _____
   f Adelaide and Darwin _____

5. Select the **most suitable unit** of measurement (cm, m or km) to measure the distance between the Earth and the moon. _____

6. Complete:

metres	kilometres
2106	

7. Complete:

kilometres	metres
4.302	

8. Use the table in question 4 to find the **distance** between Brisbane and Darwin. _____

9. Between which **two locations** in the table of question 4 do you travel 2258 km? _____

Converting lengths (1)

1. Use **decimal form** to write each of the following as **centimetres**:
   a 46 mm _____
   b 39 mm _____
   c 81 mm _____
   d 120 mm _____
   e 146 mm _____
   f 276 mm _____

2. Use **decimal form** to write each of the following as **metres**:
   a 461 cm _____
   b 738 cm _____
   c 926 cm _____
   d 1284 cm _____
   e 3695 cm _____
   f 2100 cm _____

3. Complete:

	metres	kilometres
a	1 376	
b	4 218	
c	5 798	
d	6 635	
e	9 801	
f	10 635	

4. **Complete** each of the following:
   a 55 m = _____ cm
   b 11.5 cm = _____ mm
   c 520 cm = _____ m
   d 9240 m = _____ km
   e 4.7 km = _____ m
   f $2\frac{1}{2}$ cm = _____ mm

5. Use **decimal form** to write 385 mm as **centimetres**.
   _____

6. Use **decimal form** to write 4716 cm as **metres**. _____

7. Complete:

metres	kilometres
21 763	

8. **Complete**: 2.65 m = _____ cm

9. If the running track is 400 m long and Leah runs 12 laps each day, **how far** does she run in total in:
   a metres? _____
   b kilometres? _____

Converting lengths (2)

1. Use **decimal form** to write each of the following in **centimetres**:
   a 96 mm _____
   b 27 mm _____
   c 83 mm _____
   d 129 mm _____
   e 463 mm _____
   f 3702 mm _____

2. Use **decimal form** to write each of the following in **metres**:
   a 147 cm _____
   b 218 cm _____
   c 532 cm _____
   d 8163 cm _____
   e 4790 cm _____
   f 3472 cm _____

3. Write each of the following in **metres**:
   a 7.6 km _____　　b 8.72 km _____
   c 4.832 km _____　　d 18.715 km _____
   e 46.210 km _____　　f 29.304 km _____

4. **Complete** the table:

	mm	cm	m
a			0.666
b	46		
c		83	
d			0.042
e	19		
f		24.1	

5. Use **decimal form** to write 9641 mm in **centimetres**.

   _____

6. Use **decimal form** to write 3719 cm in **metres**.

   _____

7. Write 21.03 km in **metres**. _____

8. **Complete** the table:

mm	cm	m
	13.6	

9. Calculate your **height** in mm, cm and m.

   _____

Perimeter (1)

1. Find the **perimeter** of each of the following shapes:

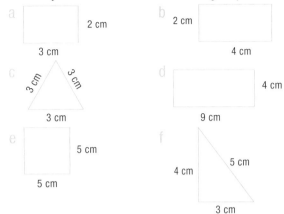

2. Find the **perimeter** of each of the following shapes:

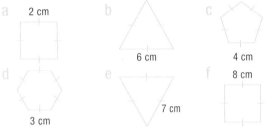

3. Complete the following table for the **rectangles**:

	Length	Breadth	Perimeter
a	12 cm	3 cm	
b	17 cm	1 cm	
c	12 cm	4 cm	
d	10.5 cm	2 cm	
e	16.5 cm	5.5 cm	
f	10 cm	9 cm	

4. Calculate the **perimeter** of each of the following shapes:
   a an equilateral triangle with sides of 6 cm _____
   b a square with sides of 20 cm _____
   c a regular hexagon with sides of 4 cm _____
   d a regular octagon with sides of 9 cm _____
   e an equilateral triangle with sides of 15 cm _____
   f a square with sides of 12 cm _____

5. Find the **perimeter**:
   7.5 cm
   6 cm

6. Find the **perimeter**:
   11 cm

7. **Complete**:

Length	Breadth	Perimeter
4 cm	2 cm	

8. Calculate the **perimeter** of a regular decagon with sides of 12 cm. _____

9. **On which polygons** can we use shortcuts to find the

Perimeter (2)

perimeter? _____

1 Circle the correct **perimeter** for each of the following rectangles:

	Length	Breadth	Perimeter		
a	4 cm	3 cm	12 cm	14 cm	16 cm
b	9 cm	7 cm	32 cm	63 cm	36 cm
c	11 m	9 m	40 m	44 m	99 m
d	6 m	3.5 m	16 m	18.5 m	19 m
e	16 km	4 km	40 km	64 km	80 km
f	20 km	15 km	70 km	150 km	300 km

2 **Complete** the table:

	Shape	Side length	Perimeter
a	square	7.2 cm	
b	equilateral triangle	19 cm	
c	regular pentagon	16 cm	
d	regular hexagon	11 cm	
e	regular octagon	14 m	
f	regular decagon	12 m	

3 Find the **perimeter** of each of the following:

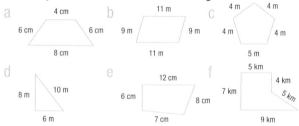

a　4 cm　6 cm　6 cm　8 cm
b　11 m　9 m　9 m　11 m
c　4 m　4 m　4 m　4 m　5 m
d　8 m　10 m　6 m
e　12 cm　6 cm　8 cm　7 cm
f　5 km　4 km　5 km　7 km　8 cm　9 km

4 Find the **side lengths** of each of the following squares with perimeters:

a　20 cm _____　b　16 m _____　c　64 km _____

d　100 mm _____　e　144 cm _____　f　96 m _____

5 Circle the correct **perimeter** for the rectangle:

Length	Breadth	Perimeter		
19 cm	7 cm	42 cm	50 cm	52 cm

6 **Complete** the table:

Shape	Side length	Perimeter
regular heptagon	4 cm	

7 Find the **perimeter** of: 3 m　3 m　5 m　5 m _____

8 Find the **side length** of a square with a perimeter of 28 m. _____

9 Draw **3 different examples** of isosceles triangles with a perimeter of 40 cm.

Area in cm²

1 **Complete** the table:

		Length (cm)	Breadth (cm)	Area (cm²)
a	4 × 4			
b	6 × 2			
c	7 × 3			
d	5 × 5			
e	2 × 1			
f	12 × 9			

2 Calculate the **area** of each of the following shapes:

a　5 cm　2 cm
b　11 cm　9 cm
c　6 cm　7 cm
d　3 cm　6 cm
e　4 cm　8 cm
f　5 cm　8 cm

_____

3 **Complete** the following:

	Length (cm)	Breadth (cm)	Area (cm²)
a	3	2	
b	7	8	
c	4	3	
d	8	5	
e	12	9	
f	15	2	

4 Calculate the **area** of each square with the following side lengths:

a　7 cm _____　b　9 cm _____　c　11 cm _____

d　3 cm _____　e　8 cm _____　f　6 cm _____

5 **Complete** the table:

	Length (cm)	Breadth (cm)	Area (cm²)
9 cm × 3 cm			

6 Calculate the **area** of: 6 cm　2 cm _____

7 **Complete** the following:

Length (cm)	Breadth (cm)	Area (cm²)
9	1	

8 Calculate the **area** of a square with side length 10 cm.

_____

9 Find the **area** of:

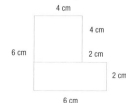

4 cm　4 cm　6 cm　2 cm　2 cm　6 cm

Excel Start Up Maths Year 6

☞ **Answers on page 14**

Area in m²

1 Circle the **correct area** for each of the following rectangles:

	Length (m)	Breadth (m)	Area (m²)		
a	10	3	17	34	30
b	5	8	13	26	40
c	9	6	40	54	63
d	4	2	8	16	20
e	7	3	20	21	23
f	11	9	40	81	99

2 Calculate the **area** of each of the following:

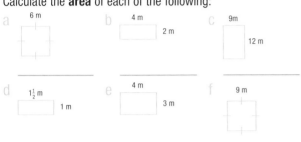

3 **Complete** the following table:

	Length (m)	Breadth (m)	Area (m²)
a	4	3	
b	9	2	
c	5	10	
d	20	4	
e	100	50	
f	60	3	

4 Find the **area** of each of the following:

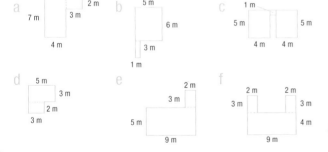

5 Circle the **correct area** for the rectangle:

Length (m)	Breadth (m)	Area (m²)		
10	12	44	120	140

6 Calculate the area: 3 m

7 **Complete** the table:

Length (m)	Breadth (m)	Area (m²)
$2\frac{1}{2}$	2	

8 Find the area: 2 m   3 m   5 m   3 m

9 Find the **side lengths** of a rectangle that has an area of 42 m². _____

Area of a triangle (1)

1 **Complete** the following table:

		Area rectangle (cm²)	Area triangle (cm²)
a	5 cm, 4 cm		
b	7 cm, 4 cm		
c	5 cm, 4 cm		
d	10 cm, 9 cm		
e	10 cm, 9 cm		
f	2 cm, 6 cm		

2 **Complete** the following table:

	Length (m)	Breadth (m)	Area rectangle (cm²)	Area triangle (cm²)
a	2	4		
b	7	6		
c	4	8		
d	9	2		
e	10	7		
f	3	6		

3 Find the **area** of each triangle:

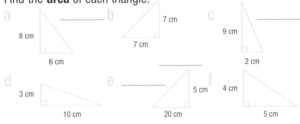

4 **Complete** the following table:

	b (cm)	$\frac{1}{2}$ b (cm)	h (cm²)	A (cm²)
a	6		3	
b	4		7	
c	8		9	
d	10		6	
e	12		10	

5 **Complete** the table:

	Area rectangle (cm²)	Area triangle (cm²)
8 cm, 4 cm		

6 **Complete** the table:

Base (m)	Height (m)	Area rectangle (m²)	Area triangle (m²)
8	6		

7 Find the **area**:   3 cm   4 cm _____

8 **Complete** the table:

b (cm)	$\frac{1}{2}$ b (cm)	h (cm²)	A (cm²)
12		7	

9 Express the formula for the **area** of the triangle in **words**:

_____

Area of a triangle (2)

1 **Complete** the following table:

	Area triangle (m²)
a 5 m, 6 m	
b 7 m, 3 m	
c 4 m	
d 9 m, 2 m	
e 10 m, 8 m	
f 6 m, 3 m	

2 Find the **area** of each of the shaded triangles:

a 6 m, 7 m

b 9 m, 4 m

c 5 m, 12 m

d 3 m, 4 m

e 5 m, 10 m

f 6 m

3 Find the **area** of each of the following triangles:

a 4 m, 8 m

b 9 m, 5 m

c 3 m, 12 m

d 5 m, 6 m

e 7 m, 6 m

f 10 m, 2 m

4 Find the **area** of each of the following triangles with:

a $b = 6$ cm and $h = 9$ cm _____

b $b = 4$ cm and $h = 8$ cm _____

c $b = 20$ cm and $h = 10$ cm _____

d $b = 4$ m and $h = 5$ m _____

e $b = 12$ m and $h = 12$ m _____

f $b = 20$ m and $h = 7$ m _____

5 **Complete** the table:

	Area triangle (m²)
7 cm, 4 cm	

6 Find the **area** of the shaded triangle: _____
8 m

7 Find the **area**: _____
12 cm, 9 cm

8 Find the **area** of a triangle with $b = 10$ cm and $h = 9$ cm. _____

9 Find the **area** of the trapezium: _____

8 cm, 12 cm, 2 cm, 2 cm

Hectares

1 Circle the places with areas which could be measured in **hectares**:

a   a backyard   b   a suburb

c   a small garden   d   a local park

e   a football stadium   f   a classroom

2 Use the **short form** to write:

a   9 hectares _____

b   4 hectares _____

c   11 hectares _____

d   47 hectares _____

e   69 hectares _____

f   47.6 hectares _____

3 Convert each of the following to **hectares** (ha):

a   30 000 m² _____

b   90 000 m² _____

c   50 000 m² _____

d   120 000 m² _____

e   140 000 m² _____

f   200 000 m² _____

4 Convert each of the following to **square metres** (m²):

a   2 ha _____

b   6 ha _____

c   7 ha _____

d   13 ha _____

e   15 ha _____

f   19 ha _____

5 Circle the places with areas which would be measured in **hectares**:

a tennis court   a beach   a farm

6 Use the **short form** to write 58.7 hectares. _____

7 Convert 150 000 m² to **hectares**. _____

8 Convert 21 hectares to **square metres** (m²).
_____

9 **Estimate** how many of each of the following will **fit into a hectare** and circle your estimate:

a a tennis court	1	2	10	40
b a suburban house block	3	5	10	20
c a bedroom	25	100	200	500

Square kilometres (1)

1 Circle the places with areas which are measured in **square kilometres**:

a a warehouse   b a country

c a state   d a sports oval

e a bedroom   f a national park

2 Convert each of the following to **hectares** (ha):

a 2 km2 _____

b 5 km2 _____

c 8 km2 _____

d 10 km2 _____

e 14 km2 _____

f 25 km2 _____

3 Convert each of the following to **square kilometres** (km^2):

a 400 ha _____   b 700 ha _____

c 300 ha _____   d 1200 ha _____

e 1500 ha _____   f 2700 ha _____

4 Find the **difference** in area between each of the following countries:

	Country 1	Area (km²)	Country 2	Area (km²)	Difference
a	Greece	132 561	Nepal	141 414	
b	Italy	301 049	Poland	311 700	
c	Iraq	435 120	Egypt	999 740	
d	Japan	370 370	Thailand	519 083	
e	Iran	1 626 520	India	3 268 580	
f	Mexico	1 972 360	Argentina	2 797 109	

5 Circle the places with areas which are measured in **square kilometres**:

a a golf course   b a national park   c a table

6 Convert 19 km2 to **hectares** (ha). _____

7 Convert 3000 ha to **square kilometres** (km^2).

_____

8 Find the **difference** in area between:

Country 1	Area (km²)	Country 2	Area (km²)	Difference
Australia	7 682 300	Canada	9 976 185	

9 Complete the measurement facts:

100 mm2 = ☐ cm^2

10 000 cm2 = ☐ m^2

10 000 m2 = ☐ ha

100 ha = ☐ km^2

Square kilometres (2)

1 Write the **most suitable unit** of measurement (m^2, ha or km^2) for the area of:

a America _____   b a swimming pool _____

c a rug _____   d a shopping centre _____

e a golf course _____ f an outback station _____

2 Complete the table:

	m²	ha
a	30 000	
b	50 000	
c	90 000	
d	110 000	
e	190 000	
f	240 000	

3 Complete the table:

	ha	km²
a	400	
b	800	
c	110	
d	468	
e	395	
f	961	

4 Complete with **< or >** to make the number statement true:

a 463 000 ha ☐ 4 km^2

b 80 000 m^2 ☐ 86 ha

c 900 000 m^2 ☐ 9.1 km^2

d 6.31 km^2 ☐ 646 000 ha

e 245 km^2 ☐ 250 000 ha

f 1.21 km^2 ☐ 120 000 m^2

5 Write the **most suitable unit** of measurement (m^2, ha or km^2) for the area of NSW.

6 Complete the table:

m²	ha
52 000	

7 Complete the table:

ha	km²
476	

8 Complete with **< or >** to make the number statement true:
949 000 m^2 ☐ 900 ha

9 What is the **total area** of France (550 634 km^2), Italy (301 049 km^2) and Germany (357 041 km^2)?

_____

Mass in grams and kilograms

1 How many **grams** are there in each of the following?

- a 0.412 kg _____
- b 0.5 kg _____
- c 0.25 kg _____
- d 0.841 kg _____
- e 0.236 kg _____
- f 0.116 kg _____

2 Use **decimal notation** to write each of the following:

- a 1 kg 720 g _____
- b 6 kg 100 g _____
- c 4 kg 250 g _____
- d 5 kg 136 g _____
- e 9 kg 648 g _____
- f 10 kg 985 g _____

3 How many **grams** are there in each of the following?

- a 3.246 kg _____
- b 1.079 kg _____
- c 4.6 kg _____
- d 8.21 kg _____
- e 9.317 kg _____
- f 5.556 kg _____

4 **Complete** the following table:

	grams	kilograms
a		2.160
b	3276	
c	4200	
d		1.05
e		7
f	9245	

5 How many **grams** are there in 0.72 kg? _____

6 Use **decimal notation** to write 7 kg 226 g.

_____

7 How many **grams** are there in 4.109 kg? _____

8 **Complete** the table:

grams	kilograms
	1.025

9 A jar of nuts has a mass of 1 kg. If the jar's mass is 180 g, what is the **mass of the nuts**? _____

Mass in tonnes

1 Select the **most suitable unit** of mass (g, kg or tonnes) for measuring each of the following:

- a a dog _____
- b a train _____
- c a man _____
- d a box of matches _____
- e a boat _____
- f a pen _____

2 How many **kilograms** are there in each of the following?

- a 2 t _____
- b 9 t _____
- c 4 t _____
- d 11 t _____
- e 15 t _____
- f 20 t _____

3 How many **tonnes** are there in each of the following?

- a 1000 kg _____
- b 5000 kg _____
- c 8000 kg _____
- d 19 000 kg _____
- e 30 000 kg _____
- f 52 000 kg _____

4 How many **kilograms** are there in each of the following?

- a 2.1 t _____
- b 7.6 t _____
- c 4.8 t _____
- d 3.215 t _____
- e 9.746 t _____
- f 21.08 t _____

5 Select the **most suitable unit** of mass (g, kg or tonnes) for measuring a truck. _____

6 How many **kilograms** are there in 27 t? _____

7 How many **tonnes** are there in 27 000 kg? _____

8 How many **kilograms** are there in 14.302 t?

9 When fully loaded, the mass of a delivery truck is 4 t 390 kg. After the first delivery, the mass of the truck is 2 t 760 kg. What was the **mass of the first delivery**?

_____

Mass in tonnes and kilograms

1 Match the **most suitable measuring device** with the item to be weighed.

a　standard balance scales　　some sugar

b　bathroom scales　　　　　a truck

c　kitchen scales　　　　　　a bag of apples

d　weighbridge　　　　　　　a suitcase

e　spring balance　　　　　　a boy

f　airport scales　　　　　　a small piece of gold

2 How many **kilograms** are there in each of the following?

a　7 t _____

b　14 t _____

c　3.5 t _____

d　11.5 t _____

e　44.25 t _____

f　1.75 t _____

3 How many **tonnes** are there in each of the following?

a　9000 kg _____

b　21 000 kg _____

c　10 500 kg _____

d　7250 kg _____

e　14 750 kg _____

f　45 500 kg _____

4 **Complete** the following table:

	kilograms	tonnes
a	6 320	
b		4.5
c		7.812
d	3 125	
e	41 600	
f		5.836

5 Circle the **most suitable measuring device** for weighing a caravan:

• weighbridge

• displacement tank

• standard balance scales

6 How many **kilograms** are there in $2\frac{1}{2}$ t? _____

7 How many **tonnes** are there in 19 250 kg? _____

8 **Complete** the table:

kilograms	tonnes
	$7\frac{1}{4}$

9 What **volume of water** would have a mass of 2 kg?

_____

Capacity in millilitres and litres (1)

1 Find the **cubic centimetres** (cm^3) in:

a　40 mL _____

b　90 mL _____

c　75 mL _____

d　250 mL _____

e　440 mL _____

f　375 mL _____

2 Find the **millilitres** (mL) in:

a　60 cm^3 _____

b　25 cm^3 _____

c　80 cm^3 _____

d　460 cm^3 _____

e　790 cm^3 _____

f　920 cm^3 _____

3 Find the **cubic centimetres** (cm^3) in:

a　2 L _____

b　4 L _____

c　9 L _____

d　12 L _____

e　17 L _____

f　22 L _____

4 Find the **litres** (L) in:

a　1000 cm^3 _____

b　7000 cm^3 _____

c　8000 cm^3 _____

d　14 000 cm^3 _____

e　16 000 cm^3 _____

f　24 000 cm^3 _____

5 Find the **cubic centimetres** (cm^3) in 650 mL.

_____

6 Find the **millilitres** (mL) in 240 cm^3. _____

7 Find the **cubic centimetres** (cm^3) in 6 L. _____

8 Find the **litres** (L) in 19 000 cm^3. _____

9 On an excursion, 22 students each drank 125 mL of juice. What was the **total amount** of juice drunk?

_____

See START UPS page 15

Capacity in millilitres and litres (2)

1 Use **decimal notation** to write each of the following as litres:

a 927 mL _____

b 446 mL _____

c 832 mL _____

d 42 mL _____

e 50 mL _____

f 100 mL _____

2 How many **millilitres** are there in each of the following?

a 0.791 L _____

b 0.398 L _____

c 0.852 L _____

d 0.017 L _____

e 0.095 L _____

f 0.04 L _____

3 How many **millilitres** are there in each of the following?

a 2.163 L _____

b 9.487 L _____

c 8.215 L _____

d 6.024 L _____

e 4.117 L _____

f 2.008 L _____

4 How many **litres** are there in each of the following?

a 2 L 375 mL _____

b 9 L 456 mL _____

c 4 L 250 mL _____

d 9701 mL _____

e 4635 mL _____

f 21 785 mL _____

5 Use **decimal notation** to write 350 mL as litres.

_____

6 How many **millilitres** are there in 0.146 L? _____

7 How many **millilitres** are there in 7.612 L? _____

8 How many **litres** are there in 31 240 mL? _____

9 **Complete** the table for water:

Capacity	Volume	Mass
1 mL		
	50 cm³	
		500 g

 See START UPS page 15

Kilograms and litres

1 What is the **equivalent mass** (kg) for each of the following quantities of water?

a 2 L _____

b 5 L _____

c 8 L _____

d 12 L _____

e 19 L _____

f 25 L _____

2 **Convert** the following masses of water to capacity:

a 3 kg _____

b 7 kg _____

c 10 kg _____

d 13 kg _____

e 15 kg _____

f 22 kg _____

3 **Convert** the following capacities of water to mass:

a 300 mL _____

b 10 mL _____

c 85 mL _____

d 450 mL _____

e 975 mL _____

f 260 mL _____

4 **Convert** these masses of water to capacity:

a 5 g _____

b 25 g _____

c 60 g _____

d 120 g _____

e 380 g _____

f 790 g _____

5 What is the **equivalent mass** (kg) for 15 L of water?

_____

6 What **capacity of water** (L) would have a mass of 17 kg?

_____

7 What is the **equivalent mass** (g) for 620 mL of water?

_____

8 What **capacity of water** (mL) would have a mass of 325 g?

_____

9 **Complete** the table for water:

Capacity	Volume	Mass
5 mL		
		400 g
	1000 cm³	

Cubic centimetres and litres

1. What are the **capacities** (mL) that the following containers can hold?
   a 20 cm³ _____
   b 60 cm³ _____
   c 85 cm³ _____
   d 500 cm³ _____
   e 150 cm³ _____
   f 825 cm³ _____

2. How many **cubic centimetres** (cm³) are there in each of the following?
   a 15 mL _____
   b 40 mL _____
   c 75 mL _____
   d 520 mL _____
   e 660 mL _____
   f 975 mL _____

3. **Convert** the following into litres:
   a 6000 cm³ _____
   b 9000 cm³ _____
   c 3000 cm³ _____
   d 1000 cm³ _____
   e 8000 cm³ _____
   f 7000 cm³ _____

4. How many **cubic centimetres** (cm³) are there in each of the following?
   a 4 L _____
   b 5 L _____
   c 2 L _____
   d 10 L _____
   e 14 L _____
   f 17 L _____

5. What is the **capacity** (mL) of a container that can hold 700 cm³? _____

6. How many **cubic centimetres** (cm³) are in 850 mL?

   _____

7. What is the **capacity** (L) of a container that can hold 11 000 cm³? _____

8. How many **cubic centimetres** (cm³) are there in 12 L?

   _____

9. Three bottles each hold 250 mL of water. If all this water was poured into a container with a capacity of 1 L, what **volume** (cm³) **remained unfilled**? _____

Cubic centimetres

1. **Complete** the table:

	Length (cm)	Breadth (cm)	Height (cm)	Volume (cm³)
a				
b				
c				
d				
e				
f				

2. Calculate the **volume** of each of the following prisms:

a (5 cm, 4 cm, 4 cm) b (2 cm, 6 cm, 7 cm) c (5 cm, 9 cm, 10 cm)

_____ _____ _____

d (4 cm, 3 cm, 7 cm) e (2 cm, 10 cm, 4 cm) f (4 cm, 8 cm, 4 cm)

_____ _____ _____

3. **Complete**:

	Length (cm)	Breadth (cm)	Height (cm)	Volume (cm³)
a	4	3	2	
b	2	1	1	
c	2	2	3	
d	4	2	1	
e	4	2	6	
f	7	3	5	

4. How many **millilitres** of water would be displaced by centicube models of the following volumes?
   a 9 cm³ _____   b 200 cm³ _____
   c 47 cm³ _____   d 1000 cm³ _____
   e 950 cm³ _____   f 1200 cm³ _____

5. **Complete** the table:

	Length (cm)	Breadth (cm)	Height (cm)	Volume (cm³)

6. Calculate the **volume** of the prism: _____

7. **Complete** the table:

Length (cm)	Breadth (cm)	Height (cm)	Volume (cm³)
4	2	2	

8. How many **millilitres** of water would be displaced by centicube models of 825 cm³ _____

9. **Sketch a prism** that has a volume of 10 cm³.

Cubic metres

1 Use the **abbreviated form** to write:

a　9 cubic metres _____

b　14 cubic metres _____

c　32 cubic metres _____

d　46 cubic metres _____

e　85 cubic metres _____

f　74 cubic metres _____

2 Tick the column which gives the **correct volume**:

	Item	Less than 1 m³	About 1 m³	More than 1 m³
a	swimming pool			
b	lunch box			
c	fruit crate			
d	telephone box			
e	CD case			
f	garbage bin			

3 Select the **most suitable unit** of volume (cm³ or m³) for each of the following:

a　a matchbox: 30 _____　b　a bathroom: 40 _____

c　a tool box: 100 _____　d　a water tank: 5000 _____

e　a trailer: 2 _____　f　a cereal box: 2500 _____

4 Find the **volume** of each of the following:

a 　b 　c

_____　_____　_____

d 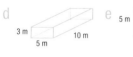　e 　f

_____　_____　_____

5 Use the **abbreviated form** to write 53 cubic metres.

_____

6 Tick the column which gives the **correct volume**:

Item	Less than 1 m³	About 1 m³	More than 1 m³
train carriage			

7 Select the **most suitable unit** of volume (cm³ or m³) for a pencil case: 300 _____

8 Find the **volume** of: _____

9 **How many boxes** 50 cm × 50 cm × 50 cm would fit inside 1 cubic metre? _____

Volume (1)

1 Select the **most suitable unit** (cm³ or m³) to find the volume of:

a　a shoe box _____　b　a briefcase _____

c　a garage _____　d　a shipping container _____

e　a school hall _____　f　an ice-cream container _____

2 What is the **volume** of each of the following?

a 　b 　c

_____　_____　_____

d 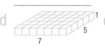　e 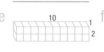　f

_____　_____　_____

3 Write each of the volumes from question 2 in **ascending order**:

a _____　b _____　c _____

d _____　e _____　f _____

4 Calculate the volume of each of the following **prisms**:

	Length (cm)	Breadth (cm)	Height (cm)	Volume (cm³)
a	8	4	2	
b	6	3	7	
c	2	1	8	
d	4	2	2	
e	1	1	2	
f	5	3	1	

5 Select the **most suitable unit** (cm³ or m³) for finding the volume of a milk crate. _____

6 Find the **volume** of:  _____

7 Write the following volumes in **ascending order**:
23 cm³, 12 cm³, 20 cm³, 18 cm³

_____

8 Calculate the volume of the **prism**:

Length (cm)	Breadth (cm)	Height (cm)	Volume (cm³)
4	2	7	

9 Find 3 different prisms that give a volume of 24 cm³ and **complete** the table:

Volume (cm³)	Length (cm)	Breadth (cm)	Height (cm)
24	2	2	
24			
24			

Volume (2)

1 Order the following items from **smallest volume** (a) **to greatest volume** (f): an apple, a basketball, a golf ball, a marble, a tennis ball and a watermelon:

a _____   b _____
c _____   d _____
e _____   f _____

2 Find the **volume** of each of the following **cubes**:

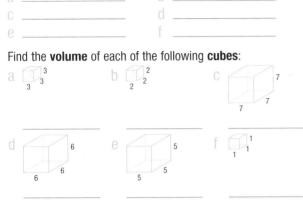

a _____   b _____   c _____

d _____   e _____   f _____

3 Find the **volume** of each of the following **shapes**:

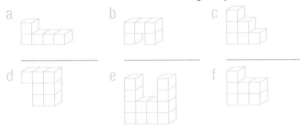

a _____   b _____   c _____

d _____   e _____   f _____

4 Find the **volume** of each of the following **prisms** (measurements in cm):

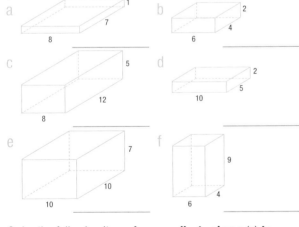

a _____   b _____

c _____   d _____

e _____   f _____

5 Order the following items from **smallest volume** (a) **to greatest volume** (c): cereal box, shoe box, matchbox

_____

6 Find the **volume** of the **cube**: 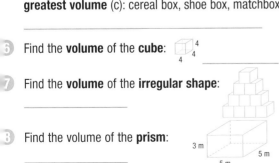 _____

7 Find the **volume** of the **irregular shape**:

_____

8 Find the volume of the **prism**:

3 m   5 m
5 m

_____

9 Which of the following 3 prisms has the **greatest volume**?

a 5 × 4 × 3   b 6 × 2 × 7   c 5 × 4 × 3

Arrangements (1)

1 Use the scale 0 to 1 to rate the **chance** of each of the following events happening:

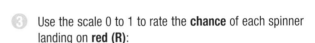

a I will have a birthday next year. _____

b I will fly to the moon next week. _____

c My first toss of a coin will be a head. _____

d My first roll of a dice will be a 6. _____

e The sun will rise tomorrow. _____

f Australia will win the next game of cricket they play.

_____

2 Are the following **correct arrangements** of △△○□?

a △○□△   b △○○□   c □○△□

d □○△△   e △○□△   f △△○□

3 Use the scale 0 to 1 to rate the **chance** of each spinner landing on **red (R)**:

a _____   b _____   c _____

d _____   e _____   f _____

4 Use the scale 0 to 1 to rate the **chance** of each of the spinners in question 3 landing on **blue (B)**:

a _____   b _____   c _____

d _____   e _____   f _____

5 Use the scale 0 to 1 to rate the **chance** that I will go to school on Christmas day. _____

6 Are the following **correct arrangements** of △△○○?

a ○○△△   b △○○△   c △△△○

7 Use the scale 0 to 1 to rate the **chance** of the spinner landing on **red (R)**. _____

8 Use the scale 0 to 1 to rate the **chance** of the spinner landing on **blue (B)**: _____

9 **List three events** that may happen tomorrow. Give them a rating of 0 to 1 for the chance of each event.

_____
_____

Arrangements (2)

1 What is the chance that:

a I will watch television today? _____

b it will snow tomorrow? _____

c the next person to enter the room will be male? _____

d I will have a haircut this month? _____

e I will have a sandwich for lunch next week? _____

f I will be prime minister when I grow up? _____

2 There are 10 coloured balls in a box. State the **likelihood** of drawing each coloured ball as a fraction:

a red (R)

b blue (B)

c yellow (Y)

d pink (P)

e white (W)

f orange (O)

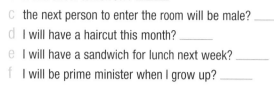

3

Which of the spinners has the **greatest chance** of landing on:

a blue (B)? _____   b white (W)? _____

c red (R)? _____   d orange (O)? _____

e green (G)? _____   f yellow (Y)? _____

4 Which spinners in question 3 have **more than a 0% and less than a 50% chance** of landing on:

a orange (O)? _____   b blue (B)? _____

c white (W)? _____   d pink (P)? _____

e green (G)? _____   f red (R)? _____

5 What is the **chance** that I will be older than 10 next year? _____

6 State the **likelihood** of selecting a purple ball as a fraction of the box in question 2. _____

7 Which of the spinners in question 3 has the **greatest chance** of landing on pink (P)? _____

8 Which of the spinners in question 3 have **more than a 0% and less than a 50% chance** of landing on yellow (Y)? _____

9 What are all the **different combinations** of rolling 2 dice? _____

Predicting

1 Hannah conducted a survey of 50 children to find their favourite drink.

Milk	Water	Juice	Soft drink	Cordial	Other
9	13	8	12	5	3

Use the information to **predict how many** children in each 100 would prefer:

a water _____   b soft drink _____   c cordial _____

d other _____   e juice _____   f milk _____

2 Using the information in question 1, **predict how many** children in each 1000 would prefer:

a juice _____   b cordial _____

c water _____   d milk _____

e soft drink _____   f other _____

3 Fifty children were surveyed to find their favourite colour:

red	blue	yellow	green	orange	pink	black
10	9	6	4	4	9	8

Use the information to **predict how many** children in each 100 would prefer:

a red _____   b green _____   c pink _____

d blue _____   e yellow _____   f orange _____

4 Use the information in question 3 to **predict how many** children in each 1000 would prefer:

a yellow _____   b green _____   c orange _____

d blue _____   e black _____   f pink _____

5 Use the information in question 1 to **predict how many** children in each 100 would prefer milk or water. _____

6 Use the information in question 1 to **predict how many** children in each 1000 would prefer soft drink or cordial.

_____

7 Use the information in question 3 to **predict how many** children in each 100 would prefer the colour black.

_____

8 Use the information in question 3 to **predict how many** children in each 1000 would prefer the colour red.

_____

9 **Draw a tree diagram** for the possibilities of spinning the spinner 3 times.

Tables and graphs

1) Mrs Jones surveyed her class to find their main use of the computer. Their use was email (E), internet (I), games (G) and homework (H). Here is the data for the class:
E, I, G, I, E, H, I, G, I, E, I, I, H, G, H, E, G, G, E, I, I, H, G, G, E, I, H, H, E, I, G, G, E, G.

Create a **tally table** from the information.

Computer use	Tally
email	c _____
a _____	d _____
b _____	e _____
homework	f _____

2) **How many** children used the computer for:
a email? _____
b homework? _____
c games? _____
d internet? _____
e email or internet? _____
f games or homework? _____

3) Use the tally table in question 1 to **complete the graph** and give a and b suitable titles:

4) **From the graph**, which computer use had:
a 5 children or more? _____
b 8 children? _____
c the most children? _____
d the least children? _____
e less than 8 children? _____
f between 5 and 9 children? _____

5) What was the **total number** of children in the class?
_____

6) **How many** children used the computer for activities other than homework? _____

7) What is a possible **title** for the graph in question 3?
_____

8) **From the graph**, which computer use has less than 6 children? _____

9) **Survey your class** about computer use and create a tally table and graph.

Bar graphs (divided)

1) On the table were 100 counters. Jo drew a bar 80 mm long, so each 0.8 mm stood for one counter.

blue	green	yellow	red

Measuring in millimetres, **how long** is the graph showing:
a green counters? _____
b red counters? _____
c yellow counters? _____
d blue counters? _____
e red or yellow counters? _____
f blue or green counters? _____

2) Measuring in millimetres, **what fraction** of the graph shows:
a yellow counters? _____
b red counters? _____
c blue counters? _____
d green counters? _____
e white counters? _____
f green or yellow counters? _____

3) Of the total number of counters, **how many** were:
a blue? _____   b red? _____
c green? _____   d yellow? _____
e blue or green? _____   f green or yellow? _____

4) Measuring in centimetres, **what fraction** of the graph shows:
a yellow counters? _____
b green counters? _____
c blue counters? _____
d red counters? _____
e blue or green counters? _____
f yellow or red counters? _____

5) Measuring in millimetres, **how long** is the graph showing green, yellow or red counters? _____

6) Measuring in millimetres, **what fraction** of the graph shows blue or green counters? _____

7) Of the total number of counters, **how many** were green, yellow or red? _____

8) Measuring in centimetres, **what fraction** of the graph shows green or yellow counters? _____

9) In a class of 20 students, here are their hair colours:

brown	blond	black	red
6	8	4	2

Construct a divided bar graph for the hair colour of the students. Each space represents two students.

Pie charts

1 For a school of 200 students, this is the breakdown of students' winter sports. **Complete the table** using the information from the pie graph:

Sport	Fraction	%	No.
football	a	37.5	75
dancing	$\frac{1}{8}$	12.5	b
indoor soccer	c	d	50
netball	$\frac{1}{4}$	e	f

2 For a school of 200 students, this is a breakdown of the students' summer sports. **Complete the table**:

	Sport	Fraction	%	No.
a	cricket			
b	netball			
c	athletics			
d	surfing			
e	swimming			
f	softball			

3 Using the information from questions 1 and 2:

a **What is** the favourite winter sport? _____

b **What is** the favourite summer sport? _____

c **How many** students play netball in both winter and summer? _____

d **Do more students** do dancing or softball? _____

e What is the **total number** of students doing water sports? _____

f What is the **total number** of students playing ball sports in winter? _____

4 The pie chart represents the city of origin of 800 people arriving at a Sydney Train Station. Each section represents 50 people. **How many** people come from:

a Melbourne? _____

b Brisbane? _____

c Adelaide? _____

d Cairns? _____

e Perth? _____

f Adelaide or Perth? _____

5 What is the **fraction** of students playing netball and football in question 1?

6 What **percentage of** students played netball in question 2? _____

7 What was the **total number of** students playing ball sports in summer and winter in questions 1 and 2? _____

8 Using the information from question 4, **how many** people arrived from Cairns or Brisbane? _____

9 **Construct a pie chart** using the information:

Preferred ice-cream flavour	No.	Degrees
chocolate	40	
vanilla	25	
strawberry	20	
caramel	10	
other	5	

Mean, median and graphs

1 Find the **mean** of each set of measurements:

a 20 mL, 80 mL, 60 mL, 80 mL _____

b 19 m, 13 m, 8 m, 11 m, 14 m _____

c 2428 mm, 3380 mm, 492 mm _____

d 38°C, 32°C, 19°C, 25°C, 26°C _____

e 42 g, 66 g, 25 g, 35 g, 71 g, 52 g _____

f 650 kg, 880 kg, 475 kg, 495 kg _____

2 What are the **means** (correct to one decimal place) of the following scores?

a 320, 640, 725, 830, 955, 756 _____

b 1128, 4326, 4980, 3620, 1175, 2246 _____

c 4280, 5600, 6325, 5920, 4955, 6892 _____

d 9980, 9762, 9543, 9029, 9785, 9421, 9360

e 22 510, 23 960, 24 785, 22 897, 27 463, 28 486, 22 435

_____

f 41 600, 43 900, 48 750, 50 210, 40 740, 48 240

_____

3 **Complete the table** and calculate the **mean** maximum temperature for the town in the 1st week of April.

Date	3/4	4/4	5/4	6/4	7/4	8/4
Temp. (°C)	a	b	c	d	e	f

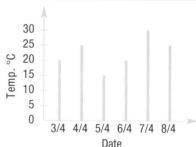

_____

4 What is the **median** of:

a 2, 4, 6, 8, 10? _____

b 1, 3, 5, 7, 9, 11, 13? _____

c 40, 60, 80, 90, 110? _____

d 1.2, 1.8, 2.3, 3.5, 4.6, 5.2? _____

e 160, 190, 250, 310, 360? _____

f 450, 320, 490, 510? _____

5 Find the **mean** of $2, $4, $10, $3 and $1. _____

6 Find the **mean** (correct to one decimal place) of 340, 520, 640, 730, 820 and 900 _____

7 If the temperature on the 9/4 is 18°C, what is the new **mean** for the week of the town in question 3? _____

8 What is the **median** of 1246, 1378, 1449 and 1500?

_____

9 The average of a set of scores is 15. None of the scores is 15 and there are 5 scores. What might these **scores** be?

Bar graphs and pie charts

1 Water, oil and detergent were used to fill a 1000 mL container. In the container, what is the **volume** of:

a   oil? _____

b   detergent? _____

c   water? _____

What fraction of the container has:

d   water? _____

e   oil? _____

f   detergent? _____

```
detergent
700 mL
          oil
500 mL

          water
```

2 Of a survey of 240 people, here is a graph of their favourite shape. **What fraction** of people chose:

a   triangle?

b   circle?

c   square?

d   rectangle?

e   other?

f   square or rectangle?

```
        triangle

                  square
  circle   rectangle
           other
```

3 Of the results in question 2, **how many** people chose:

a   circle? _____   b   rectangle? _____

c   square? _____   d   triangle? _____

e   other? _____   f   circle or square? _____

4

dogs	cats	birds	fish

Of 500 people surveyed, this is the breakdown of the most popular types of pets.

How many people preferred:

a   cats? _____   b   dogs? _____

c   birds? _____   d   fish? _____

e   dogs or cats? _____   f   birds or fish? _____

5 **What fraction** of the container in question 1 has oil or detergent? _____

6 **What fraction** of people in question 2 chose circles or triangles? _____

7 **How many** people in question 2 chose rectangles or circles? _____

8 **How many** people preferred cats, fish or birds in question 4? _____

9 Draw the container of question 1 as a **divided bar graph**.

Line graphs

1 Yuko travels 900 km to work 4 times a year. Find the **time** it takes to travel:

a   900 km _____

b   500 km _____

c   200 km _____

d   700 km _____

e   100 km _____

f   400 km _____

```
Distance (km)
900
800
700
600
500
400
300
200
100
    1 2 3 4 5 6 7 8 9 10 11 12
           Time (hours)
```

2 Find **how far** Yuko travels in the first:

a   1 hour _____   b   4 hours _____

c   9 hours _____   d   6 hours _____

e   3 hours _____   f   7 hours _____

3 Here is the temperature for two days:

Time	Noon	1 pm	2 pm	3 pm	4 pm	5 pm
Day 1 temp.	24°C	26°C	27°C	27°C	29°C	28°C
Day 2 temp.	27°C	28°C	29°C	32°C	33°C	33°C

Plot the 2 sets of data on the same graph:

4 **Which day** had:

a   the greatest temperature at 3 pm? _____

b   the greatest temperature at noon? _____

c   the greatest temperature in the afternoon? _____

d   the lowest temperature in the afternoon? _____

e   the greatest increase in temperature in an hour? _____

f   the greatest decrease in temperature in an hour? _____

5 **How long** is Yuko's break after driving 300 km in question 1? _____

6 What is the **largest distance** Yuko travels without a break in question 1? _____

7 Give the graph in question 3 a **title**.

_____

8 What is the **difference** in temperature between day 1 and day 2 at 3 pm in question 3?

_____

9 A walker covers 100 m every minute and a jogger covers 200 m every minute. **Draw a graph** to show the walker and the jogger's travel over the first 1000 m.

Tally marks and graphs

1 Here is a list of animals seen in a national park in the evening. Using the list, **complete the tally table**:

C, K, R, P, M, R, B, K,
M, R, D, C, B, R, K, B,
C, P, R, B, K, M, K, M,
D, B, R, C, K, R, M, B,
R, D, C

Animal	Tally	Total
a rabbit	!!!! !!!	8
b cat		
c kangaroo		
d possum		
e dog		
f bird		
g mouse		

2 Create a **bar graph** from the tally table:

3 **How many** of the following animals were there?

a rabbits and mice _____

b cats and dogs _____

c kangaroos, possums and birds _____

Which animal(s) was/were seen:

d more than 6 times? _____

e less than 3 times? _____

f 6 times? _____

4 **Use the graph** to find the answer to each of the following:

a $3 \times 6 =$ _____

b $1.5 \times 6 =$ _____

c $1\frac{3}{4} \times 6 =$ _____

d $2\frac{1}{2} \times 6 =$ _____

e $3\frac{1}{4} \times 6 =$ _____

f $2.75 \times 6 =$ _____

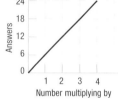

Six times table

5 In question 1, how many winged animals **were counted**?

_____

6 What was the **total number** of animals counted in question 1? _____

7 What was the **total number** of four-legged animals counted in question 1? _____

8 **What** is 3.5×6 using the graph in question 4? _____

9 **Draw a graph** for the first five of the 9 times table.

Reading graphs

1 Eye colour of Year 6 students was noted and the following graph produced. **How many** students had:

a brown eyes? _____

b grey eyes? _____

c green eyes? _____

What category had:

d the **least number** of students? _____

e the **most number** of students? _____

f **between** 6 and 12 students? _____

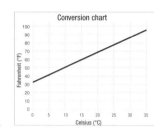

Eye colour

2 The following graph allows us to convert between Celsius and Fahrenheit temperatures.

Use the graph to **convert**:

a 15°C to °F _____

b 30°C to °F _____

c 90°F to °C _____

Which is the **greater** temp.?

d 5°C or 35°F _____

e 20°C or 70°F _____

f 75°F or 27°C _____

Conversion chart

3 Jordan drew a graph to show her school day.

a **What activities** took up the most time?

b **What activity** took up the least time?

c Was **more time** spent reading or doing art?

d **Which activity** was closest to reading?

e Was **less time** spent in assembly or maths?

f **Which sections** used $\frac{1}{4}$ of the school day?

4 What was the:

a **maximum temperature** for Friday?

b **maximum temperature** for Wednesday?

c **minimum temperature** for Tuesday?

d **minimum temperature** for Thursday?

e day that had the **greatest difference** between maximum and minimum temperature?

f day that had the **least difference** between maximum and minimum temperature?

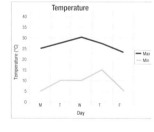

Temperature

5 What was the **total number** of students surveyed in question 1? _____

6 Which is the **lowest temperature**—0°C or 32°F—using the information of question 2? _____

7 **Which two activities** in question 3 use the least amount of time? _____

8 What was the **difference** between the maximum and minimum temperature on Tuesday in question 4?

9 List **one advantage** and **one disadvantage** of a pie chart.

_____

                           ☞ Answers on page 15

Collected data

1 **Using the graph** of the population of Australia,

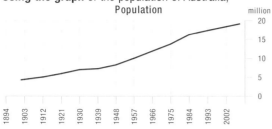

Population

Source: Australian Demographic Statistics (3101.0); Australian Demographic Trends (3102.0); Official Year Book of the Commonwealth of Australia 1901–1910.

when:

a did the population reach 5 million? _____

b did the population reach 10 million? _____

c did the population reach 15 million? _____

d was the population approximately 7 million? _____

e was the population approximately 12 million? _____

f was the population approximately 18 million? _____

2 **What was** the population:

a in 1930? _____   b in 1980? _____

c in 1990? _____   d in 2000? _____

e difference between 1900 and 2000? _____

f difference between 1900 and 1950? _____

3 Here is a table of totals of different insect types:
Complete the **tally** table.

Insect type	Tally	Total
a butterfly		9
b ant		14
c fly		8
d flea		13
e grasshopper		5
f beetle		12

4 Construct a **suitable graph** using the question 3:

5 **Using the graph** of question 1, do you think the population is now greater than or less than 20 million? Explain. _____

6 When was the **greatest** population growth in a ten year period? _____

7 What was the **total number** of insects found in question 3? _____

8 Which type of insect had **more than** 13 found in question 4? _____

9 Use 2 coins and collect 20 pieces of information. Create a **tally chart** and **graph** your results.

Addition and subtraction practice

1 Find the **total** of:

a 42 146 + 38 491 + 2468 _____

b 1076 + 49 830 + 211 063 _____

c 110 439 + 204 117 + 841 735 _____

d 1 096 423 + 408 291 + 441 055 _____

e 4 639 805 + 221 176 + 449 851 _____

f 369 725 + 11 063 + 1185 _____

2 **Complete**:

a	b	c
9000	10 000	30 000
− 4287	− 1 569	− 26 483

d	e	f
22 000	140 000	321 000
− 14 892	− 26 487	− 46 987

3 **Complete**:

a	b	c
11 640	42 103	846 931
20 143	89 487	257 486
+ 1 764	+ 143 243	+ 110 798

d	e	f
421 103	463 981	468 295
98 467	24 836	110 763
11 042	44 997	43 685
+ 4 385	+ 10 436	+ 11 994

4 Complete the **missing boxes**:

a
```
  5 1 ☐ 4
−  3 ☐ 0 6
  ☐ 6 1 ☐
```

b
```
    4 0 9 ☐
−   3 ☐ ☐ 6
      5 2 6
```

c
```
  9 6 2 ☐ 6
−   3 ☐ 5 2 ☐
  ☐ 7 ☐ 2 5
```

d
```
  ☐ 2 ☐ 8 0
− 1 9 8 ☐ 3
  2 ☐ 8 1 ☐
```

e
```
  ☐ 3 ☐ 7 9
−   ☐ 8 4 ☐
  6 7 ☐ 0
```

f
```
  2 1 ☐ 9 ☐
− 1 ☐ 3 ☐ 6
  3 1 3 6
```

5 Find the **total** of: 36 924 + 216 852 + 1 093 845 _____

6 **Complete**:
```
  46 000
−  7 385
```

7 **Complete**:
```
  167 935
  246 013
+  98 443
```

8 Complete the **missing boxes**:
```
  4 ☐ 1 0 ☐
−  ☐ 9 ☐ 3 0
  1 6 2 ☐ 7
```

9 In one week, James deposited into his account $348 and $526. He also withdrew $249, $399 and $107. Did James's account **increase** or **decrease** and by **how much**?

_____

Multiplication and division practice

1 **Complete:**

a $\begin{array}{r} 438 \\ \times\ 20 \\ \hline \end{array}$ b $\begin{array}{r} 691 \\ \times\ 40 \\ \hline \end{array}$

c $\begin{array}{r} 426 \\ \times\ 60 \\ \hline \end{array}$ d $\begin{array}{r} 3248 \\ \times\ 30 \\ \hline \end{array}$

e $\begin{array}{r} 1469 \\ \times\ 50 \\ \hline \end{array}$ f $\begin{array}{r} 2487 \\ \times\ 80 \\ \hline \end{array}$

2 **Find:**

a $60\,)\overline{\,4285\,}$ b $70\,)\overline{\,1107\,}$

c $50\,)\overline{\,3560\,}$ d $80\,)\overline{\,2448\,}$

e $20\,)\overline{\,4165\,}$ f $30\,)\overline{\,1109\,}$

3 **Complete:**

a $29 \times 47 =$ _____

b $46 \times 33 =$ _____

c $62 \times 81 =$ _____

d $19 \times 36 =$ _____

e $24 \times 44 =$ _____

f $95 \times 86 =$ _____

4 **Find:**

a $4\,)\overline{\,37\,980\,}$ b $9\,)\overline{\,911\,763\,}$

c $8\,)\overline{\,42\,116\,}$ d $7\,)\overline{\,43\,684\,}$

e $5\,)\overline{\,21\,104\,}$ f $3\,)\overline{\,278\,496\,}$

5 **Complete:** $\begin{array}{r} 2178 \\ \times\ 70 \\ \hline \end{array}$

6 **Find:**

$40\,)\overline{\,2486\,}$

7 **Complete:** $73 \times 45 =$ _____

8 **Find:**

$6\,)\overline{\,248\,963\,}$

9 479 packets of 6 boxes of sultanas need to be divided evenly into 3 crates. **How many** boxes of sultanas are in each crate?

Fractions practice

1 **Complete the equivalent fractions:**

a $\frac{5}{9} = \frac{\Box}{18}$ b $\frac{6}{10} = \frac{18}{\Box}$ c $\frac{2}{3} = \frac{\Box}{30}$

d $\frac{80}{100} = \frac{\Box}{10}$ e $\frac{49}{56} = \frac{7}{\Box}$ f $\frac{35}{50} = \frac{\Box}{10}$

2 **Find:**

a $\frac{2}{5}$ of 20 _____   b $\frac{3}{4}$ of 48 _____

c $\frac{5}{9}$ of 45 _____   d $\frac{2}{7}$ of 84 _____

e $\frac{2}{3}$ of 27 _____   f $\frac{5}{6}$ of 60 _____

3 **Complete:**

a $\frac{2}{5} + \frac{7}{10} =$ _____   b $\frac{6}{9} - \frac{1}{3} =$ _____

c $\frac{5}{10} + \frac{2}{3} =$ _____   d $2 - \frac{5}{6} =$ _____

e $\frac{3}{4} + \frac{5}{16} =$ _____   f $\frac{9}{12} - \frac{1}{4} =$ _____

4 **Complete:**

a $\frac{3}{5} \times \frac{2}{3} =$ b $\frac{4}{10} \times \frac{2}{3} =$

c $\frac{5}{6} \times \frac{1}{7} =$ d $\frac{3}{4} \times \frac{5}{8} =$

e $\frac{1}{4} \times \frac{8}{9} =$ f $\frac{2}{7} \times \frac{1}{2} =$

5 Complete the **equivalent fraction** for:

$$\frac{9}{12} = \frac{\Box}{4}$$

6 **Find:** $\frac{3}{5}$ of 40 _____

7 **Complete:** $\frac{2}{3} + \frac{4}{9} =$ _____

8 **Complete:** $\frac{3}{4} \times \frac{4}{5} =$ _____

9 **Draw a diagram** to show 4 groups of $\frac{3}{4}$ and find the answer.

Decimals practice

1. **Complete:**

a   4.601
   + 2.4

b   9.365
   + 2.194

c   11.245
   + 9.67

d   18.246
   + 13.487

e   21.486
   + 19.577

f   36.98
   + 21.073

2. Find the **difference** between:

a 5 and 2.18 _____
b 9 and 7.365 _____
c 4 and 3.467 _____
d 21 and 14.921 _____
e 14 and 9.625 _____
f 11 and 10.739 _____

3. **Complete:**

a $4.21
   ×   3

b $9.75
   ×   6

c $8.32
   ×   4

d $9.98
   ×   2

e $2.75
   ×   8

f $1.99
   ×   7

4. **Find:**

a 4.62 ÷ 10 = _____
b 9.265 ÷ 100 = _____
c 21.48 ÷ 1000 = _____
d 123.245 ÷ 1000 = _____
e 49.3 ÷ 10 = _____
f 0.46 ÷ 100 = _____

5. **Complete:**   9.281
              + 7.365

6. Find the **difference** between: 7 and 3.872 _____

7. **Complete:** $11.46
                 ×   5

8. **Find:** 1.025 ÷ 100 = _____

9. Jorge has four hundred and thirty-five 10 cent coins and ninety-two $1 coins. **How much** money does Jorge have? _____

Problem solving – inverse operations

1. **Complete** the boxes:

a 46 + 19 = 50 + ☐
b 198 + 245 = 360 + ☐
c 56 + 135 = 126 + ☐
d 328 + ☐ = 109 + 248
e 411 + ☐ = 512 + 346
f 245 + ☐ = 456 + 173

2. **Complete** the boxes:

a 4 × 70 = 560 ÷ ☐
b 90 ÷ ☐ = 5 × 6
c 1210 ÷ ☐ = 10 × 11
d 49 ÷ ☐ = 350 ÷ 50
e 12 × ☐ = 432 ÷ 3
f 75 ÷ 3 = 5 × ☐

3. **Solve** each of the following:

a 3 + ☐ = 8 − 5
b 7 × ☐ = 14 × 2
c 100 ÷ ☐ = 25 − 5
d 144 ÷ 6 = 6 × ☐
e 45 + 11 = 7 × ☐
f 198 − ☐ = 12 × 11

4. What was the **starting number** if I:

a subtracted 6, multiplied by 5, then added 9 to give 34? ___
b multiplied by 8, added 429, divided by 5 to get 105? ___
c added 57, multiplied by 2, divided by 20 to get 11? ___
d divided by 3, added 17, multiplied by 3 to get 90? ___
e subtracted 248, divided by 4, subtracted 100 to get 88? ___
f multiplied by 7, added 20, divided by 30 to get 10? ___

5. **Complete** the box: 956 + ☐ = 452 + 896

6. **Complete** the box: 400 ÷ ☐ = 100 ÷ 5

7. **Solve:** 46 + ☐ = 9 × 6

8. What was the **starting number** if I halved it, subtracted 236 and multiplied by 2 to give 528. ___

9. 5 balls were placed in a pyramid. One ball was at the top. **How many** balls were on the bottom? ___

Problem solving – money

1 Recently I bought some plants for my vegetable garden. I bought 6 strawberry plants for $4.85, a tomato plant for $2.35, a packet of 20 carrot seeds for $6.50, a box of 8 lettuces for $7.55 and a small lemon tree for $10.15.

  a Which single plant **cost the most**? _____

  b Which single plant **cost the least**? _____

  c **How much** was each strawberry plant? _____

  d **How much** was each lettuce plant? _____

  e What was the **total cost** of the lemon tree and tomato plant? _____

  f If only 15 carrots grew, **how much** did each one cost?

  _____

2 Doreen is paid $11.25 an hour. If she works for 5 hours, circle the **correct pay**:

  a $54.95   b $53.50   c $55.75

  d $55.00   e $52.15   f $56.25

3 **Calculate** the following:

  a $3 \times \$7.56 =$ _____

  b $\$46.20 \div 2 =$ _____

  c $\$15.75 + \$4.85 =$ _____

  d $\$40.00 - \$16.85 =$ _____

  e $\$100 - \$78.22 =$ _____

  f $\$20.15 + \$2.75 + \$3.20 =$ _____

4 Find the **missing amount**:

  a $\$3.26 + \$4.30 + \boxed{} = \$10.00$

  b $\$75.26 + \$11.15 + \boxed{} = \$100.00$

  c $\$50.25 = \$42.98 + \$1.56 + \boxed{}$

  d $\$32.48 = \$11.37 + \$12.65 + \boxed{}$

  e $\$75.50 = \$100.00 - \boxed{}$

  f $\$45.52 = \$70.85 - \boxed{}$

5 What was the **total cost** of all of the items in question 1?

  _____

6 **True or false**? Doreen is paid more than $56.00 in question 2. _____

7 **Calculate** the following totals:

  a $\$45.79 + \$15.36 + \$7.56 =$ _____

  b $\$80.65 - \$12.91 =$ _____

  c $(\$4.45 \times 15) + \$20.45 =$ _____

8 Find the **missing amount**:

  $\$98.52 = \$75.26 + \$3.47 + \boxed{}$

9 **Write a word question** that has the answer $11.17.

Problem solving

1 Witches' hats are placed in a straight line one metre apart. Find **how many** witches' hats are used if the line extends:

  a 10 m _____   b 85 m _____

  c 36 m _____   d 47 m _____

  e 93 m _____   f 127 m _____

2 I have 8 coloured pencils that vary in length from 14.7 cm to 17.3 cm. Circle the amount which could be the **total** of their lengths:

  a 96.7 cm   b 112.9 cm   c 111.9 cm

  d 125.5 cm   e 116.7 cm   f 140.2 cm

3 Here is the breakdown of 64 people's favourite fruit snack.

  a **How many** people selected pears? _____

  b **How many** people selected apples? _____

  c **How many** people selected bananas? _____

  d **How many** people selected oranges? _____

  e Which was the **most popular** fruit snack? _____

  f Which fruit snack or snacks had a **popularity** of 8 people? _____

4 Children link hands to form a chain. Find **how many** hands are held if there are:

  a 3 children in the chain _____

  b 5 children in the chain _____

  c 6 children in the chain _____

  d 9 children in the chain _____

  e 10 children in the chain _____

  f 15 children in the chain _____

5 Witches' hats are placed in a straight line, one metre apart. **How many** witches' hats are used if the line extends 50 m? _____

6 I have 3 coloured pencils that vary in length from 10.6 cm to 15.3 cm. Circle the amount which is the **total** of their lengths:

  29.8 cm   37.9 cm   43.5 cm   47.9 cm

7 Object A has a mass of 120 g and object B has a mass of 190 g. Object C has a mass more than A but less than B. Which of the following is the **total mass** of the three objects?

  420 g   475 g   510 g _____

8 20 children link hands to form a chain. **How many** hands are held? _____

9 A snail is climbing a wall which is 21 m high. It climbs up 4 m every night and slides down 3 m every night. **How long** does it take the snail to reach the top of the wall?

---

1 The **value** of the 5 in 2458 is:
A fifty   B 5 million
C 500 thousand   D 50 thousand

UNIT 1 Q3 / 3 Q1 / 3 Q4

2 Circle the **largest** number:
A −4   B −1   C −3   D −8

6 Q2

3 **True or false**?
104 395 > 140 395 _____

2 Q3

4 **True or false**?
There are 42 thousands in 42 891. _____

5 Q4

5 Write 368 502 in **words**.
_____

2 Q2

6 Arrange the following in **ascending order**:
6 384 971   6 583 942   6 395 211   647 853
_____

3 Q2 / 4 Q1

7 Write 400 000 + 90 000 + 6000 + 20 + 5 as a number in **words**. _____

2 Q2 / 5 Q1

8 What is the **number** represented?

HTh   TTh   Th   H   T   U

2 Q1

9 Write a **rule** for the number pattern:
250, 50, 10, 2, $\frac{1}{5}$ _____

4 Q4

10 **Complete**:

−7 + 4 = _____

1 Q1 / 6 Q4

11 Round nine hundred and seventy-two thousand, eight hundred and eleven to the **nearest million**.
_____

3 Q3

12 **How many tens** are there in:
1 000 000 + 40 000 + 600 000 + 900 + 20 + 4?
_____

5 Q2 / 5 Q3

Score = ____ /12

---

1 700 + 400 =
A 110 000   B 2800
C 1200   D 1100

UNIT 7 Q1

2 The **best estimate** of 785 + 901 is:
A 1700   B 100   C 1800   D 7200

7 Q3

3 **True or false**?

```
    4 5 6
    2 8 1
+   3 7 5
-------
  1 1 1 2
```
_____

7 Q4 / 8 Q4

4 **True or false**?
The missing number in the following is 9.

```
  4 8 6 □ 5 4
  3 2 9 7 6 2
+ 8 1 6 6 1 6
```
_____

8 Q3

5 Find the **total** of $4 632 150.85 and $7 728 105.46 _____

9 Q3

6 **Complete**:

```
  438 511
  469 824
+  98 634
---------
```

9 Q1

7 **Complete**: 576 + 79 = _____

7 Q2

8 Find the **total** of $68 721 and $3496.
_____

8 Q2

9 At a Christmas tree farm, there were 976, 4385 and 2479 Christmas trees in each of three paddocks. What was the **total number** of Christmas trees?
_____

8 Q4

10 Find the **total**:

4850 L   2198 L   3156 L   7981 L

9 Q4

11 Give the answer to the equation in question 5 in **words**. _____

9 Q2

12 **Complete**:

+	468	110	946	1187	32 345
721					

7 Q1 / 7 Q2 / 7 Q3 / 7 Q4

Score = ____ /12

1 4876 rounded to the **nearest ten** is:
UNIT 12 Q1

  A 4870 B 4900
  C 4880 D 5000

2 197 − 59 =
11 Q4

  A 138 B 39 C 148 D 136

3 **True or false?**
10 Q4 / 11 Q2 / 13 Q4

The difference between 6421 and 19 048 is 12 627. _____

4 **True or false?**
12 Q1

127 118 rounded to the nearest thousand is 128 000. _____

5 **Find:**
14 Q1

$$1\ 729\ 000 - 563\ 000$$

6 **Complete** the missing boxes:
10 Q3

$$\begin{array}{r} 4\ 6\ \square\ 2 \\ -\ 3\ \square\ 4\ 8 \\ \hline 9\ 3\ \square \end{array}$$

7 Find the **difference** between 9000 and 785.
11 Q3

_____

8 Find the **difference** between the two masses:
13 Q3 / 14 Q4

| 147 385 t | 85 621 t | _____

9 Estimate the answer by rounding each amount to the **nearest dollar**:
12 Q2 / 15 Q3

$$\$425\,.98 - \$269\,.22$$

10 **Complete:**
10 Q1 / 11 Q4

−	72	83	107	124	141
56					

11 What is the **difference** in area between NSW (800 642 km²) and Tasmania (68 401 km²)?
14 Q3

_____

12 **Estimate** the answer by rounding each number to the nearest 1000. Then check the answer with an addition equation.
14 Q3 / 15 Q2 / 15 Q4

$$367\ 428 - 119\ 107$$

1 The **product** of 6 and 12 is:
UNIT 17 Q1 / 18 Q1

  A 62 B 84 C 50 D 72

2 The **total** number of days in 9 weeks is:
17 Q4

  A 63 B 56 C 72 D 81

3 **True or false?**
16 Q3

The missing number is 7 in:
$$6 \times \square = 42$$

4 **True or false?**
17 Q2

$3 \times 8 = 7 \times 4$ _____

5 **Complete:**
17 Q3 / 18 Q2

$$\begin{array}{r} 11 \\ \times\ \underline{0} \end{array}$$

6 **Complete** the boxes:
18 Q3

$5 \times 8 = \square = 4 \times \square$

7 Find: six **multiplied by** zero. _____
18 Q1 / 18 Q4

8 **Find:**
16 Q2

$8 \times 10 =$ _____

9 Find the **total cost** of 5 movie tickets at $12 each plus 5 packets of popcorn at $3 each. _____
16 Q4

10 **Complete:**
16 Q2

×	4	7	12	9	8
3					

11 Complete with **< or >** to make the number statement true:
16 Q2

$6 \times 5\ \square\ 7 \times 4$

12 Find the **total** number of pieces of fruit in:
16 Q4

- 3 baskets with 8 pieces in each _____
- 7 boxes with 12 pieces in each _____
- 5 bags with 6 pieces in each _____

_____

Score = /12

Score = /12

 Answers on page 15

Multiplication of tens, hundreds and thousands (1)
Multiplication of tens, hundreds and thousands (2)
Multiplication of tens, hundreds and thousands (3)
Multiplication

The **product** of 196 and 100 is:

1.96	1960
19 600	196 000

6×7 hundreds = ☐ hundreds: 19 Q1

13	42	48

True or false?

$80 \times 30 = 240$ _____

True or false?
$$\begin{array}{r} 67 \\ \times \quad 3 \\ \hline 201 \end{array}$$

Complete:
$$\begin{array}{r} 927 \\ \times \quad 5 \\ \hline \end{array}$$

Find the **total** number of 20 groups of 40 students.

_____

Find the **product** of 9763 and 7.

_____

Complete: $4000 \times 8 =$ _____

Describe the pattern in the answers to:

$10 \times 15 =$
$20 \times 15 =$
$30 \times 15 =$ _____

Complete the chart:

×	32
10	
100	
1000	

Find the **product** of:

one hundred and eighty and fifty _____

Find the **total** number of plants if there are 6 plants in each of 1295 containers.

_____

The **value** of the missing box in:

$14 \times 25 = (10 \times 25) + (4 \times 25) =$ ☐

64	290	250	350

The next answer in the **pattern:**

$8 \times 20 = 160$
$80 \times 20 = 1600$
$800 \times 20 = 16\,000$
$8000 \times 20 =$ ☐

16 000 000	160 000	1600	1 600 000

True or false?
$$\begin{array}{r} 17\,32 \\ \times \quad 7 \\ \hline 71\,24 \end{array}$$

True or false?
The product of 22 and 57 is 1254. _____

Complete:
$$43 \times 72 = \begin{array}{r} 72 \\ \times 40 \\ \hline \boxed{} \end{array} + \begin{array}{r} 72 \\ \times 3 \\ \hline \boxed{} \end{array} = \boxed{}$$

Find: 36×1420 _____

Find the **total** cost of 27 books at $89 each:

_____

Complete:

×	6	60	600	6000
8				

What is the **total cost** of 3 televisions at $1500 each and 3 DVD players at $89 each? _____

Circle the **larger** amount:

$16 \times 33 =$ ☐ $\begin{array}{r} 1\,8 \\ \times \quad 3\,0 \\ \hline \boxed{} \end{array}$

Find the **missing number:**

$14 \times$ ☐ $= 28 + 280 = 308$

What is the **difference** between these two number sentences? $(15 \times 6) \times 8$ and $15 \times (6 \times 8)$

_____

Score =   **Score =**

REVIEW TESTS: Units 28 – 34

1. Which of the following numbers is **divisible** by 3? (UNIT 28 Q1)
   A 735   B 103   C 1276   D 199

2. Which of the following is **not a factor** of 100? (28 Q2 28 Q3)
   A 10   B 5   C 8   D 4

3. **True or false?** (28 Q2 28 Q3)
   7 is a factor of 24. _____

4. **True or false?** (29 Q1)
   $40 \times 8 = 320$ _____

5. Find an estimate by first rounding to the **nearest ten**: $68 \times 89 =$ _____ (30 Q2)

6. List the first 8 **multiples** of 4. (28 Q4)
   _____

7. Find $46 \times 10 =$ _____ (29 Q2)
   and then $46 \times 5 =$ _____

8. Round the first number to the **nearest ten** and the second number to the **nearest hundred** to **estimate** the answer to: 26×408 _____ (30 Q4)

9. **Complete** with < or >: (29 Q2 29 Q3 29 Q4)
   63×4 ☐ 45×5

10. By rounding each number to the **nearest ten**, **estimate** the answer to: forty-one multiplied by eighteen _____ (30 Q2)

11. Is 589 x 11 **less than or greater than** 6000? (30 Q3)
    _____

12. Each of 23 shops donated an average of 67 toys. **Estimate** how many toys were donated altogether. (30 Q2)
    _____

Score = /12

1. The **missing number** in $11 \times$ ☐ $= 132$ is: (UNIT 31 Q3)
   A 10   B 13   C 11   D 12

2. The **remainder** of 4 children sharing 25 cards is: (32 Q2)
   A 6   B 1   C 4   D 2

3. **True or false?** (32 Q3)
   $120 \div 4 = 30$ _____

4. **True or false?** (31 Q2)
   $11 \div 11 = 0$ _____

5. **Complete**: (33 Q2)
   $5 \overline{)325}$

6. Write the answer as a **mixed number**: (34 Q3)
   $9 \overline{)438}$

7. **Find**: (31 Q4)
   $4 \overline{)692}$

8. What is the **remainder** of: (33 Q3)
   $3 \overline{)2747}$?

9. Find the **fair share** of 103 pieces of fruit between 12 children: _____ (33 Q4 34 Q1)

10. **Complete** the table: (32 Q4)

Question	Quotient	Remainder
☐ ÷ 7	11	4

11. Find, writing the **remainder as a fraction**: two thousand four hundred and seventy-three divided by five. _____ (34 Q4)

12. **Find**: (34 Q1)
    $7 \overline{)3}$

Score = /12

110 · Excel Start Up Maths Year 6 · Answers on page 15

Division with zeros in the answer
Division with zeros in the divisor
Division by numbers with zeros
Division of numbers larger than 999
Extended division

The number of **tens** in 2198 is:

2198   219   19   12

520 mm written as **centimetres** is:

52 cm   5.2 cm

0.52 cm   5200 cm

True or false?

$$80 \overline{)4800}$$ gives 60 _____

True or false?

$$10 \overline{)492}$$ gives $49\frac{1}{5}$ _____

Complete:

$$6 \overline{)72\,436}$$

Find:

$$14 \overline{)364}$$

Write the answer as a **decimal**:

$$10 \overline{)42\,103}$$

There were 1554 runs scored during a round robin competition. If there were 12 games, what was the **average number** of runs scored per game? _____

Find the **missing number**:
46 r 2 = ☐ ÷ 3

Find:
sixty-seven thousand **divided by** one hundred.

_____

True or false?

$$90 \overline{)3030}$$ > 33 _____

What is 148 ÷ 14? _____
Give the remainder as a fraction.

Averages (1)
Averages (2)
Inverse operations and checking answers
Number lines and operations

The correct **inverse equation** of 5 × * = 160 is:

160 − 5 = *   160 ÷ 5 = *

* = 160 × 5   * = 160 + 5

The **average** of 27 and 29 is:

56   29   28   27

True or false?
A number line for start at 70 and count backward by 4s is: _____

70   74   78   82

True or false?
A multiplication equation which checks:
132 ÷ 12 = 11 is 11 × 12 = 132. _____

Draw a **number line** to find 468 − 34 =

Find the **average** of $1, $7, $9, $3, $7 and $3.

_____

Write the remainder as a **decimal** of:
391 ÷ 5 _____

Write an **addition equation** to check:
921 − 385 = 535 _____

Write an **equation** from the number line:

+10   +10
1056 1060   1080

_____

The **average speed** of travelling 550 kilometres in 5 hours is _____.

List 3 numbers which would give an average of 30.

_____

Find the **answer** to 43 × 5 and check with a suitable equation. _____

Score = ___ /12   Score = ___ /12

REVIEW TESTS: Units 44 – 54

1 $30 \div 2 \div 2 \div 2$ is the **same as**:

  A $30 - (2 \times 2 \times 2)$ B $30 \times (2 \times 2 \times 2)$

  C $30 - 2 - 2 - 2$ D $30 \div (2 \times 2 \times 2)$

2 In order of operations, the **operation completed first** is:

  A addition   B brackets

  C subtraction   D multiplication

3 **True or false?**

Working left to right:

$9 \times 4 \div 2 = 17$ _____

4 **True or false?**

$(2 \times 5 \times 3) + 6 = 21$ _____

5 Complete the **multiplication and division first**:

$40 + 12 \times 12 \div 2 =$ _____

6 **Complete:**

$(48 \div 8) \times (12 - 2) =$ _____

7 **Find:**

$19 \times 6 \times (4 \times 0) \times (3 \times 1) =$ _____

8 **Find:**

$(\frac{1}{2} \times 8) \times (\frac{1}{5} \times 20) =$ _____

9 **Find:**

$(9.3 + 2.7) \times (4 - 3.5) =$ _____

10 **Add brackets** to make the equation true:

$36 \div 9 \times 4 + 6 = 40$

11 **Find:**

(seven multiplied by three) plus

(fifty divided by five) _____

12 **Explain** each step performed to solve:

$(5.3 + 2.7) \times 3 \div 6 =$ _____

_____

Score = _____ /12

---

1 The **value** of M in: $M - 4.2 = 6.8$ is:

  A 11.0   B 10.0   C 2.6   D 24.6

2 20 written as a **binary number** is:

  A 11001   B 10100

  C 10101   D 11100

3 **True or false?**

$9.73 rounded to the nearest 5 cents

is $9.70 _____

4 **True or false?**

$(100 \div 5) \times (4 - 4) = 0$ _____

5 **Complete:**
$$\begin{array}{r} 721\,000 \\ \times \quad\quad 6 \\ \hline \end{array}$$

6 Find the **value** of D in:

$90 - 76 = 2 \times D$ _____

7 Write the **rule** for the number pattern:

2, 4, 8, 16, 32, 64 _____

8 Find the **value** of V in:

when I subtract 4×7 from the difference of 100 and 16 my answer is V _____

9 Write the **first five terms** for the number pattern:

start at 500 and multiply by $\frac{1}{5}$

_____

10 **Complete:**

$769\,000 + 472\,000 - 35\,000 =$ _____

11 Write the equation and its solution in **binary notation**:

$23 - 12$ _____

_____

12 Find the **change** from $95 if Jan spent four lots of $19.65 _____

_____

Score = _____ /12

Excel Start Up Maths Year 6   ☞ Answers on page 1

Equations with numbers and words
Substituting values
Number sentences (1)
Number sentences (2)
Number sentences (3)

Square and cube numbers
Working with numbers
Change of units
Negative numbers
Prime and composite numbers

The **value** of the letter W in $W \times W \times W = 64$ is:

16   8   3   4

$11^2 =$

100   132   22   121

The **value** of the missing number in:

$(7 \times \boxed{}) + 5 = 54$ is:

8   7   6   9

5 hours is the **same as**:

300 minutes   30 minutes

3 minutes   3000 minutes

True or false?
If $50 \div \boxed{} + 7 = 17$ then $\boxed{} = 10$ _____

True or false?
41 087 392 is the number immediately after 41 087 393 _____

True or false?
$14.2 - \triangle = 9$ then $\triangle = 6.2$ _____

True or false?
87 is a prime number. _____

Find the **value** of the missing number:
$49 - \boxed{} = 7 \times 4$

Place the set of numbers in **ascending order**:
5, –2, 3, 8, 0, –4, –6, –1, 1

_____

Complete the table:

$\triangle$	4.5
$\square$	2.3
$\square + \triangle$	
$\triangle - \square$	

Find **two prime numbers** that add to give 20.

_____

Complete the **tree diagram**:   176

Find the **missing number**:

298
× ⬚
2384

Change 20 000 mm to **metres**. _____

Write a number sentence and **solve** it for:
the quotient of a number and 6 is 12

_____

Find: $12^2 - 4^2$ _____

Write an **equation** to show if the following is correct:
Albert had 436 coins in his collection, but after he sold 179 he had 528 left.

_____

Write the **answer**:

$\boxed{}$ –5   0   _____

Find the **value** of * in:
* + three quarters = two _____

List all the **composite numbers** between 110 and 120.

_____

Explain the following equation in **words**, giving the answer: $9 \times 10 - (7 \times 12) = 6$ _____

_____

Complete the following to find the **pattern**:

$2^2 + 1^2 =$ _____

$3^2 + 2^2 =$ _____

$4^2 + 3^2 =$ _____

$5^2 + 4^2 =$ _____

$6^2 + 5^2 =$ _____

$7^2 + 6^2 =$ _____ _____

I think of a number, add 5, multiply by 11, square root the amount, then subtract (3 + 2). The answer is 6. What is the **starting number**?

_____

Score = _____ /12

Score = _____ /12

1 The **equivalent fraction** for $\frac{3}{5}$ is:

A $\frac{5}{3}$ B $\frac{8}{10}$ C $\frac{2}{5}$ D $\frac{6}{10}$

UNIT
68 Q1
68 Q2
68 Q3
69 Q1
69 Q2
70 Q1
70 Q2
70 Q4

2 $\frac{80}{90}$ reduced to its **simplest form** is:

A $\frac{70}{80}$ B $\frac{9}{8}$ C $\frac{8}{9}$ D $\frac{1}{10}$

3 **True or false?**

$\frac{1}{2}$ of the shape has been shaded. _____

65 Q1

4 **True or false?**

The mixed number of $\frac{20}{7}$ is $2\frac{6}{7}$. _____

71 Q3
71 Q4

5 What is $\frac{1}{5}$ of:

○○○○○
○○○○○
○○○○○ _____

66 Q1
66 Q2
67 Q2

6 Complete with **< or > or =** to make the number statement true: $\frac{1}{3}$ ☐ $\frac{1}{4}$

70 Q3

7 Write the **improper fraction** for $3\frac{3}{8}$ _____

71 Q3

8 **Find:** $\frac{1}{4}$ of 48. _____

66 Q3
67 Q1

9 Draw a **diagram** to show $\frac{4}{9}$ of 18. _____

67 Q2
67 Q4

10 Write 3 **equivalent fractions** for $\frac{2}{3}$:

69 Q4

11 Circle the **largest fraction**:

$1\frac{3}{4}$ $1\frac{7}{8}$ $\frac{16}{8}$ $\frac{10}{4}$

68 Q1
68 Q2
68 Q3
69 Q1
70 Q1
70 Q2
71 Q3

12 There were 24 cards in a set. Joseph had collected $\frac{7}{8}$ of them. **How many more** cards did he need for the whole set? _____

66 Q4
67 Q3

UNIT
75 Q2

1 $\frac{18}{8}$ written as a **mixed number** is:

A $1\frac{10}{8}$ B $2\frac{1}{4}$ C $2\frac{3}{8}$ D $1\frac{1}{4}$

2 $3\frac{2}{5}$ written as an **improper fraction** is:

75 Q1

A $\frac{10}{5}$ B $\frac{30}{5}$

C $\frac{17}{5}$ D $\frac{15}{5}$

3 **True or false?**

72 Q1

$\frac{7}{12} > \frac{1}{3}$ _____

4 **True or false?**

74 Q4

The difference between $\frac{9}{10}$ and $\frac{2}{5}$ is $\frac{1}{2}$. _____

5 **Complete:** $\frac{4}{5} + \frac{2}{5} + \frac{3}{5} =$

72 Q2
73 Q1
73 Q3

6 **Complete:** $\frac{5}{6} - \frac{1}{3} =$

72 Q3
74 Q2
74 Q3
75 Q4

7 **Find:** $7 \times \frac{3}{8} =$

72 Q4

8 **Add** one sixth and one quarter.

73 Q4
75 Q3

9 Circle the **simplest form** of $\frac{60}{80}$:

74 Q1

$\frac{6}{8}$ $\frac{30}{40}$ $\frac{3}{4}$

10 Draw a number line to show $\frac{2}{5} + \frac{4}{5}$.

73 Q2
73 Q4
75 Q4

11 Complete with **< or > or =:**

72 Q3
74 Q2
74 Q3
75 Q3
75 Q4

$\frac{2}{5} + \frac{1}{10}$ ☐ $\frac{4}{5} - \frac{2}{10}$

12 Insert the **correct sign** from +, − or × to make the number statement true:

72 Q3
73 Q4
74 Q2
74 Q3
75 Q3
75 Q4

$\frac{2}{8}$ ☐ $\frac{3}{4}$ ☐ $\frac{1}{8} = \frac{7}{8}$

Score = ☐ /12

Score = ☐ /12

1 $\frac{9}{12}$ **simplified** is:

A $\frac{3}{4}$ B $\frac{3}{4}$ C $\frac{2}{4}$ D $\frac{1}{3}$

2 $\frac{11}{4}$ written as a **mixed number** is:

A $1\frac{3}{4}$ B $2\frac{1}{2}$ C $2\frac{3}{4}$ D $2\frac{1}{4}$

3 **True or false?**

The missing number in $\frac{\square}{5} = 4\frac{2}{5}$ is 22.

4 **True or false?**

$\frac{1}{3}$ x 5 is $\frac{5}{3} = 1\frac{2}{3}$ _____

5 Find 7 **lots of** $\frac{1}{8}$ of a bar of chocolate.

_____

6 **Complete:** $\frac{4}{5} \times \frac{3}{4} = $ _____

7 Complete with **< or >:**

$4 \times \frac{2}{3} \ \square \ 7 \times \frac{1}{6}$

8 **Find** $\frac{1}{7}$ of 56. _____

9 What is the product of $\frac{3}{4}$ and $\frac{6}{10}$?

10 **Complete** the boxes:

$\frac{2}{10} \times \frac{\square}{3} = \frac{8}{\square}$

11 Of 660 pencils, $\frac{1}{4}$ were red, $\frac{1}{3}$ were blue and the rest were other colours. **How many** pencils were neither red nor blue? _____

12 Find: $\frac{5}{12}$ of 1.008 t _____

1 The **value** of the 3 in 6.035 is:

A 3 tenths   B 3 hundredths
C 3 thousandths   D 3 units

2 2.365 × 10 is:

A 23   B 0.2365   C 23.65   D 236.5

3 **True or false?**

$\frac{8}{100}$ written as a decimal is 0.8 _____

4 **True or false?**
321.09 ÷ 1000 = 0.32109 _____

5 **Complete:**   2.7
                        3.86
                      + 1.09

6 Find the **total length** of 5 lengths of 2.81 m of ribbon: _____

7 Find the **difference** between 106.9 and 77.28:

_____

8 What is 192.87 **divided by** 3? _____

9 Write 21.046 in **words.**

_____

10 What is the **total cost** of 3 books at $12.95 and 7 pens at $2.76 each? _____

11 Which is **cheaper:**
a packet of 4 toilet rolls costing $3.75 or a packet of 6 toilet rolls costing $4.98?

_____

12 **Explain** what happens to the decimal point when multiplying by 10, 100 or 1000.

_____

Score = ⬡ /12

Score = ⬡ /12

1. 19% expressed as a **decimal** is:

   A 0.019   B 1.9   C 19   D 0.19

2. 4.681 **rounded** to one decimal place is:

   A 4.7   B 4.6   C 4.68   D 4

3. **True or false**?

   $\frac{142}{100}$ = 142% _____

4. **True or false**?

   The smallest number of notes and coins needed to make $9.45 is $5, $2, $2, 20c, 10c and 5c. _____

5. Express 0.36 as a **percentage**. _____

6. **Find** 20% of 60 children. _____

7. Find the **total** of the following items and **round** to the nearest 5 cents. _____

   $1.55 $2.27 $4.69 $6.71

8. If A$1 = HK$4.20 in Hong Kong, what does a A$40 T-shirt **cost** in Hong Kong? _____

9. If 1 can of soft drink costs 33 cents, how much do 24 cans **cost**? And what is the change from $10.00?

   _____

10. Find the **discounted price** on a $80 computer game with a 20% discount. _____

11. **Complete** the table:

Fraction	Decimal	Percentage
$\frac{3}{4}$		

12. Draw a **diagram** to show 25%.

---

1. A square has _____ **lines of symmetry**.

   4   6   2   0

2. This **line** ——————— is known as:

   A horizontal   B vertical
   C perpendicular   D parallel

3. **True or false**?

   has rotational symmetry.

   _____

4. **True or false**?

   has 4 diagonals.

   _____

5. Draw the **lines of symmetry**:

6. Add to the shape so it has **rotational symmetry**:

7. Circle the number which has **parallel lines**:

   1   2   3   4   11   15   13

8. Complete the diagram so it is **symmetrical**:

9. Draw a quadrilateral (4-sided shape) that has **no axis of symmetry**:

10. What are these **lines** called?

    _____

11. Do the following contain **vertical** lines?

12. Mark the **axes of symmetry** on the following letters:

   # M E X W

Score = ___ /12

Score = ___ /12

Angles
Reading angles (1)
Reading angles (2)
Drawing angles
Triangles

3D objects
Drawing 3D objects
Properties and views of 3D objects
Cylinders, spheres and cones
Parallelograms and rhombuses

The name of the **angle**   is:
   reflex   straight
   full revolution   right

The closest **estimate** of the angle   is:

   60°   90°   180°   270°

True or false?
An example of an acute angle is:

_____

True or false?
The missing angle of the triangle is 50°.

_____   65°   65°

Measure the angle
to the **nearest degree**:

_____

Complete the angle so that it measures 195°.

To measure an angle, the instrument used is
a _____ .

Draw a **straight angle**.

Are the following angles **obtuse**? _____

Measure the **reflex angle**:

_____

Find the value of the **missing angle**, a.   60°
_____   \ a

The angles together make a   \ 120°
straight angle. Find the **missing**
angle, a _____

The **name** of the shape is:
   rhombus   parallelogram
   square   kite

An example of a **cylinder** is:

True or false?
The shapes that make up a cube are squares
and rectangles. _____

True or false?
A pyramid is an object that meets at a point.

_____

Complete the table:

Object	Faces	Edges	Vertices
triangular prism			

Which of the following is the correct **view** of a cone?

Draw the **cross-section**:   \

Complete the **rhombus**:

How many **faces** does a hexagonal prism have?

_____

True or false?
Every rectangle is a parallelogram. _____

Which of the following shapes is not a **prism**?

Draw a **stack** of 3 rows by 3 columns by 3 deep
of cubes.

Score =

Score =

UNIT

1 Which of the following shapes **tessellate**? 114 Q1

A   B   C   D

2 The **point** in the middle of a circle is known as the: 110 Q2

A centre   B circumference
C arc   D sector

3 **True or false?** 111 Q3

is a net that makes a triangular prism. _____

4 **True or false?** 112 Q1

If the scale is 1 cm : 3 km, then a line 3 cm long 112 Q2
represents 9 kilometres. _____

5 **Complete** the table: 109 Q1
109 Q2
109 Q3

No. of hexagons	1	2	3	4
No. of sides				

6 Draw the **top view** of a rectangular pyramid. 111 Q2

7 **Rotate** the triangle clockwise through 90° around 114 Q4
the dot.

8 For the square, what happens to the 113 Q4
total number of squares when the side
lengths are made twice as long? _____

9 The **diameter** of a circle is twice the length of 110 Q1
the _____. 110 Q2

10 Has the **shape** been translated/rotated/reflected? 114 Q2
114 Q3
114 Q4
_____

11 Draw the **net** of a rectangular pyramid. 111 Q3

12 **Rotate** the pattern 90° to the right about the dot. 114 Q4

Score = /12

UNIT

1 What is the **direction** between north and west? 115 Q1

A east   B north-west
C south-west   D south-east

2 If you are facing north, the **direction** to your 115 Q2
right is:

A north   B south
C east   D west

3 **True or false?** 117 Q1
The **coordinate** of the 119 Q2
diamond is 1C. 120 Q2

1
0
A B C D

4 **True or false?** 115 Q3

The shape south of the
star is the triangle.

5 Mark a **dot** at the coordinate C2. 117 Q2
118 Q3
119 Q1
120 Q1

2
1
0
A B C D E

6 Give the **direction** of the square from the circle. 116 Q2
119 Q3

7 State the **direction** while 116 Q2
travelling directly from A to C. 119 Q3

A   C
B

8 What **direction** is directly opposite south-east? 115 Q1
115 Q2

9 Do the pairs of **coordinates** (4, 7) and (7, 4) 117 Q2
show the same position? _____ 119 Q1
120 Q1

10 Name the **coordinate** that is 117 Q4
3 spaces south-west of X.

4
3
2
1
0
0 1 2 3 4

11 Give the **coordinates** of the 117 Q1
vertices of the triangle. 119 Q2
120 Q2

4
3
2
1
0
A B C D

12 If ↑ represents north and → is east, 115 Q1
what does ↗ represent? _____ 115 Q2
115 Q3

Score = /12

Excel Start Up Maths Year 6

☞ Answers on page 15

Analog time
Digital time
Digital and analog time
24-hour time (1)
24-hour time (2)

Stopwatches
Timelines
Timetables
Time zones (1)
Time zones (2)
Travelling speed

Quarter to five written as a **digital time** is:

5:15   4:45   5:45   6:15

written as a **digital time** is:

12:55   10:55
11:50   11:55

True or false?
1:29 in the afternoon is the same as 1:29 am _____

True or false?
4:35 pm is the same as 1635. _____

Draw 27 minutes to 6
on the **clock face**.

Write 2314 as an **am** or **pm** time.

_____

Draw 1711 on the **clock face**.

Find the **difference** between 1420 and 2310.

_____

Write the time which is **15 minutes after** 1:55 am.

_____

An alarm clock read 8:52 am, when the power
went off. It read 9:14 am when the power was
restored. Was the power off **more or less** than
half an hour? _____

What will the **time** be in 8 hours?

_____

How do we write a pm time in **24-hour time**?

Use 7:15 pm as an example. _____

6 minutes = _____ **seconds**?

600   36   3600   360

9:50 pm in **24-hour time** is:

0950   2150   2250   1950

True or false?
It will take 2 hours to travel 2 kilometres at
1 km/h. _____

True or false? _____

Distance	Time	Average speed
50 m	10 s	5 m/s

If it is 9:50 am in Melbourne, it will be _____
in Hobart.

Using the map on page 83, if it is noon at
Greenwich what is the **time** at 120°E?

_____

If it is 11:50 am in Sydney, show
time on the **clock face** in Adelaide
for daylight saving.

Find the **difference** between 07:47:39 and 09:36:19

_____

A train runs every 7 minutes. **How many** will have
run in 2 hours? _____

Add Veronica's birthday, the 20th November to
the **timeline**.

Jan.   Dec.

A bus leaves Sydney at 1050 and arrives in
Canberra at 1600. **How long** does it take to
travel between the two cities? _____

Circle the correct answer.
To change 3 **years to days** we:

× 365   ÷ 365   × 52   ÷ 52

Score = _____

Score = _____

119

1 4683 m written in **decimal notation** is:

   A 4.683 m   B 468.3 m
   C 46.83 km   D 4.683 km

2 4.2 cm =

   A 42 mm   B 0.42 km
   C 420 mm   D 4 mm

3 **True or false?**
Metres would be the most suitable measurement to measure your foot length. _____

4 **True or false?**
There are 170 cm in 1.7 m. _____

5 Order from the **shortest to longest**:
29 cm   1.26 m   1 m   30 cm   89 cm   0.96 m

_____

6 **Complete:**

mm	cm	m
		0.3

7 Find the **total height**:

_____

8 **Round** 156 mm to the nearest centimetre.

_____

9 Circle the **correct answer**.
7.07 m means:

7 m 700 cm   7 m 70 cm
7 m 7 cm   7 km 7 m

10 **How many** 60 cm lengths of ribbon can be cut from a 5 m roll (if the excess is discarded)? _____

11 0.75 of 1 km **is** _____.

12 I have 38 cm of tape. **How much more** is needed to make 1 metre? _____

Score = (/12)

---

1 The **perimeter** of a square with side lengths 5 cm is:

   A 25 cm   B 20 cm
   C 10 cm   D 50 cm

2 The **area** of a square with side lengths of 6 m is:

   A 36 m²   B 24 m²
   C 12 m²   D 60 m²

3 **True or false?**
A unit of area is square units. _____

4 **True or false?**
The area of a triangle is half the area of the related square or rectangle. _____

5 Find the **perimeter** of:

6 cm   7 cm   7 cm   10 cm

_____

6 Find the **area**:

2 m   10 m

_____

7 Find the **area**:

5 cm   6 cm   2 cm   1 cm

_____

8 Find the **area** of a triangle with base of 10 cm and perpendicular height of 7 cm. _____

9 If a square had an area of 100 cm², what is the **length of its side**? _____

10 **Draw a diagram** to show the area of a triangle as half that of a square with side length 8 cm, and find the **area** of the triangle.

11 Find the **perpendicular height** of a triangle with base 70 m and area of 1330 m².

_____

12 Find the **area** of the shaded part of the diagram. _____

8 cm   5 cm   8 cm   5 cm

Score = (/12)

Hectares
Square kilometres (1)
Square kilometres (2)

Mass in grams and kilograms
Mass in tonnes
Mass in tonnes and kilograms

19.2 hectares written in **short form** is:

19.2 h	19.2 H
19.2 Ha	19.2 ha

The area which would be measured in **hectares** is:

a rug	a national park
America	a small garden

True or false?
400 ha = 4 km² _____

True or false?
90 000 m² > 9.2 km² _____

Convert 400 000 m² to **hectares**. _____

Find the **difference** in area between India
(3 268 580 km²) and Nepal (141 414 km²).

Complete the table:

m²	ha	km²
	110	

19 ha = _____ m²

What is the **most suitable unit of measurement**
for the area of Western Australia? _____

Find the **total area** of 400 ha + 300 ha + 200 ha.

_____

Complete with **> or <** to make the number
statement true:

one point two square
kilometres ☐ one hundred and twenty-
four square metres

Complete:

10 000 cm² = ☐ m²

☐ m² = 1 ha

100 ha = ☐ km²

A bag of potatoes would be **weighed with**:

a displacement tank	a spring balance
a weighbridge	standard scales

5 kg 250 g can be **written as**:

525 g	52.5 g	5.25 kg	525 kg

True or false?
There are 29 tonnes in 29 000 kg. _____

True or false?
There are 315 g in 9.315 kg. _____

What would be the **best unit** for measuring the
mass of a mobile phone? _____

How many **kilograms** are there
in 2.69 t? _____

Complete the table:

g	kg	t
		0.851

Complete with **< or >**:
0.469 t ☐ 470 g

Find the **total mass**:

6.3 t   7.6 t   1.8 t

_____

Complete the table:

kg	t
6 t 135 kg	

Which item would have the **greater mass**:
a truck or 10 boxes of fruit? _____

A container of nuts has a mass of 2 kg. If the
mass of the container is 115 g, what is the
mass of the nuts? _____

Score =

Score =

REVIEW TESTS: Units 150 – 163

1 The most **suitable unit** of volume for a lunchbox is:
A m³   B cm³   C cm²   D km³

2 What **capacity** of water would have a mass of 20 g?
A 200 mL   B 20 kL   C 200 L   D 20 mL

3 **True or false?**
There are 60 L in 60 cm³. _____

4 **True or false?**
19 cubic metres = 19 m³ _____

5 Find the **volume**:
2 m, 6 m, 6 m
_____

6 Write 9.216 L as **mL**. _____

7 What is the **equivalent mass of water** for 32 L?
_____

8 **Complete** the table:

Length (cm)	Breadth (cm)	Height (cm)	Volume (cm³)
6	2		24

9 Circle the **correct answer**.
A delivery van has a volume:
less than 1 m³   about 1 m³   greater than 1 m³

10 Find the **volume** of a cube whose edges measure 15 mm. _____

11 The capacity of a rectangular prism is 6000 mL. Its length is 20 cm and its width is 30 cm. What is the **depth** in centimetres? _____

12 Write the volume in L and mL.
1000 mL / 750 mL / 500 mL / 250 mL
_____
_____

1 Another **arrangement** of △☆△□ is:
A □□△△   B △△☆□
C □△☆□   D ☆☆△△

2 What is the **chance** that I will become shorter in old age?
A definite   B impossible
C likely   D equal chance

3 **True or false?**
0.5 = equal chance _____

4 **True or false?**
There is a 50% chance of landing on the number 2. _____

5 If 10 out of 50 children prefer the colour red, **predict** how many children in 1000 would prefer the colour red. _____

6 Add the **tally 15** to the table:

Shape	Tally
△	

7 The **length** of the bar showing the letter B is:
[ ] mm or [ ] cm
A   B   C

8 What **fraction** of the pie chart shows 400?   400 / 100 / 100 / 200

9 What is the **most popular** pet?
Number — dog cat fish → Pet

10 There are 6 doughnuts in the box. What is the **likelihood** (as a **fraction**) of selecting a yellow one? b y p / b y p

11 **Label** the information on the pie chart:
red = $\frac{2}{8}$ blue = $\frac{4}{8}$
orange = $\frac{1}{8}$ yellow = $\frac{1}{8}$

12 What is the **chance** of selecting a vowel from a packet of alphabet cards? _____

Score = /12   Score = /12

1 The **mean** of 10 kg, 60 kg and 80 kg is:

A 60 kg   B 50 kg   C 150 kg   D 30 kg

2 The **median** of 1, 3, 5, 7 and 11 is:

A 9   B 27   C 6   D 5

3 **True or false?**
The volume of water in the container is more than oil. _____

oil
water

4 **True or false?**
8 squares were counted.

Shape	Tally	Total
square	IIII III	
triangle	IIII IIII	

_____

5 What number is the **most common**? _____

Total
10
5

1 2 3 4
Numbers

6 Draw a **bar graph** of the information opposite:

Animal	No.
dog	2
cat	5
chicken	14
cow	20
sheep	17

7 What was the **most common** letter? _____

E A
D B
C

8 What is the **difference** between a line graph and a bar graph? _____

9 What was the **temperature** at 6 minutes?

_____

(Temp. °C)
10
4
2

4 8 10
Time (min)

10 Of 60 pencils **how many** were pink? _____

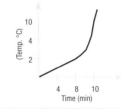

pink   blue   yellow

11 **Which** of the pie charts would represent this data?
There are 60 teams:
20 play soccer, 10 play netball and the rest play cricket.

A B C

12 **True or false?**
This is an example of a divided bar graph:

_____

1 The missing number of the **equivalent fraction**

$\frac{45}{50} = \frac{\square}{10}$ is:

A 4   B 4.5   C 5   D 9

2 0.47 ÷ 10 =

A 470   B 47   C 4.7   D 0.047

3 **True or false?**
$4 \times 70 = 560 - 280$ _____

4 **True or false?**
14 witches' hats are placed in a straight line 1 m apart and the line extends for 12 m.

_____

5 Find: 190 000
        − 26 429

6 **Complete**:

20) 4685

7 **Find** the missing number:
$(4 \times 100) + 6 = 750 - \square$

8 Complete with **< or >**:
$17.21 + $19.85 \square 3 \times 9.60

9 **Find** three fifths of fifty. _____

10 What is the **difference** between the two number sentences?
$(20 \times 6) + 3$ and $20 \times (6 + 3)$ _____

11 **Add** 192 846, 110 796.24 and 384 108.95

_____

12 I have 5 straws that vary in length from 5 cm to 19.5 cm. Give the **range** (lowest to highest) that could be the **total of the lengths**. _____

Score = ___ /12

Score = ___ /12

Unit 1 Page 19

1. a 521 702 b 900 576 c 250 820 d 611 465 e 108 239 f 95 891

2.

HTh	TTh	Th	H	T	U
5	2	1	7	0	2
9	0	0	5	7	6
2	5	0	8	2	0
6	1	1	4	6	5
1	0	8	2	3	9
0	9	5	8	9	1

3. a 8 tens b 6 units c 7 hundred Th d 8 Th e 7 TTh f 6 H

4. a 456 957, 454 957, 452 957 b 742 115, 742 215, 742 315
c 907 126, 907 136, 907 146 d 852 105, 862 105, 872 105
e 223 467, 323 467, 423 467 f 831 046, 841 046, 851 046

5. 798 462

6.

HTh	TTh	Th	H	T	U
7	9	8	4	6	2

7. 4 tens

8. 110 734, 110 744, 110 754

9. one hundred and ten thousand, seven hundred and ninety-three

Unit 2 Page 19

1. a–f

2. a eighty thousand, four hundred and eleven b ninety thousand c one hundred and seventy thousand, two hundred and forty-one
d nine hundred and ninety-eight thousand, six hundred and forty-two e three hundred and eighty-four thousand and sixty-one
f eight hundred and seventy thousand, four hundred

3. a < b > c > d < e < f <

4. a 19 221 b 198 921 c 51 010 d 89 270 e 24 879 f 456 285

5.

6. two hundred and seventy thousand, eight hundred and fifty

7. <

8. 31 795

9. a 4 b 23 c 204 d 219

Unit 3 Page 20

1. a 5 units b 5 million c 5 thousands d 5 hundred thousands e 5 thousands f 5 ten thousands

2. a 1 243 819, 1 308 925, 1 346 721 b 2 487 905, 2 635 921, 2 711 809 c 4 105 907, 4 246 385, 4 365 111
d 7 621 505, 7 921 300, 8 051 987 e 5 021 486, 5 121 352, 5 296 837 f 6 842 859, 7 932 481, 8 110 425

3. a 2 000 000 b 6 000 000 c 1 000 000 d 1 000 000 e 8 000 000 f 5 000 000

4.

Number	Place value	Total value
398 421	9 tens of thousands	90 000
8 710 486	8 millions	8 000 000
2 198 704	7 hundreds	700
3 947 825	7 thousands	7000
21 843 211	1 millions	1 000 000
427 806 921	20 millions	20 000 000

5. 5 ten thousands

6. 2 085 921, 2 127 460, 2 196 380

7. 3 000 000

8.

Number	Place value	Total value
1 438 216	4 hundred thousand	400 000

9. 50 000 000 50 000 000 60 000 000

Unit 4 Page 20

1. a 10, 12 b 100, 120 c 136, 145 d 391, 381 e 32, 64 f 880, 868

2. a add 2 b add 20 c add 9 d subtract 10 e multiply by 2 f subtract 12

3. a

1st No.	4	5	6	7	8
2nd No.	36	45	54	63	72

b

1st No.	26	36	46	56	66
2nd No.	45	55	65	75	85

c

1st No.	1.5	2.5	3.5	4.5	5.5
2nd No.	15	25	35	45	55

d

1st No.	7	17	27	37	47
2nd No.	35	85	135	185	235

e

1st No.	46	56	66	76	86
2nd No.	38	48	58	68	78

f

1st No.	64	54	44	34	24
2nd No.	80	70	60	50	40

4. a 1st number × 9 b 1st number + 19 c 1st number × 10 d 1st number × 5 e 1st number − 8 f 1st number + 16

5. 13, $15\frac{1}{4}$

6. start at $6\frac{1}{4}$ and add $2\frac{1}{4}$

7.

1st No.	100	90	80	70	60
2nd No.	20	18	16	14	12

1st number ÷ 5

8. 1, 4, 9, 16 i.e. $1^2, 2^2, 3^2, 4^2$ $10^2 = 100$

Unit 5 Page 21

1. a 142 561 b 295 629 c 453 785 d 608 096 e 870 807 f 952 003

2. a 50 000 + 6000 + 400 + 9 b 200 000 + 10 000 + 3000 + 800 + 40 + 7 c 400 000 + 60 000 + 2000 + 1 d 800 000 + 90 000 + 6000 + 300 + 20 + 5
e 1 000 000 + 200 000 + 20 000 + 4000 + 300 + 80 + 7 f 1 000 000 + 900 000 + 5000 + 600 + 20 + 1

3. a 428 b 917 c 4863 d 2748 e 21 368 f 72 499

4. a 4 b 21 c 92 d 847 e 123 f 1428

5. 429 026

6. 4 000 000 + 600 000 + 30 000 + 2000 + 500 + 80 + 9

7. 432 684

8. 468

9. a < b <

Unit 6   Page 21

1 a −3, −1, 0, 5, 6, 7, 9, 10 b −7, −3, −2, 0, 1, 2, 4, 8 c −8, −5, −4, −2, 0, 1, 5, 10 d −10, −6, 0, 1, 2, 13, 14 e −10, −5, −4, −2, 0, 3, 5 f −4, −3, −1, 0, 2, 3, 5, 8 2 a 10 b 5 c 0 d 11 e −1 f 0 3 a 8, 10, 12 b 9, 12, 15 c 4, 2, 0 d −1, −3, −5 e −3, −6, −9, 4, 6, 8 4 a −2 b −5 c 1 d −2 e −3 f −9 5 −10, −7, −3, −2, 0, 2, 5, 10 6 −2 7 −6, −10, −14 8 1

9

$$\xrightarrow{\qquad \underset{-3}{|} \qquad \underset{-1\frac{1}{2}}{|} \qquad \underset{0\ \ 0.5}{|} \qquad \underset{-2\frac{1}{4}}{|} \qquad \underset{4}{|} \qquad}$$

Unit 7   Page 22

1 a 110 b 120 c 120 d 1000 e 900 f 1500 2 a 195 b 394 c 913 d 285 e 193 f 351 3 a 800 b 800 c 1200 d 1300 e 1900 f 3300 4 a 1412 b 1423 c 9083 d 13 655 e 7764 f 8267 5 11 000 6 485 7 4400 8 10 883 9 27 846 + 39 468 = 67 314

Unit 8   Page 22

1 a 1760 b 1443 c 2215 d 4935 e 13 538 f 17 134 2 a $58 661 b $129 977 c $861 081 d $178 602 e $785 333 f $1 018 256 3 a

```
    3 5 5 6 4
  +   4 8 4 5
  ─────────────
    4 0 4 0 9
```
b
```
    6 3 2 9 8 6
  + 2 0 1 2 6 4
  ─────────────
    8 3 4 2 5 0
```
c
```
    1 0 7 9 3 2
  + 4 6 5 1 8 7
  ─────────────
    5 7 3 1 1 9
```
d
```
    4 6 7 3 2 6
  + 4 2 2 7 3 6
  ─────────────
    8 9 0 0 6 2
```
e
```
    3 2 9 1 8 4
  + 4 6 2 7 7 3
  ─────────────
    7 9 1 9 5 7
```
f
```
    6 2 7 8 5 4
  + 2 5 6 4 3 7
  ─────────────
    8 8 4 2 9 1
```

4 a $10 050 b 85 763 cows c 4450 caps d 2401 km e 614 cm f 1476 pieces 5 1889 6 $943 028 7
```
    4 5 3 7 8 4
  + 5 3 6 8 4 8
  ─────────────
    9 9 0 6 3 2
```
8 54 172 avocados 9 1 003 961

Unit 9   Page 23

1 a 1 511 935 b 1 478 643 c 1 122 143 d 1 649 274 e 1 339 666 f 938 838 2 a 308 175 b 6 235 754 c 2 276 103 d 11 528 000 e 17 383 000 f 13 730 000 3 a $644 688.43 b $5 653 635.79 c $11 284 181.38 d $2 400 878.60 e $9 790 564.09 f $12 241 973.30 4 a 54 208 g b 21 702 cm c 85 294 tonnes d 16 309 L e 39 313 km f 1 549 522 ha 5 1 151 669 6 11 292 428 7 $3 560 539.35 8 6490 9 $35 085

Unit 10   Page 23

1 a 427 b 834 c 374 d 261 e 139 f 519 2 a 4622 b 884 c 271 d 2887 e 1638 f 606 3 a
```
    5 6 1 7
  − 4 3 1 3
  ─────────
    1 3 0 4
```
b
```
    5 1 6 4
  − 3 1 2 7
  ─────────
    2 0 3 7
```
c
```
    9 5 4 1
  − 2 6 7 2
  ─────────
    6 8 6 9
```
d
```
    8 7 6 3
  − 2 4 0 8
  ─────────
    6 3 5 5
```
e
```
    8 5 7 0
  −   7 2 3
  ─────────
    7 8 4 7
```
```
    8 2 0 0
  − 7 0 0 4
  ─────────
    1 1 9 6
```
4 a 2401 b 7252 c 5520 d 5484 e 842 f 2281 5 547 6 2555 7
```
    4 0 1 6
  − 1 3 2 5
  ─────────
    2 6 9 1
```
8 2123 9 $3192 − $2385 = $807 profit

Unit 11   Page 24

1 a 110 b 290 c 190 d 180 e 160 f 140 2 a 147 b 38 c 142 d 180 e 192 f 448 3 a 5514 b 7202 c 2891 d 3473 e 8105 f 4789 4 a 36 b 129 c 147 d 129 e 79 f 44 5 290 6 246 7 6373 8 244 9 177 cards

Unit 12   Page 24

1 a 50 b 60 c 100 d 110 e 260 f 490 2 a 100 b 400 c 900 d 1300 e 5000 f 4500 3 a 1000 b 1000 c 3000 d 18 000 e 30 000 f 126 000 4

	Question	Rounded	Estimate
a	5778 + 3697	6000 + 4000	10 000
b	2866 + 3105	3000 + 3000	6000
c	1249 + 2958	1000 + 3000	4000
d	35977 + 6104	36 000 + 6000	42 000
e	55394 + 5106	55 000 + 5000	60 000
f	9999 + 27108	10 000 + 27000	37 000

5 730 6 52 800 7 135 000 8

Question	Rounded	Estimate
4687 + 3721	5000 + 4000	9000

9 a 9 k b 14 k c 21 k d 51 k e 37 k f 85 k

Unit 13 Page 25

1 a 36 461 b 44 237 c 37 719 d 34 640 e 25 270 f 4250

2
a	b	c	d	e
47 000	83 000	92 000	67 000	60 000
− 21 000	− 68 000	− 43 000	− 41 000	− 17 000
26 000	15 000	49 000	26 000	43 000

f
43 000
− 11 000
32 000

3 a 554 406 kg b 366 568 m c 123 433 L d 49 274 t e 146 227 ha f 452 279 cm

4 a 780 838 b 341 597 c 26 966 d 252 781 e 488 463 f 222 055 **5** 8638 **6** 64 000 **7** 62 713 mm **8** 542 423
− 40 000
24 000

9 various

Unit 14 Page 25

1 a 1 254 000 b 6 686 000 c 3 528 000 d 1 889 000 e 4 529 000 f 1 049 000 **2** a $3 923 225 b $2 926 290 c $517 253
d $4 462 314 e $1 970 304 f $1 822 528 **3** a 159 619 km² b 182 950 km² c 1 541 119 km² d 1 353 846 km² e 798 300 km²
f 554 745 km² **4** a 310 713 kg b 11 153 L c 375 225 t d $582 756 e 631 474 cm f 705 313 g **5** 481 000 **6** $1 460 795
7 573 915 km² **8** 12 335 686 L **9** WA − ACT = 2 523 170 km²

Unit 15 Page 26

1
a	b	c	d	e	f
46 200	17 600	24 800	142 900	429 100	873 100
+ 38 000	+ 19 300	+ 46 000	+ 173 100	+ 140 300	+ 117 800
84 200	36 900	70 800	316 000	569 400	990 900

2
a	b	c
42 000	26 000	47 000
− 20 000	− 8 000	− 34 000
22 000	18 000	13 000

d
129 000
− 114 000
15 000

e
168 000
− 123 000
45 000

f
850 000
− 328 000
522 000

3 a $422 + $62 = $484 b $122 + $157 = $279 c $643 + $249 = $892
d $479 − $136 = $343 e $846 − $138 = $708 f $649 − $378 = $271

4
a	b	c	d	e	f
4300	7400	8800	4900	6200	9600
+ 2000	+ 1300	+ 4100	+ 3900	+ 7500	+ 1000
6300	8700	12900	8800	13700	10600

5
721 100
+ 385 200
1 106 300

6
478 000
− 169 000
309 000

7 $733 − $458 = $275

8
47 900
+ 23 500
71 400

9 2 144 000 − 1 794 000 = 350 000

Unit 16 Page 26

1 a 28 b 27 c 120 d 40 e 54 f 4 **2** a 24 b 36 c 77 d 40 e 18 f 49 **3** a 3 b 9 c 8 d 7 e 4 f 12 **4** a $90 b $12
c $84 d $15 e $24 f $32 **5** 108 **6** 121 **7** 9 **8** $55 **9**

×	4	7	9	11	12
6	24	42	54	66	72

Unit 17 Page 27

1 a 100 b 42 c 36 d 10 e 0 f 33 **2** a true b false c false d true e false f true **3** a 24 b 60 c 72 d 21 e 60 f 0
4 a 42 days b 7 days c 70 days d 28 days e 84 days f 49 days **5** 24 **6** true **7** 44 **8** 63 days
9 0,99,110,132,77,66,121,88

Unit 18 Page 27

1 a 63 b 16 c 55 d 84 e 48 f 144 **2** a 96 b 0 c 28 d 45 e 35 f 6 **3** a 6 × 2 = 12 = 12 × 1
b 9 × 8 = 72 = 6 × 12 c 8 × 3 = 24 = 6 × 4 d 6 × 5 = 30 = 3 × 10 e 2 × 9 = 18 = 6 × 3
f 5 × 4 = 20 = 10 × 2 **4** a twenty-seven b forty-eight c seven d one hundred and thirty-two e one hundred and eight
f zero **5** 70 **6** 108 **7** 5 × 10 = 50 = 25 × 2 **8** fifty-six **9** 60 cows, 6 horses, 4 pigs, 50 chickens = 120 animals

Unit 19 Page 28

1 a 8 b 27 c 42 d 25 e 32 f 56 **2** a 280 b 150 c 600 d 450 e 280 f 480 **3** a 1400 b 1600 c 1800 d 4000 e 5400
3500 **4** a 32 000 b 24 000 c 6000 d 27 000 e 14 000 f 30 000 **5** 16 **6** 270 **7** 6300 **8** 81 000
9 700 × 7 = 4900 L

Unit 20 Page 28

1 a 230, 460, 690 b 140, 280, 420 c 760, 1520, 2280 d 340, 680, 1020 e 520, 1040, 1560 f 170, 340, 510
2 a 200, 400, 600 b 500, 1000, 1500 c 900, 1800, 2700 d 700, 1400, 2100 e 400, 800, 1200 f 800, 1600, 2400
3 a 3600 b 4000 c 2700 d 2800 e 5400 f 1400 **4** a 1200 books b $560 c 600 students d 3600 words e 1500 biscuits
700 L of milk **5** 260, 520, 780 **6** 300, 600, 900 **7** 2500 **8** 1200 Easter eggs **9** 1480 left

Unit 21 Page 29

1 a 15 000 b 16 000 c 24 000 d 45 000 e 27 000 f 28 000 **2**

×	10	100	1000
a	40	400	4000	40 000
b	70	700	7000	70 000
c	83	830	8300	83 000
d	29	290	2900	29 000
e	200	2000	20 000	200 000
f	167	1670	16 700	167 000

3 a 3600 b 10 000 c 2200 d 35 000 e 8800 f 4200
4 a 700 b 80 000 c 42 300 d 126 000 e 47 000 f 9300
5 42 000 **6**

×	10	100	1000
123	1230	12 300	123 000

7 8400 **8** 98 000 **9** 519 × 30 = 15 570 students approximately

Unit 22 Page 29

1 a 84 b 57 c 378 d 185 e 441 f 324 **2** a 447 b 1032 c 1505 d 4950 e 4998 f 4416 **3** a 8622 b 7443 c 32 204
5960 e 32 112 f 7364 **4** a 14 580 b 36 960 c 5350 d 121 800 e 387 000 f 36 000 **5** 136 **6** 2740 **7** 14 728
8 108 300 **9** a 3600 s b 21 600 s c 36 000 s

Unit 23 Page 30

1 a 520 × 4 = 2080 b 260 × 4 = 1040 c 300 × 5 = 1500 d 830 × 6 = 4980 e 710 × 7 = 4970 f 550 × 8 = 4400
2 a 13 × 61 = (10 × 61) + (3 × 61) = $\boxed{793}$ b 23 × 47 = (20 × 47) + (3 × 47) = $\boxed{1081}$
29 × 58 = (20 × 58) + (9 × 58) = $\boxed{1682}$ d 32 × 76 = ($\boxed{30}$ × 76) + ($\boxed{2}$ × 76) = $\boxed{2432}$
17 × 63 = ($\boxed{10}$ × 63) + ($\boxed{7}$ × 63) = $\boxed{1071}$ f 43 × 85 = ($\boxed{40}$ × 85) + ($\boxed{3}$ × 85) = $\boxed{3655}$

3 a 27 × 63 =   b 53 × 87 =   c 37 × 96 =   d 47 × 26 =

63 63	87 87	96 96	26 26
× 20 × 7	× 50 × 3	× 30 × 7	× 40 × 7
$\boxed{1260}$ + $\boxed{441}$ = $\boxed{1701}$	$\boxed{4350}$ + $\boxed{261}$ = $\boxed{4611}$	$\boxed{2880}$ + $\boxed{672}$ = $\boxed{3552}$	$\boxed{1040}$ + $\boxed{182}$ = $\boxed{1222}$

22 × 78 =   f 45 × 53 =

78 78	53 53
× 20 × 2	× 40 × 5
$\boxed{1560}$ + $\boxed{156}$ = $\boxed{1716}$	$\boxed{2120}$ + $\boxed{265}$ = $\boxed{2385}$

4 a 12 750 b 34 320 c 41 750 d 23 133 e 6734 f 5029
5 860 × 4 = 3440 **6** 17 × 26 = ($\boxed{10}$ × 26) + ($\boxed{7}$ × 26) = $\boxed{442}$
7 72 × 75 =   75   75   **8** 8085
          × 70   × 2
       $\boxed{5250}$ + $\boxed{150}$ = $\boxed{5400}$

9 1126 × 37 = 41 662

Unit 24 Page 30

1 a 420 b 1800 c 3200 d 180 e 30 000 f 1500 **2** a 120, 1200, 12 000 b 630, 6300, 63 000 c 400, 4000, 40 000
d 2800, 28 000, 280 000 e 1200, 12 000, 120 000 f 4800, 48 000, 480 000 **3** a 28 882 b 66 872 c 4108 d 23 115 e 32 100
f 39 816 **4** a

43	73	96	65
× 25	× 48	× 37	× 53
215 (5 × 43)	584 (8 × 73)	672 (7 × 96)	195 (3 × 65)
+ 860 (20 × 43)	+ 2920 (40 × 73)	+ 2880 (30 × 96)	+ 3250 (50 × 65)
1075	3504	3552	3445

e	f
59	88
× 17	× 66
413 (7 × 59)	528 (6 × 88)
+ 590 (10 × 59)	+ 5280 (60 × 88)
1003	5808

5 3200 **6** 1500, 15 000 **7** 21 380
8
86
× 14
344 (4 × 86)
+ 860 (10 × 86)
1204

9 1800 eggs

Unit 25 Page 31

1 a

92	73	56	28
× 17	× 25	× 49	× 75
644 (7 × 92)	365 (5 × 73)	504 (9 × 56)	140 (5 × 28)
+ 920 (10 × 92)	+ 1460 (20 × 73)	+ 2240 (40 × 56)	+ 1960 (70 × 28)
1564	1825	2744	2100

e	f
63	37
× 82	× 53
126 (2 × 63)	111 (3 × 37)
+ 5040 (80 × 63)	+ 1850 (50 × 37)
5166	1961

2 a 1152 b 1950 c 1134 d 1012 e 1512 f 969
3 a 1008 b 4940 c 672 d 1386 e 2075 f 2173
4 a $792 b $1083 c $1020 d $680 e $950 f $774

5
45
× 63
135 (3 × 45)
+ 2700 (60 × 45)
2835

6 3024 **7** 2295 **8** $507 **9** (32 + 5) × 12 = $444

Unit 26 Page 31

1 a 816 b 608 c 4171 d 7696 e 46 782 f 32 775 **2** a 672 b 1947 c 1875 d 4232 e 5355 f 3196 **3** a 32 b 65 c 26
d 27 e 35 f 19 **4** a 1470 bananas b 2241 avocados c 2912 oranges d 198 apples e 3150 mandarins f 1273 pineapples
5 3266 **6** 1533 **7** 43 **8** 2210 plums **9** 19 550 km

Unit 27 Page 32

1 a 14 445 b 23 112 c 15 281 d 19 928 e 3043 f 26 622 **2** a $1106 b $2028 c $9812 d $4500 e $10 530 f $213 150
3 a 247 380 b 166 400 c 60 900 d 134 400 e 170 240 f 183 160 **4** a $1666 b $4984 c $5280 d $3276 e $2720
f $3220 **5** 32 148 **6** $9724 **7** 83 430 **8** $3354 **9** 179 × 26 = 4654 eggs

Unit 28 Page 32

1

a	Divisible by 2	(302)	491	(682)	1105	(6234)	8255	95253
b	Divisible by 3	173	(735)	828	(1143)	1276	(7827)	(23412)
c	Divisible by 4	423	(536)	(984)	(1364)	1649	6385	(26424)
d	Divisible by 5	(105)	621	898	1462	(1700)	(9515)	83966
e	Divisible by 8	(256)	452	(984)	1076	1935	(6456)	73265
f	Divisible by 9	(198)	356	899	(1368)	8753	(9981)	(12420)

2 a true b false c false d true e false f true
3 a 1, 12, 2, 6, 3, 4 b 1, 18, 2, 9, 3, 6 c 1, 24, 2, 12, 3, 8, 4, 6
d 1, 30, 2, 15, 3, 10, 5, 6 e 1, 48, 2, 24, 3, 16, 4, 12, 6, 8
f 1, 60, 2, 30, 3, 20, 4, 15, 5, 12, 6, 10
4 a 7, 14, 21, 28, 35, 42, 49, 56 b 6, 12, 18, 24, 30, 36, 42, 48
c 11, 22, 33, 44, 55, 66, 77, 88 d 12, 24, 36, 48, 60, 72, 84, 96
e 10, 20, 30, 40, 50, 60, 70, 80 f 8, 16, 24, 32, 40, 48, 56, 64
5 321, (460), 703, 1011, (4200), (9090), 12345 **6** true **7** 1, 100, 2, 50, 4, 35, 5, 20, 10 **8** 9, 18, 27, 36, 45, 54, 63, 72
9 5000, 1, 2500, 2, 1250, 4, 5, 1000, 8, 625, 10, 500, 20, 250, 25, 200, 40, 125, 50, 100

Unit 29 Page 33

1 a 180 b 320 c 420 d 2000 e 1500 f 7200 2 a 80 b 120 c 180 d 230 e 190 f 270 3 a 64 b 72 c 96 d 176 e 264
f 376 4 a 252 b 225 c 370 d 252 e 675 f 2178 5 3600 6 215 7 152 8 1052 9 a 288 b 384 c 528

Unit 30 Page 33

1 a 30 × 6 = 180 b 50 × 7 = 350 c 50 × 5 = 250 d 100 × 9 = 900 e 200 × 8 = 1600 f 300 × 4 = 1200
2 a 80 × 20 = 1600 b 50 × 30 = 1500 c 40 × 60 = 2400 d 40 × 20 = 800 e 50 × 70 = 3500 f 30 × 70 = 2100
3 a 80 × 400 = 32 000 b 80 × 700 = 56 000 c 20 × 500 = 10 000 d 600 × 10 = 6000 e 40 × 600 = 24 000
f 60 × 900 = 54 000 4 a 30 000, 29 281 b 16 000, 14 668 c 9000, 11 303 d 14 000, 14 076 e 12 000, 13 317
f 15 000, 11 475 5 400 × 7 = 2800 6 70 × 30 = 2100 7 60 × 400 = 24 000 8 28 000, 25 467
9 23 × 379 ≃ 20 × 400 = 8000 newspapers

Unit 31 Page 34

1 a 9, 8 b 6, 5 c 7, 4 d 12, 8 e 8, 6 f 12, 3 2 a 9 b 8 c 1 d 8 e 7 f 10 3 a 2 b 9 c 10 d 12 e 8 f 9
4 a 32 b 9 c 12 d 23 e 22 f 12 5 12, 6 6 12 7 0 8 11 9 41 pencils in each box

Unit 32 Page 34

1 a 6 b 4 c 3 d 12 e 2 f 8 2 a 4 r 4 b 3 r 3 c 2 r 6 d 2 r 4 e 1 r 4 f 2 r 2 3 a 60 b 90 c 40 d 50 e 50 f 40

4

	Question	Quotient	Remainder
	20 ÷ 3	6	2
a	30 ÷ 4	7	2
b	51 ÷ 7	7	2
c	38 ÷ 4	9	2
d	40 ÷ 9	4	4
e	55 ÷ 10	5	5
f	63 ÷ 6	10	3

5 4 6 2 r 2 7 70 8

Question	Quotient	Remainder
14 ÷ 6	2	2

9

Question	Quotient	Remainder
32 ÷ 6	5	2
14 ÷ 8	1	6
28 ÷ 3	9	1
60 ÷ 7	8	4

Unit 33 Page 35

1 a 8 r 4 b 13 r 1 c 7 r 7 d 4 r 6 e 6 r 8 f 8 r 2 2 a 324 b 123 c 112 d 122 e 132 f 126 3 a 72 r 2 b 65 r 5
c 109 r 2 d 330 r 4 e 3008 r 2 f 303 r 8 4 a $46.50 b 82 with 5 eggs over c 159 cars with 3 tyres over d 106 mL e 197 cm
f 1342 tacks with 1 left over 5 8 r 3 6 235 7 580 r 5 8 1071 letters 9 $\frac{48 + 52 + 64}{3}$ = 54.67 cm

Unit 34 Page 35

1 a 1 b 1 r 1 c 2 d 1 r 2 e 2 r 2 f 4 r 3 2 a $21\frac{1}{2}$ 2)43 b $10\frac{1}{3}$ 3)31 c $7\frac{1}{4}$ 4)29 d $13\frac{2}{6} = 13\frac{1}{3}$ 6)8²0 e $18\frac{4}{5}$ 5)9⁴4 f $7\frac{1}{7}$ 7)50

3 a $150\frac{2}{6} = 150\frac{1}{3}$ 6)9³02 b $125\frac{3}{4}$ 4)5¹0²3 c $89\frac{6}{7}$ 7)62⁶9 d $74\frac{2}{8} = 74\frac{1}{4}$ 8)59³4 e $28\frac{4}{9}$ 9)25⁷6 f $86\frac{3}{5}$ 5)43³3 4 a $1210\frac{5}{6}$ 6)7¹265 b $1206\frac{2}{8} = 1206\frac{1}{4}$ 8)9¹650 c $1823\frac{2}{3}$ 3)5²47¹1
d $1335\frac{5}{7}$ 7)9²3²5⁴0 e $274\frac{2}{9}$ 9)24⁶6³8 f $1340\frac{3}{4}$ 4)5¹3¹63 5 3 r 1 6 $9\frac{3}{8}$ 7 $82\frac{1}{3}$ 8 $1061\frac{2}{5}$ 9 a $\frac{7}{10}$ b $\frac{1}{4}$ c $\frac{5}{7}$

Unit 35 Page 36

1 a 39 b 85 c 40 d $67\frac{1}{10}$ e $34\frac{9}{10}$ f 85 2 a 1045 b 1011 c 912 d 1202 e 703 f 2090 3 a $503\frac{1}{4}$ b $1403\frac{4}{5}$ c 535
d $10\,200\frac{1}{3}$ e $8826\frac{7}{8}$ f 6017 4 a 709 in each row b $195 each c 207 in each pile d 102 per rack e 507 trays f 1201 weeks
5 $25\frac{9}{10}$ 6 1002 7 $306\frac{1}{7}$ 8 834 lengths 9 51 523

Unit 36 Page 36

1 a 430.1 b 743.8 c 506 d 849.7 e 663.5 f 901 2 a 436 b 2107 c 4600 d 2104 e 3911 f 6127 3 a 2468 b 7102
c 8763 d 19 041.6 e 48 795.1 f 84 731.5 4 a 960 cm b 1750 cm c 49 cm d 871 cm e 3842 cm f 112 cm 5 437.1
6 1426 7 47 180.5 8 3910 cm 9 35 000 boxes

Unit 37 Page 37

1 a 576 b 249 c 310 d 2300 e 4690 f 4870 2 a 21 b 37 c 29 d 480 e 520 f 390 3 a 21 b 120 c 70 d 600 e 119
f 30 4 a 33.7 b 35.5 c 35.7 d 95.4 e 92.7 f 182.2 5 432 6 107 7 30 8 33.8 9 a 154.375, 154 b 168.64, 169

Unit 38 Page 37

1 a 1438 b 518 c 1443 d 484 e 1062 f 1035 2 a 9022.71 b 3162 c 5948.5 d 4268.1 e 7940.3 f 8436.6

3 a 500 students b 706 L in each container c 149 265 m² per paddock d 11 598 km e 141 t per boat f 66 points

4 a 3702 b 6126 c 4417 d 7218 e 8464 f 5912 5 711 6 5790.13 7 $1787 8 8655 9 16 896

Unit 39 Page 38

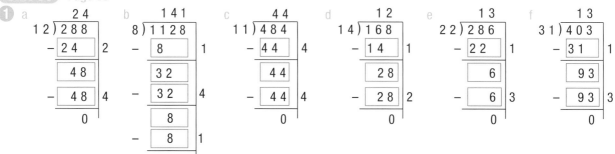

2 a 31 r 2 b 17 r 6 c 38 r 2 d 12 e 10 r 20 f 48 r 1 3 a 16 r 11 b 50 c 19 r 21 d 11 r 4 e 49 f 5 r 8 4 a 275 b 646
c 365 d 1369 e 951 f 9723 5 [division layout: 83, 6)498, −48 |8, 18, −18 |3] 6 37 r 9 7 11 r 10 8 487 9 15 cartons with 4 eggs left over

Unit 40 Page 38

1 a 5 b 13 c 50 d 100 e 162.5 f 7.5 2 a 5 b 38 c 22⅓ d 449 e $3.43 f $9.00 3 a 50 b 0.9 c 2.4 d 252 e 2.5
f 1200 4 a 25°C b 27°C c 24.3°C d 20.5°C e 25.2°C f 23.86°C 5 21.5 6 32 7 2 8 23.3°C 9 example: 26, 27, 28

Unit 41 Page 39

1 a 38.5 b 37.5 c 9.25 d 49.6 e 59.25 f 79.2 2 a 10 b 78 c 10 d 21 e 50 f 20

3

	Team	Score	Average
a	Numbers	0, 3, 4, 2, 1, 2	2
b	Totals	6, 5, 2, 1, 3, 1	3
c	Dividers	0, 2, 1, 3, 0, 0	1
d	Multipliers	4, 6, 3, 7, 1, 3	4
e	Adders	5, 7, 3, 9, 1, 2	4.5
f	Subtracters	5, 6, 7, 8, 3, 3	5.3

4 a 31.25°C b 116 marbles c 31.8 runs d 13.6 fruit e 10.7 pencils
f 81.8 matches 5 49.6 6 16 7

Team	Score	Average
Powers	4, 7, 3, 8, 5, 3	5

8 $22.20 9 17

Unit 42 Page 39

1 a correct b 171 c correct d 293 e 1378 f correct 2 a 20 b correct c 3 d correct e correct f correct 3 a false b true
c false d true e true f false 4 a D b F c E d A e C f B 5 1791 6 correct 7 true 8 12 × 8 = * 9 16 birds

Unit 43 Page 40

1 a [number line: 10 17 24 31 38] b [number line: 50 53 56 59 62] c [number line: 113 118 123 128 133] d [number line: 68 74 80 86 92] e [number line: 348 357 366 375]
f [number line: 0 250 500 750 1000] 2 a 739 b 1258 c 1194 d 2066 e 1407 f 2797 3 a 291 b 441 c 66 d 689 e 219 f 934

4 a 78 b 110 c 225 d 15 e 17 f 26 5 [number line: 1126 1134 1142 1150] 6 5787 7 1889 8 210 9 a [number line: 1 1¼ 1½ 1¾ 2 2¼ 2½ 2¾ 3]
b i ¾ ii 8 iii 2 iv 2¼

Unit 44 Page 40

1 a 150 b 36 c 33 d 16 e 27 f 77 2 a 36 b 33 c 18 d 10 e 8 f 8 3 a 35 b 41 c 56 d 80 e 7 f 24

4 a 52 b 3 c 53 d 197 e 2 f 56 5 41 6 15 7 83 8 72 9 17 + (3 + 5) × 4 = 16 − 7 + (8 × 5) = 49

Unit 45 Page 41

1 a 31 b 13 c 60 d 6 e 16 f 37　2 a 22 b 40 c 7 d 1422 e 4480 f 142　3 a 11 b 15 c 110 d 15 e 100 f 70
4 a 32 b 0 c 0 d 20.8 e 171 f 380　5 19　6 142　7 48　8 40
9 a same answer as starting number b inverse operations

Unit 46 Page 41

1 a 4 b 12 c 420 d 20 e 0 f 10　2 a 36 b 36 c 36 d 4 e 26 f 26　3 a 40 b 80 c 110 d 70 e 40 f 40
4 a 25 b 25 c 27 d 27 e 2 f 2　5 188　6 400, 4　7 10, 10　8 15, 15　9 example: $(10 \times 9) + (5 \times 6) = 120$
$(10 \times 9) - (5 \times 6) = 60$

Unit 47 Page 42

1 a 3.5 b 3 c 1.2 d 21 e 1 f 6　2 a 11 b 4 c 1.4 d 1.2 e 8.4 f 7.7　3 a 28.2 b 109.5 c 5 d 21.9 e 13.5 f 75
4 a 7 b $\frac{3}{5}$ or 0.6 c 3 d 5 e $2\frac{3}{4}$ or $\frac{11}{4}$ f 45　5 1　6 5　7 10.1　8 2　9 $(0.4 + 0.3) \times 12 - 0.2 - 1.0 = 7.2$

Unit 48 Page 42

1 a

1st No.	64	60	56	52	48
2nd No.	32	30	28	26	24

b

1st No.	7	8	9	10	11
2nd No.	56	64	72	80	88

c

1st No.	70	63	56	49	42
2nd No.	10	9	8	7	6

d

1st No.	60	54	48	42	36
2nd No.	10	9	8	7	6

e

1st No.	1	2	3	4	5
2nd No.	$\frac{1}{2}$	1	$1\frac{1}{2}$	2	$2\frac{1}{2}$

f

1st No.	0.5	0.6	0.7	0.8	0.9
2nd No.	5	6	7	8	9

2 a divide by 2 b multiply by 8 c divide by 7 d divide by 6 e divide by 2 f multiply by 10

3 a 44, 22 b 12, 96 c 35, 5 d 30, 5 e 6, 3 f 1.0, 10　4 a 28, 14 b 16, 128 c 7, 1 d 6, 1 e 10, 5 f 1.4, 14

5

1st No.	9	19	29	39	49
2nd No.	26	36	46	56	66

6 add 17　7 59, 76　8 99, 116　9

No. of triangles	1	2	3	4
No. of sides	3	6	9	12

Unit 49 Page 43

1 a 12, 17, 23 b 25, 36, 49 c 7, 9.5, 12.5 d 37, 26, 17 e 32, 47, 65 f 64, 216, 2048　2 a add 1, 2, 3, ...
b add 1 and square c add 0.5, 1, 1.5, ... d subtract 19, 17, 15, ... e add 3, 6, 9, ... f multiply by 8, divide by 2

3

a 1st No.	2nd No.		b 1st No.	2nd No.		c 1st No.	2nd No.		d 1st No.	2nd No.		e 1st No.	2nd No.		f 1st No.	2nd No.
3	4		10	8		5	50		4	16		100	84		60	75
6	7		11	9		7	70		5	20		99	83		55	70
9	10		12	10		9	90		6	24		98	82		50	65
12	13		13	11		11	110		7	28		97	81		45	60
15	16		14	12		13	130		8	32		96	80		40	55
18	19		15	13		15	150		9	36		95	79		35	50

4

a 1st No.	2nd No.		b 1st No.	2nd No.		c 1st No.	2nd No.		d 1st No.	2nd No.		e 1st No.	2nd No.		f 1st No.	2nd No.
100	101		48	46		24	240		100	400		16	0		10	25

5 $1\frac{1}{4}$, $1\frac{1}{2}$, $1\frac{3}{4}$　6 add $\frac{1}{4}$　7

1st No.	2nd No.
7	35
6	30
9	45
12	60
10	50
15	75

8

1st No.	2nd No.
100	500

9

□	2	4	6	8	10	12	14
△	9	13	17	21	25	29	33

Unit 50 Page 43

1 a 486 b 0 c 574 d 381 e 3.4 f 3784　2 a 6 b 700 c 5 d 100 e 0 f 560　3 a 2 b 3 c 99 d 57 e 13.4 f 13
4 a M = 10 + (7 × 3 × 2) M = 52 b △ = (16 + 17 + 18) ÷ 3 △ = 17 c (11 + 9) ÷ 4 × 7 = 35
d V = (100 − 4) − (3 × 7) V = 75 e T = (11 × 12) ÷ 2 + 4, T = 70 f * = 12 × 6 − 8 × 7 = 16　5 122　6 8　7 144
8 (60 × 3) − 120 = D = 60　9 * = ((9.8 ÷ 2) + 0.1) ÷ 8 = 0.625 or $\frac{5}{8}$

Unit 51 — Page 44

1 a 0 b 0 c 0 d 0 e 0 f 0
2 a 1 689 599 b 1 184 000 c 11 533 000 d 187 000 e 777 500 f 61 250 000
3 a 1 230 810 b 4 859 400 c 67 128 000 d 26 850 e 1 526 400 f 362 300

4 a
```
  1 0 1 7 6 0
+ 3 2 8 3 3 7
  4 3 0 0 9 7
```
b
```
  4 7 1 2 9 9 4
- 1 6 6 4 6 8 4
  3 0 4 8 3 1 0
```
c
```
     1 1 8 6 8 0
5 ) 5 9 4 3 3 4 0 0
```
d
```
    5 0 7
  ×  4 2
  1 0 1 4
+ 2 0 2 8 0
  2 1 2 9 4
```
e
```
    3 0 7
  ×  4 7
  2 1 4 9
+ 1 2 2 8 0
  1 4 4 2 9
```
f
```
    8 0 8
  ×  6 3
  2 4 2 4
+ 4 8 4 8 0
  5 0 9 0 4
```

5 0 **6** 1 170 500

7 1 964 800 **8**
```
  1 0 7 4 8 0
-   3 8 4 6 0
    6 9 0 2 0
```
9 11 352 000 packets per year

Unit 52 — Page 44

1 a 51 b 19 c 10 d 9.2 e 26 f 7
2 a 21 b 56 c 6 d 27 e 35 f $\frac{121}{144}$
3 a 3 b 8 c 1.5 d 160 e 3.7 f $1\frac{1}{3}$
4 a $42.50 ÷ 5 = $8.50 b apples + 4 + 6 = 13, apples = 3 c 60 ÷ (4 × 3) = 5 trays d $25.50 + bf = $27.25, bf = $1.75
e 6 × 6 = area, area = 36 cm² f (5 × 7) + (6 × L) = 71, 6 lettuce plants per row **5** 2.9 **6** 6 **7** $\frac{6}{10} = \frac{2}{5}$
8 6.3 cm − 2.9 cm = 3.4 cm **9** x ÷ (7 + 3) + 50 − 7 = 9 × 5, starting number was 20

Unit 53 — Page 45

1

		2^4 (16)	2^3 (8)	2^2 (4)	2^1 (2)	2^0 (1)
a	5			1	0	1
b	26	1	1	0	1	0
c	17	1	0	0	0	1
d	9		1	0	0	1
e	11		1	0	1	1
f	21	1	0	1	0	1

2 a 11 b 110 c 1010 d 10 000 e 1111 f 10 011
3 a 7 b 9 c 14 d 12 e 21 f 29 **4** a 7 + 5 = 12 b 9 ÷ 3 = 3
c 21 − 11 = 10 d 31 − 13 = 18 e 8 × 4 = 32 f 5 + 10 = 15

5

	2^4 (16)	2^3 (8)	2^2 (4)	2^1 (2)	2^0 (1)
2				1	0

6 10 111 **7** 24 **8** 12 ÷ 3 = 4 **9** 21, 34, 55, 89, 144

Unit 54 — Page 45

1 a $4.75 b $3.00 c $81.65 d $100.00 e $3.45 f $1010.90 **2** a $13.07 b $14.28 c $16.86 d $0.22 e $9.46 f $13.77
3 a $32.00 b $65.03 c $39.15 d $2.85 e $2.55 f $2.39 **4** a $4.65 b $10.55 c $10.30 d $6.03 e $1.71 f $3.85
5 $7.80 **6** $52.10 **7** $22.95 **8** $0.68 **9** (39 × $3.25) + (4 × $4.99) + (2 × $2.45) = $34.61

Unit 55 — Page 46

1 a 30 b 14 c 9 d 25 e 48 f 9 **2** a (5 × 100) − (7 × 6) = 458 b (49 ÷ 7) + (8 × 2) = 23 c (15 + 9) × 3 ÷ 8 = 9
d (11.9 + 6) − 9.3 = 8.6 e 5^2 × (4 × 1) = 100 f (22 ÷ 2) × 12 + 8 = 140 **3** a 92 b 12 c 12.3 d 394 e 129 f 120

4

Δ	2.3	6	7.8	9.05
□	1.7	4.2	c 3.5	6.11
Δ + □	a 4	c 10.2	11.3	15.16
Δ − □	b 0.6	1.8	e 4.3	f 2.94

5 94 **6** 9 × 7 − (8 × 3) = 39 **7** 14 **8**

Δ	4.6
□	1.07
Δ + □	a 5.67
Δ − □	b 3.53

9 A 12 B 11 C 10 D 11, answer C. There are 10 small squares.

Unit 56 — Page 46

1 a true b false c true d false e false f false **2** a 77 b 189 c 16 d 180 e 6 f 50
3 a
```
  6 0 7
+ 7 8 2
1 3 8 9
```
b
```
4 3 2 6
- 7 8 9
3 5 3 7
```
c
```
    4 6 1
  ×  8 7
3 2 2 7
```
d
```
      1 5 6 2
2 ) 1 7 8 1
```
e
```
  9 5 6
+ 7 7 8
1 7 3 4
```
f
```
2 6 3 9 0 0
1 4 6 5 0 0
1 1 7 4 0 0
```

4 a x × 2 + 6 = 50, x = 22 b x × 7 − 15 = 62, x = 11 c (x + 100) ÷ 5 = 40, x = 100 d (x − 13) × 3 = 237, x = 92
e (x ÷ 2) − 57 = 50, x = 214 f (x ÷ 3) + 47 = 69, x = 66 **5** false **6** 48 **7**
```
  1 2 3 4
×       8
9 8 7 2
```
8 x × x + 9 = 90, x = 9
9 1 × 18, 18 × 1, 9 × 2, 2 × 9, 6 × 3, 3 × 6

Unit 57   Page 47

1 a true b false c true d false e false f true   **2** a 68 b 12 c 55 d 4 e 84 f 30   **3** a 7 b 4 c 19 d 12 e 1 f 13
4 a false $135 b true c false 23 d true e true f false 156   **5** true   **6** 35   **7** 8   **8** false 67   **9** $x \div 25 \times 20 = 80$, $x = 100$

Unit 58   Page 47

1 a true b false c true d true e false f false   **2** a 3.3 b $1\frac{1}{2}$ $\left(\frac{6}{4}\right)$ c 2.2 d $6\frac{3}{8}$ e 1.1 f 5.7   **3** a $* - 12$ b $\frac{1}{3}*$ c $*^2$ d $9 \times *$
$76 + *$ f $11 + *$ **4** a $8 \times x = 24$, $x = 3$ b $x^2 = 100$, $x = 10$ c $x + 6 = 14$, $x = 8$ d $x - 21 = 35$, $x = 56$ e $\frac{x}{4} = 12$, $x = 48$
$x - 17 = 45$, $x = 62$ **5** true   **6** $\frac{1}{2}$ **7** $* - 40$ **8** $x + 72 = 95$, $x = 23$ **9** $10 - 2 = 4 \times 2$; $8 + 6 = 20 - 12 \div 2$

Unit 59   Page 48

1 a 12 b 424 c 116 d 40 e $\frac{1}{2}$ f 90   **2** a true b false c false d true e true f false   **3** a $(x + 10) \times 6 = 600$, $x = 90$
$(x - 5) \div 10 = 50$, $x = 505$ c $x \div 11 + 6 = 15$, $x = 99$ d $x \times 7 + 40 = 96$, $x = 8$ e $x^2 + 9 = 90$, $x = 9$
$(x - 102) \div 4 = 24$, $x = 198$ **4** a 1 b 8 c 1 d 8 e 4 f 32   **5** 827   **6** true   **7** $(x + 67) \div 4 = 40$, $x = 93$ **8** 21
9 a 9.1 b 3 c 4 d 9.2

Unit 60   Page 48

1 a 81 b 400 c 196 d 27 e 1000 f 64   **2** a 64 b 216 c 49 d 125 e 144 f 8000
3

Number	1	2	3	4	5	6
Squared	1	4	9	16	25	36
Cubed	1	8	27	64	125	216

4 a $16 + 9 = 25$ b $4 - 1 = 3$ c $81 - 25 = 56$ d $16 + 25 = 41$
e $144 - 64 = 80$ f $49 + 1 + 9 = 59$ **5** 216   **6** 900
7

Number	7
Squared	49
Cubed	343

8 $121 - (16 + 4) = 101$

9 3, 5, 7, 9, 11, 13 increasing by 2 each time

Unit 61   Page 49

1 a > b > c > d < e = f >   **2** a 46 201 500 b 46 790 208 c 21 703 d 399 999 e 245 296 200 f 27 486 295
3 a 21 428 and 31 428 b 14 986 and 24 986 c 31 489 and 41 489 d 56 725 and 66 725 e 70 921 and 80 921
100 675 and 110 675   **4** For example: a 400 b 1000 c 256 d 96

200 2	250 4	8 32	6 16

| 5 | 40 | | 25 | 10 | 2 | 2 | | 2 | 4 | 8 | 4 | | 2 | 3 | 4 | 4 |

e 450 f 1400

| 18 25 | 50 28 |

| 9 | 2 | 5 | 5 | | 25 | 2 | 7 | 4 |

5 >   **6** 28 999 999   **7** 110 052 and 120 052
8 For example: 81 000   **9** a 4 (million) b 4 c 0.07

900 90

| 100 | 9 | 9 | 10 |

Unit 62   Page 49

1 a 0.96 m b 20 000 m c 50 m d 10 m e 6120 m f 0.98 m   **2** a 4 kg b 0.09 kg c 4000 kg d 7200 kg e 2.967 kg
f 800 kg   **3** a 360 min b 7 min c 4680 min d 1440 min e 90 min f 7200 min   **4** a > b < c < d < e < f <   **5** 4.6 m
6 0.65 kg   **7** 25 min   **8** <   **9** For example:

4500 g

6 kg

1 kg	200 g	400 g
200 g	50 g	100 g
5 kg	5 g	1 tonne

Unit 63   Page 50

1 a −5, −3, −2, −1, 0, 1, 3, 4, 6 b −10, −5, −3, −1, 0, 1, 2, 5, 6 c −6, −4, −2, 0, 2, 4, 6 d −5, −3, −1, 0, 1, 3, 5, 7
e −30, −20, −15, −10, 0, 5, 10, 20 f −15, −13, −10, −6, 0, 13, 14, 15, 18, 19   **2** a 9°C b 0°C c 3°C d 15°C e −2°C f −6°C
3 a $5 b $8 c $0 d −$5 e −$24 f −$57   **4** a −5 b 5 c 7 d −2 e −6 f −7   **5** −23, −21, −14, −11, 0, 10, 20, 25   **6** −4°C
7 −$28   **8** 3   **9** a 3 b 9 c −8 d 2

Unit 64 Page 50

1 a c b c c p d p e c f p **2**

	Divisor					
a	2	(16)	(38)	91	(156)	(344)	1029
b	3	(21)	(54)	80	122	(225)	1471
c	4	(40)	(88)	102	(164)	490	1562
d	5	(60)	76	(95)	(120)	581	1247
e	6	(72)	(90)	110	149	(684)	1436
f	7	(77)	(105)	149	(196)	485	(1260)

3 sample: a 73 + 5 = 78 b 19 + 5 = 24 c 97 + 3 = 100 d 53 + 7 = 60 e 23 + 7 = 30 f 83 + 7 = 90 **4** a 6, 8, 9, 10, 12, 14
b 18, 20, 21, 22 c 51, 52, 54, 55, 56, 57, 58 d 81, 82, 84, 85, 86, 87, 88, 90, 91, 92, 93, 94, 95, 96, 98, 99
e 116, 117, 118, 119, 120, 121, 122, 123, 124 f 152, 153, 154, 155, 156, 158, 159 **5** c

6

Divisor						
8	(56)	68	106	(248)	(1480)	(1560)

7 17 + 2 = 19
8 192, 194, 195, 196, 198, 200, 201, 202, 203, 204, 205, 206, 207, 208, 209
9 2, 3, 5, 7, 11, 13, 17, 19, 23, 29, 31, 37, 41, 43, 47

Unit 65 Page 51

1 a $\frac{4}{6} = \frac{2}{3}$ b $\frac{2}{4} = \frac{1}{2}$ c $\frac{7}{8}$ d $\frac{1}{3}$ e $\frac{4}{5}$ f $\frac{7}{10}$ **2** a $\frac{1}{3}$ b $\frac{1}{2}$ c $\frac{1}{8}$ d $\frac{2}{3}$ e $\frac{1}{5}$ f $\frac{3}{10}$ **3** a $\frac{4}{8}$ b $\frac{1}{4}$ c $\frac{9}{10}$

d $\frac{2}{5}$ e $\frac{1}{2}$ f $\frac{5}{6}$ **4** a $\frac{5}{6}$ b $\frac{3}{4}$ c $\frac{3}{8}$ d $\frac{3}{6} = \frac{1}{2}$ e $\frac{7}{12}$ f $\frac{8}{10} = \frac{4}{5}$ **5** $\frac{3}{5}$ **6** $\frac{2}{5}$ **7** **8** $\frac{6}{9} = \frac{2}{3}$

9 $\frac{3}{4} \times 24 = 18$ broken, 6 not broken

Unit 66 Page 51

1 a 6 b 4 c 3 d 8 e 2 f 12 **2** a 2 b 3 c 2 d 4 e 3 f 5 **3** a 11 b 12 c 11 d 20 e 4 f 6 **4** a 5 postcards
b 35 bears left c 9 marbles d 20 cars e 56 blank f 16 stamps left **5** 1 **6** 4 **7** 24 **8** 24 balls left
9 a 60 b 100 c 40 d 25

Unit 67 Page 52

1 a 4 b 75 c 8 d 12 e 48 f 6 **2** a 4 b 3 c 6 d 2 e 9 f 8 **3** a 10 letters b 12 songs c 9 DVDs d 91 emails e 35 mins
f 15 s **4** a 9 b 15 c 16 d 12 e 18 f 40 **5** 6 **6** 8 **7** $20.00 **8** 14 **9** No. $\frac{4}{5} \times 90 = 72$

Unit 68 Page 52

1 a $\frac{2}{8}$ b $\frac{2}{6}$ c $\frac{10}{12}$ d $\frac{2}{4}$ e $\frac{4}{6}$ f $\frac{6}{20}$ **2** a 4 b 4 c 4 d 2 e 4 f 6 **3** a 12 b 10 c 25 d 8 e 9 f 15
4 a true b true c false d false e true f true **5** $\frac{10}{16}$ **6** 9 **7** 10 **8** true **9** $\frac{5}{10} = \frac{20}{40}, \frac{3}{8} = \frac{15}{40}; \frac{5}{10}$ is larger

Unit 69 Page 53

1 a $\frac{6}{8}$ b $\frac{4}{8}$ c $\frac{3}{12}$ d $\frac{5}{50}$ e $\frac{6}{15}$ f $\frac{12}{18}$ **2** a $\frac{3}{12}$ b $\frac{3}{15}$ c $\frac{6}{9}$ d $\frac{12}{15}$ e $\frac{9}{12}$ f $\frac{15}{18}$ **3** a 2 b 4 c 2 d 2 e 3 f 2

4 a $\frac{1}{2} = \frac{2}{4} = \frac{3}{6} = \frac{4}{8}$ b $\frac{1}{4} = \frac{2}{8} = \frac{3}{12} = \frac{4}{16}$ c $\frac{1}{3} = \frac{2}{6} = \frac{3}{9} = \frac{4}{12}$ d $\frac{1}{5} = \frac{2}{10} = \frac{3}{15} = \frac{4}{20}$ e $\frac{1}{6} = \frac{2}{12} = \frac{3}{18} = \frac{4}{24}$

f $\frac{1}{8} = \frac{2}{16} = \frac{3}{24} = \frac{4}{32}$ **5** $\frac{6}{16}$ **6** $\frac{15}{24}$ **7** 2 **8** $\frac{1}{10} = \frac{2}{20} = \frac{3}{30} = \frac{4}{40}$ 1 = 2 = 3 = 4 **9** e.g. $\frac{3}{12} = \frac{1}{4} = \frac{2}{8} = \frac{4}{16} = \frac{6}{24}$

Unit 70 Page 53

1 a $\frac{8}{12}$ b $\frac{10}{12}$ c $\frac{5}{15}$ d $\frac{10}{60}$ e $\frac{9}{12}$ f $\frac{24}{30}$ **2** a $\frac{1}{2}$ b $\frac{1}{2}$ c $\frac{3}{4}$ d $\frac{3}{5}$ e $\frac{1}{3}$ f $\frac{2}{4}$ **3** a < b > c < d < e = f =
4 a $\frac{2}{3}$ b $\frac{2}{3}$ c $\frac{1}{4}$ d $\frac{3}{4}$ e $\frac{3}{4}$ f $\frac{1}{8}$ **5** $\frac{16}{24}$ **6** $\frac{5}{6}$ **7** = **8** $\frac{5}{6}$ **9**

Item	Amount	Fraction	Simplest form
Movies	$12	$\frac{12}{60}$	$\frac{1}{5}$
Food/drink	$15	$\frac{15}{60}$	$\frac{1}{4}$
Bus fares	$ 9	$\frac{9}{60}$	$\frac{3}{20}$
Books	$10	$\frac{10}{60}$	$\frac{1}{6}$
Go-Karts	$14	$\frac{14}{60}$	$\frac{7}{30}$

Unit 71 — Page 54

1 a $\frac{3}{2}, 1\frac{1}{2}$ b $\frac{7}{4}, 1\frac{3}{4}$ c $\frac{12}{8}, 1\frac{1}{2}$ d $\frac{24}{8}, 3$ e $\frac{13}{10}, 1\frac{3}{10}$ f $\frac{9}{4}, 2\frac{1}{4}$
2 a $1\frac{4}{5}$ b $2\frac{2}{3}$ c $2\frac{1}{2}$ d $1\frac{3}{5}$ e $1\frac{1}{3}$ f $1\frac{4}{6}=1\frac{2}{3}$
3 a $\frac{5}{2}$ b $\frac{7}{5}$ c $\frac{7}{3}$ d $\frac{23}{5}$ e $\frac{21}{8}$ f $\frac{22}{5}$
4 a $1\frac{7}{8}$ b $2\frac{1}{10}$ c $3\frac{2}{3}$ d $1\frac{7}{10}$ e $2\frac{3}{6}=2\frac{1}{2}$ f $3\frac{4}{5}$
5 $\frac{9}{4}, 2\frac{1}{4}$
6 $1\frac{2}{4}=1\frac{1}{2}$
7 $\frac{14}{3}$
8 $2\frac{6}{10}=2\frac{3}{5}$
9 $\frac{11}{4}, \frac{16}{4}, 1\frac{14}{4}, \frac{12}{4}, \frac{10}{4}, 1\frac{10}{4}, 2\frac{3}{4}, 3, \frac{14}{4}, \frac{16}{4}$

Unit 72 — Page 54

1 a false b false c true d true e true f true
2 a $\frac{4}{10}+\frac{1}{10}=\frac{5}{10}=\frac{1}{2}$ b $\frac{6}{8}+\frac{3}{8}=\frac{9}{8}=1\frac{1}{8}$ c $\frac{8}{10}=\frac{4}{5}$ d $\frac{5}{6}$ e $\frac{9}{10}$ f $\frac{7}{8}$
3 a $\frac{5}{6}-\frac{2}{6}=\frac{3}{6}=\frac{1}{2}$ b $\frac{7}{10}-\frac{4}{10}=\frac{3}{10}$ c $\frac{3}{8}$ d $\frac{2}{12}=\frac{1}{6}$ e $\frac{1}{4}$ f $\frac{4}{10}=\frac{2}{5}$
4 a $\frac{6}{5}=1\frac{1}{5}$ b $\frac{4}{3}=1\frac{1}{3}$ c $\frac{10}{12}=\frac{5}{6}$ d $\frac{18}{10}=1\frac{4}{5}$ e $\frac{15}{4}=3\frac{3}{4}$ f $\frac{12}{8}=1\frac{1}{2}$
5 false
6 $\frac{11}{10}=1\frac{1}{10}$
7 $\frac{5}{12}$
8 $1\frac{1}{5}$
9 $\frac{1}{6}, \frac{2}{6}, \frac{2}{3}, 1, 1\frac{1}{3}, 2\frac{1}{3}$

Unit 73 — Page 55

1 a $\frac{10}{12}=\frac{5}{6}$ b $\frac{6}{9}=\frac{2}{3}$ c $\frac{6}{8}=\frac{3}{4}$ d $\frac{2}{4}=\frac{1}{2}$ e $\frac{3}{5}$ f $\frac{8}{10}=\frac{4}{5}$
2 a $\frac{13}{10}=1\frac{3}{10}$ b $\frac{15}{10}=1\frac{1}{2}$ c $\frac{17}{10}=1\frac{7}{10}$ d $\frac{12}{10}=1\frac{1}{5}$ e $\frac{15}{10}=1\frac{1}{2}$ f $\frac{19}{10}=1\frac{9}{10}$
3 a $\frac{7}{5}=1\frac{2}{5}$ b $\frac{14}{8}=1\frac{6}{8}=1\frac{3}{4}$ c $\frac{6}{4}=1\frac{1}{2}$ d $\frac{17}{10}=1\frac{7}{10}$ e $\frac{7}{4}=1\frac{3}{4}$ f $\frac{11}{5}=2\frac{1}{5}$
4 a $\frac{3}{12}+\frac{7}{12}=\frac{10}{12}=\frac{5}{6}$ b $\frac{5}{10}+\frac{3}{10}=\frac{8}{10}=\frac{4}{5}$ c $\frac{1}{6}+\frac{4}{6}=\frac{5}{6}$
$\frac{3}{10}+\frac{8}{10}=\frac{11}{10}=1\frac{1}{10}$ $\frac{3}{6}+\frac{5}{6}=\frac{8}{6}=1\frac{1}{3}$ $\frac{3}{9}+\frac{2}{9}=\frac{5}{9}$
5 $\frac{6}{8}=\frac{3}{4}$
6 $\frac{13}{10}=1\frac{3}{10}$
7 $\frac{9}{6}=1\frac{3}{6}=1\frac{1}{2}$
8 $\frac{1}{8}+\frac{6}{8}=\frac{7}{8}$
9 $\frac{3}{4}+\frac{1}{2}=\frac{3}{4}+\frac{2}{4}=\frac{5}{4}=1\frac{1}{4}$ cups

Unit 74 — Page 55

1 a $\frac{2}{3}$ b $\frac{3}{4}$ c $\frac{7}{8}$ d $\frac{1}{5}$ e $\frac{1}{3}$ f $\frac{1}{3}$
2 a $\frac{3}{10}$ b $\frac{2}{12}=\frac{1}{6}$ c $\frac{2}{8}=\frac{1}{4}$ d $\frac{1}{6}$ e $\frac{2}{6}=\frac{1}{3}$ f $\frac{3}{9}=\frac{1}{3}$
3 a $\frac{9}{10}-\frac{4}{10}=\frac{5}{10}=\frac{1}{2}$ b $\frac{7}{8}-\frac{2}{8}=\frac{5}{8}$ c $\frac{5}{6}-\frac{4}{6}=\frac{1}{6}$
$\frac{8}{10}-\frac{1}{10}=\frac{7}{10}$ $\frac{7}{9}-\frac{3}{9}=\frac{4}{9}$ $\frac{10}{12}-\frac{3}{12}=\frac{7}{12}$
4 a $\frac{6}{10}-\frac{4}{10}=\frac{2}{10}=\frac{1}{5}$ b $\frac{7}{12}-\frac{6}{12}=\frac{1}{12}$ c $\frac{6}{9}-\frac{4}{9}=\frac{2}{9}$ d $\frac{8}{10}-\frac{4}{10}=\frac{4}{10}=\frac{2}{5}$ e $\frac{3}{8}-\frac{2}{8}=\frac{1}{8}$
$\frac{4}{6}-\frac{3}{6}=\frac{1}{6}$
5 $\frac{9}{10}$
6 $\frac{3}{5}$
7 $\frac{5}{8}-\frac{4}{8}=\frac{1}{8}$
8 $\frac{7}{8}-\frac{6}{8}=\frac{1}{8}$
9 $\frac{7}{10}-\frac{3}{10}=\frac{1}{5} \Rightarrow \frac{4}{10}-\frac{2}{10}=\frac{2}{10}=\frac{1}{5}$ left

Unit 75 — Page 56

1 a $\frac{16}{10}$ b $\frac{9}{4}$ c $\frac{11}{3}$ d $\frac{37}{8}$ e $\frac{15}{2}$ f $\frac{14}{5}$
2 a $1\frac{1}{3}$ b $1\frac{2}{5}$ c $2\frac{1}{10}$ d 2 e $2\frac{1}{8}$ f $2\frac{2}{6}=2\frac{1}{3}$
3 a $\frac{1}{4}+\frac{2}{4}=\frac{3}{4}$ b $\frac{4}{6}+\frac{4}{6}=\frac{8}{6}=1\frac{1}{3}$ c $\frac{3}{8}+\frac{2}{8}=\frac{5}{8}$
$\frac{7}{10}+\frac{4}{10}=\frac{11}{10}=1\frac{1}{10}$ $\frac{1}{9}+\frac{6}{9}=\frac{7}{9}$ $\frac{4}{12}+\frac{5}{12}=\frac{9}{12}=\frac{3}{4}$
4 a $\frac{5}{8}-\frac{2}{8}=\frac{3}{8}$ b $\frac{9}{10}-\frac{8}{10}=\frac{1}{10}$ c $\frac{5}{6}-\frac{4}{6}=\frac{1}{6}$ d $\frac{11}{12}-\frac{9}{12}=\frac{2}{12}=\frac{1}{6}$ e $\frac{8}{10}-\frac{5}{10}=\frac{3}{10}$
$\frac{7}{9}-\frac{6}{9}=\frac{1}{9}$
5 $\frac{41}{5}$
6 $2\frac{2}{5}$
7 $\frac{6}{10}+\frac{4}{10}=1$
8 $\frac{7}{8}-\frac{4}{8}=\frac{3}{8}$
9 $\frac{6}{8}+\frac{5}{8}=\frac{11}{8}=1\frac{3}{8}$

Unit 76 — Page 56

1 a $2\frac{2}{5}$ b $3\frac{2}{3}$ c $1\frac{1}{6}$ d $1\frac{1}{2}$ e $2\frac{1}{4}$ f $2\frac{1}{2}$
2 a $\frac{8}{6}$ b $\frac{15}{4}$ c $\frac{17}{3}$ d $\frac{29}{8}$ e $\frac{67}{10}$ f $\frac{17}{5}$
3

Question	Repeated addition	Fraction	Simplified fraction
a $2\times\frac{3}{4}$	$\frac{3}{4}+\frac{3}{4}$	$\frac{6}{4}$	$1\frac{1}{2}$
b $3\times\frac{1}{4}$	$\frac{1}{4}+\frac{1}{4}+\frac{1}{4}$	$\frac{3}{4}$	$\frac{3}{4}$
c $4\times\frac{2}{3}$	$\frac{2}{3}+\frac{2}{3}+\frac{2}{3}+\frac{2}{3}$	$\frac{8}{3}$	$2\frac{2}{3}$
d $3\times\frac{3}{5}$	$\frac{3}{5}+\frac{3}{5}+\frac{3}{5}$	$\frac{9}{5}$	$1\frac{4}{5}$
e $2\times\frac{6}{8}$	$\frac{6}{8}+\frac{6}{8}$	$\frac{12}{8}$	$1\frac{1}{2}$
f $4\times\frac{2}{10}$	$\frac{2}{10}+\frac{2}{10}+\frac{2}{10}+\frac{2}{10}$	$\frac{8}{10}$	$\frac{4}{5}$

4 a $\frac{5}{4}=1\frac{1}{4}$ b $\frac{8}{6}=1\frac{1}{3}$ c $\frac{9}{2}=4\frac{1}{2}$ d $\frac{3}{5}$ e $\frac{10}{8}=1\frac{1}{4}$ f $\frac{5}{3}=1\frac{2}{3}$
5 $4\frac{1}{5}$
6 $\frac{17}{5}$
7

Question	Repeated addition	Fraction	Simplest form
$5\times\frac{2}{5}$	$\frac{2}{5}+\frac{2}{5}+\frac{2}{5}+\frac{2}{5}+\frac{2}{5}$	$\frac{10}{5}$	2

8 $\frac{15}{10}=1\frac{1}{2}$
9 $9\times\frac{1}{4}=\frac{9}{4}=2\frac{1}{4}$; $2\frac{1}{4}$ metres

Unit 77 — Page 57

1 a $\frac{1}{8}$ b $\frac{2}{3}$ c $\frac{3}{10}$ d $\frac{1}{4}$ e $\frac{3}{4}$ f $\frac{3}{10}$
2

Question	Repeated addition	Fraction	Mixed number
a $3\times\frac{2}{5}$	$\frac{2}{5}+\frac{2}{5}+\frac{2}{5}$	$\frac{6}{5}$	$1\frac{1}{5}$
b $3\times\frac{5}{8}$	$\frac{5}{8}+\frac{5}{8}+\frac{5}{8}$	$\frac{15}{8}$	$1\frac{7}{8}$
c $2\times\frac{2}{3}$	$\frac{2}{3}+\frac{2}{3}$	$\frac{4}{3}$	$1\frac{1}{3}$
d $2\times\frac{7}{10}$	$\frac{7}{10}+\frac{7}{10}$	$\frac{14}{10}$	$1\frac{2}{5}$
e $8\times\frac{1}{6}$	$\frac{1}{6}+\frac{1}{6}+\frac{1}{6}+\frac{1}{6}+\frac{1}{6}+\frac{1}{6}+\frac{1}{6}+\frac{1}{6}$	$\frac{8}{6}$	$1\frac{1}{3}$
f $10\times\frac{3}{4}$	$\frac{3}{4}+\frac{3}{4}+\frac{3}{4}+\frac{3}{4}+\frac{3}{4}+\frac{3}{4}+\frac{3}{4}+\frac{3}{4}+\frac{3}{4}+\frac{3}{4}$	$\frac{30}{4}$	$7\frac{1}{2}$

3 a $\frac{9}{8}=1\frac{1}{8}$ b $\frac{6}{10}=\frac{3}{5}$ c $\frac{10}{5}=2$ d $\frac{8}{3}=2\frac{2}{3}$ e $\frac{18}{4}=4\frac{1}{2}$ f $\frac{45}{6}=7\frac{1}{2}$
4 a $\frac{12}{3}=4$ bags b $\frac{15}{8}=1\frac{7}{8}$ of cake
c $\frac{8}{5}=1\frac{3}{5}$ bags of sweets
d $\frac{8}{6}=1\frac{1}{3}$ bars of chocolates e $\frac{9}{2}=4\frac{1}{2}$ pineapples
f $\frac{36}{10}=3\frac{3}{5}$ boxes of pencils
5 $\frac{1}{3}$
6

Question	Repeated addition	Fraction	Mixed number
$6\times\frac{3}{8}$	$\frac{3}{8}+\frac{3}{8}+\frac{3}{8}+\frac{3}{8}+\frac{3}{8}+\frac{3}{8}$	$\frac{18}{8}$	$2\frac{1}{4}$

7 $\frac{21}{4}=5\frac{1}{4}$
8 $\frac{75}{6}=12\frac{1}{2}$ egg cartons
9 $\frac{18}{4}=4\frac{1}{2}$ or $5\frac{1}{4}$; $5\frac{1}{4}$

Unit 78 Page 57

1. a $\frac{8}{5} = 1\frac{3}{5}$ b $\frac{12}{10} = 1\frac{1}{5}$ c $\frac{3}{2} = 1\frac{1}{2}$ d $\frac{15}{4} = 3\frac{3}{4}$ e $\frac{30}{6} = 5$ f $\frac{10}{3} = 3\frac{1}{3}$ 2. a $\frac{8}{5} = 1\frac{3}{5}$ b $\frac{8}{3} = 2\frac{2}{3}$ c $\frac{6}{4} = 1\frac{1}{2}$
d $\frac{5}{2} = 2\frac{1}{2}$ e $\frac{27}{5} = 5\frac{2}{5}$ f $\frac{42}{10} = 4\frac{1}{5}$ 3. a $\frac{2}{12} = \frac{1}{6}$ b $\frac{20}{30} = \frac{2}{3}$ c $\frac{10}{40} = \frac{1}{4}$ d $\frac{6}{32} = \frac{3}{16}$ e $\frac{9}{20}$ f $\frac{8}{30} = \frac{4}{15}$
4. a $\frac{7}{4} = 1\frac{3}{4}$ h b $\frac{5}{10} = \frac{1}{2}$ my money c $\frac{4}{3} = 1\frac{1}{3}$ of a year d $\frac{5}{6}$ metre e $\frac{55}{6} = 9\frac{1}{6}$ kg f $\frac{18}{5} = 3\frac{3}{5}$ of a day
5. $\frac{4}{3} = 1\frac{1}{3}$ 6. $\frac{21}{8} = 2\frac{5}{8}$ 7. $\frac{9}{20}$ 8. $\frac{42}{8} = 5\frac{1}{4}$ apples 9. a 8 b 18 c 18 d 18

Unit 79 Page 58

1. a 9 b 32 c 5 d 23 e 21 f 73 2. a 8 b 12 c 7 d 12 e 8 f 20 3. a $6 b $40 c 1.5 m d 90 mL e 3000 L f 3 eggs
4. a $\frac{12}{24} = \frac{1}{2}$ b $\frac{5}{30} = \frac{1}{6}$ c $\frac{21}{80}$ d $\frac{1}{27}$ e $\frac{9}{25}$ f $\frac{3}{24} = \frac{1}{8}$ 5. 14 6. 7 7. 10 min 8. $\frac{4}{9}$ 9. $60

Unit 80 Page 58

1.
a 15.281 b 32.605 c 49.018 d 27.116 e 63.21 f 0.295

2. a 9.6 b 9.27 c 19.014 d 90.052 e 90.002 f 19.20 3. a 7 hundredths b 7 thousandths c 7 units d 7 units e 7 hundredths
f 7 tenths 4. a 0.22 b 0.19 c 0.4 d 0.236 e 0.04 f 0.143 5. [abacus] 26.150 6. 901.021 7. 7 thousandths
8. 0.006 9. 3.267

Unit 81 Page 59

1. a 7.84 b 12.16 c 13.77 d 10.705 e 7.137 f 16.053 2. a 14.41 b 14.91 c 14.89 d 18.422 e 65.441 f 45.843
3. a $99.30 b $116.05 c $117.05 d $61.40 e $176.85 f $197.15 4. a $42.78 b $174.74 c $294.22 d $125.87 e $370.97
f $552.55 5. 12.101 6. 25.255 7. $323.45 8. $125.62 9. 22.89 km

Unit 82 Page 59

1. a 0.2 b 1.1 c 1.02 d 2.13 e 3.3 f 4.87 2. a 0.64 b 4.77 c 20.88 d 2.575 e 2.522 f 3.459 3. a $6.15 b $85.53
c $155.73 d $236.58 e $81.50 f $36.53 4. a 57.78 b 0.93 c 4.595 d 4.674 e 8.57 f 3.649 5. 4.29 6. 5.371
7. $85.25 8. 3.81 9. 3.92 m

Unit 83 Page 60

1. a 13.83 b 15.96 c 19.52 d 4.611 e 12.43 f 153.712 2. a $8.25 b $20.50 c $12.30 d $12.91 e $9.89 f $18.77
3. a $41.70 b $21.81 c $103.30 d $91.60 e $1202.31 f $1286.60 4. a 7.56 m b 5.25 m c 74.25 m d 76.45 m
e 264.95 m f 50.52 m 5. 173.34 6. $21.29 7. $101.92 8. 85.04 m 9. 2 L

Unit 84 Page 60

1. a 3.43 b 4.31 c 4.05 d 9.21 e 3.064 f 4.341 2. a 8.1 b 5.4 c 4.125 d 3.24 e 2.7 f 2.31 3. a $9.28 b $5.34 c $11.25
d $6.12 e $12.11 f $7.23 4. a $1.23 b 87c c 67c d 75c e 78c f 33c 5. 5.04 6. 2.025 7. $13.07 8. 78c 9. 12.49

Unit 85 Page 61

1. a 4.36 b 21.76 c 61.73 d 9 e 463.5 f 0.71 2. a 631 b 47.2 c 8179 d 6421 e 110 421 f 26 500 3. a 0.0452 b 0.671
c 1.296 d 13.021 e 42.1639 f 21.4853 4. a 0.004 21 b 6.973 c 0.0491 d 0.321 01 e 1.049 85 f 0.024 691 5. 216.3
6. 4928.5 7. 74.521 8. 6.9312 9.

× 1000	× 100	× 10	Number	÷ 10	÷ 100
46 830	4683	468.3	46.83	4.683	0.4683
924 100	92410	9241	924.10	92.41	9.241
4630	463	46.3	4.63	0.463	0.0463
10 480	1048	104.8	10.48	1.048	0.1048
110 216	11021.6	1102.16	110.216	11.0216	1.10216
30 050	3005	300.5	30.05	3.005	0.3005

ANSWERS: Units 86 – 89

Unit 86 Page 61

1 a 0.84 b 1.61 c 1.68 d 0.058 e 0.066 f 0.084 **2** a 0.84 b 1.61 c 1.68 d 0.058 e 0.066 f 0.084
3 a 7.11 b 7.23 c 12.33 d 4.98 e 4.12 f 3.88 **4** a 7.11 b 7.23 c 12.33 d 4.98 e 4.12 f 3.88 **5** 102, 1.02 **6** 1.02 **7** 12.47
8 12.47 **9** 0.48 and 0.48. They are the same as it is the same equation expressed in a different way.

Unit 87 Page 62

1 a 0.63 b 0.246 c 0.8 d 0.09 e 0.042 f 0.6 **2** a $\frac{2}{10}$ b $\frac{85}{100}$ c $\frac{326}{1000}$ d $\frac{4}{100}$ e $\frac{406}{1000}$ f $\frac{1}{1000}$ **3** a $\frac{2}{10}=0.2$ b $\frac{1}{20}=\frac{5}{100}=0.05$
c $\frac{3}{4}=\frac{75}{100}=0.75$ d $\frac{1}{8}=\frac{125}{1000}=0.125$ e $\frac{3}{5}=\frac{60}{100}=0.6$ f $\frac{3}{8}=\frac{375}{1000}=0.375$

4

		Fraction of 100	Decimal
a		$\frac{19}{100}$	0.19
b		$\frac{25}{100}$	0.25
c		$\frac{80}{100}$	0.8
d		$\frac{52}{100}$	0.52
e		$\frac{73}{100}$	0.73
f		$\frac{22}{100}$	0.05

5 0.56 **6** $\frac{123}{1000}$ **7** $\frac{7}{20}=\frac{35}{100}=0.35$

8

	Fraction of 100	Decimal
	$\frac{35}{100}$	0.35

9

Unit 88 Page 62

1 a 6.2 b 4.7 c 1.1 d 143.5 e 28.0 f 18.0 **2** a 6.49 b 8.02 c 7.40 d 211.09 e 42.12 f 879.64 **3** a 10 + 3 + 106 = 119
b 2 + 4 + 19 = 25 c 903 + 19 + 15 = 937 d 7 + 9 + 4 = 20 e 421 + 1 + 5 = 427 f 13 + 3 + 19 = 35 **4** a 17.478, 17.5
b 49.967, 50.0 c 99.879, 99.9 d 144.19, 144.2 e 413.164, 413.2 f 424.265, 424.3 **5** 17.1 **6** 96.22 **7** 47 + 22 + 8 = 77
8 141.075, 141.1 **9** $4 + $3 + $4 + $3 + $4 = $18

Unit 89 Page 63

1 a 20% b 90% c 60% d 81% e 36% f 2% **2** a 0.47 b 0.63 c 0.98 d 0.04 e 0.07 f 1.25
3

	Fraction	Decimal	Percentage
a	$\frac{3}{10}$	0.3	30%
b	$\frac{9}{10}$	0.9	90%
c	$\frac{41}{100}$	0.41	41%
d	$\frac{73}{100}$	0.73	73%
e	$\frac{27}{100}$	0.27	27%
f	$\frac{14}{100}$	0.14	14%

4 a 61% b 26% c $\frac{41}{100}$ d 90% e 50% f 0.77 **5** 7%

6 1.63 **7**

Fraction	Decimal	Percentage
$\frac{22}{100}$	0.22	22%

8 0.17 **9** a $\frac{20}{100}=20\%$ b $\frac{3}{4}=\frac{75}{100}=75\%$ c $2\frac{50}{100}=250\%$

Unit 90 Page 63

1 a 6 b 90 c 10 d 35 e 16 f 27 2 a $2 b $10 c $12 d $32 e $18 f $8 3 a 50% b 25% c 5% d 20% e 75% f 10%
4 a $30 b $9.50 c $20 d $12 e $30 f $45 5 7 6 $13.20 7 a 40% b 100% c 30% 8 $40
9 a 90 b 96 c 5.6 d 3.75

Unit 91 Page 64

1 a [circle] 120 — 25% = 30 b [square] 500 — 25% = 125 c [triangle] 360 — 50% = 180 d [rectangle] 90 — 20% = 18

e [pentagon] 1000 — 20% = 200 f [rectangle] 410 — 50% = 205 2 a $2.50 b $8.50 c $9.00 d $11.00 e $1.90 f $76.50

3 a 8 pigs b 9 goats c 25 cats d 18 chickens e 7 horses f 11 birds

4

	a	b	c	d	e	f
Price	$20	$50	$30	$80	$900	$120
% off	10	50	20	25	5	20
Discount	$2	$25	$6	$20	$45	$24
Discount price	$18	$25	$24	$60	$855	$96

5 [circle] 150 — 30 6 $120.00 7 130 cows

8

Price	$300
% off	90
Discount	$270
Discount price	$30

9 $20.00

Unit 92 Page 64

1 a 20% b 90% c 1% d 12% e 56% f 130% 2 a 0.07 b 0.03 c 0.4 d 0.59 e 0.63 f 1.21 3 a 40% b 80% c 8%
d 90% e 47% f 136% 4 a $\frac{89}{100}$ b 34% c 0.5 d $\frac{100}{100}$ e 123% f 7.6 5 126% 6 2.46 7 229% 8 4.23
9 a $\frac{20}{100} = \frac{1}{5}$ b $\frac{16}{100} = \frac{4}{25}$ c $\frac{140}{100} = 1\frac{2}{5}$ d $\frac{290}{100} = 2\frac{9}{10}$

Unit 93 Page 65

1 a $2, $1, 50c, 20c, 5c b $10, $1, 50c, 20c, 10c c $20, $5, $2, 10c, 5c d $20, $20, $2, $1, 50c, 20c, 20c, 5c
e $50, $20, $10, $5, $2, 50c, 20c f $100, $20, $5, $1, 20c, 20c, 5c 2 a $16.60 b $22.15 c $5.85 d $28.10 e $32.95 f $13.20
3 a $7.00 b $19.40 c $11.80 d No e B f $5.65 4 a $15.02, $15.00 b $24.85 c $16.68, $16.70 d $12.29, $12.30
e $14.27, $14.25 f $13.17, $13.15 5 $50, $20, $5, 50c, 20c, 20c 6 $20.40 7 $17.85 8 $16.36, $16.35
9 bag of oranges

Unit 94 Page 65

1 a $1529.55 b $1682.29 c $700.00 d $347.26 e $100.00 f $92.76 2 a $2039.53 b $1919.23 c $1719.23 d $1732.48 e
$2158.48 f $2175.33 3

4 a false b true c false d false e true f false
5 $440.02 6 $2175.33 7

8 false 9 a €1500 b $5000

	A$1 =	$28 souvenir =
a	C$.83	C$23.24
b	NZ$1.12	NZ$31.36
c	€0.60	€16.80
d	£0.42	£11.76
e	S$0.93	S$26.04
f	HK$4.20	HK$117.60

A$1 =	$28 souvenir =
Bht22.16	Bht620.48

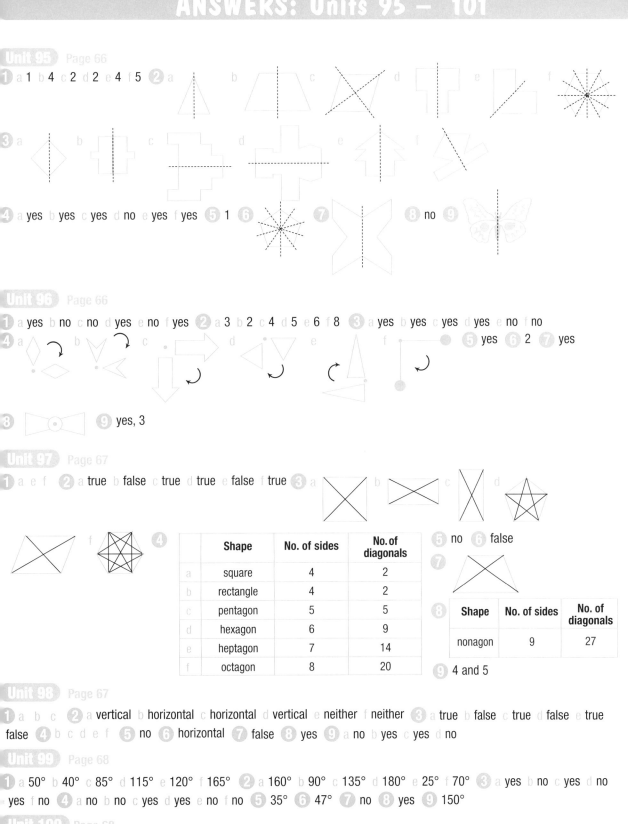

Unit 95 Page 66

1 a 1 b 4 c 2 d 2 e 4 f 5 2 a ... 3 a ... 4 a yes b yes c yes d no e yes f yes 5 1 6 7 8 no 9

Unit 96 Page 66

1 a yes b no c no d yes e no f yes 2 a 3 b 2 c 4 d 5 e 6 f 8 3 a yes b yes c yes d yes e no f no 4 a ... 5 yes 6 2 7 yes 8 9 yes, 3

Unit 97 Page 67

1 a e f 2 a true b false c true d true e false f true 3 a ... 4

	Shape	No. of sides	No. of diagonals
a	square	4	2
b	rectangle	4	2
c	pentagon	5	5
d	hexagon	6	9
e	heptagon	7	14
f	octagon	8	20

5 no 6 false 7 8

Shape	No. of sides	No. of diagonals
nonagon	9	27

9 4 and 5

Unit 98 Page 67

1 a b c 2 a vertical b horizontal c horizontal d vertical e neither f neither 3 a true b false c true d false e true f false 4 b c d e f 5 no 6 horizontal 7 false 8 yes 9 a no b yes c yes d no

Unit 99 Page 68

1 a 50° b 40° c 85° d 115° e 120° f 165° 2 a 160° b 90° c 135° d 180° e 25° f 70° 3 a yes b no c yes d no e yes f no 4 a no b no c yes d yes e no f no 5 35° 6 47° 7 no 8 yes 9 150°

Unit 100 Page 68

1 a yes b no c yes d no e no f yes 2 a yes b no c no d yes e no f no 3 sample: a 30° b 90° c 100° d 15° e 140° f 175° 4 a 40° acute b 95° obtuse c 132° obtuse d 360° revolution e 300° reflex f 310° reflex 5 no 6 no 7 50° 8 180°, straight 9 the same, 108°

Unit 101 Page 69

1 a 30° b 50° c 60° d 100° e 80° f 150° 2 a 310° b 280° c 320° d 345° e 260° f 225° 3 a acute b right c full revolution d obtuse e obtuse f reflex 4 a 220° b 220° c 300° d 340° e 270° f 260° 5 120° 6 200° 7 straight 8 195° 9 60°

ANSWERS: Units 102 – 105

Unit 102 Page 69

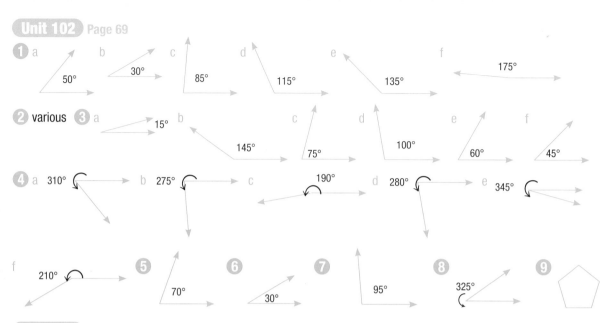

2 various **3** a 15° b 145° c 75° d 100° e 60° f 45°

4 a 310° b 275° c 190° d 280° e 345°

f 210° **5** 70° **6** 30° **7** 95° **8** 325° **9** (pentagon)

Unit 103 Page 70

1 a 129° b 39° c 70° d 103° e 137° f 91° **2** a 41° b 20° b 10° b 40o ° 13° b 48°

3 a 90° b 60° c 30° d 50° e 40° f 45° **4** a 90° b 100° b 125° b 30° b 50° b 40° **5** 55° **6** 12

7 120° **8** 105° **9** 140°

Unit 104 Page 70

1 a rectangular prism b pentagonal prism c hexagonal pyramid d triangular prism e triangular pyramid f cube **2** a cylinder
b cone c triangular prism d hexagonal prism e square pyramid f rectangular pyramid **3** a triangular pyramid b cube
c pentagonal prism d rectangular prism e triangular prism f hexagonal pyramid

4

	Object	Faces	Edges	Vertices
a	cube	6	12	8
b	rectangular prism	6	12	8
c	triangular prism	5	9	6
d	hexagonal prism	8	18	12
e	square pyramid	5	8	5
f	triangular pyramid	4	6	4

5 square pyramid **6** octagonal prism **7** circle

8

Object	Faces	Edges	Vertices
rectangular pyramid	5	8	5

9 square pyramid

Unit 105 Page 71

1 a rectangle b square, triangle c square d rectangle, triangle e triangle, rectangle f hexagon, rectangle
2 a b c d e f

4 a octagonal prism b triangular pyramid c rectangular pyramid d cylinder e square prism
f hexagonal pyramid **5** pentagon, rectangle **6**

8 triangular prism **9** a cube b rectangular prism

140   Excel Start Up Maths Year 6

Unit 106 Page 71

1

a	**Name**	cube	cone	cylinder	tri. prism
b	**No. of surfaces**	6	2	3	4
c	**No. of edges**	12	1	2	6
d	**No. of vertices**	8	1	0	4
e	**No. of curved surfaces**	0	1	1	0
f	**Front view**	square	triangle	rectangle	triangle

2 a cone and cylinder b cone c cylinder
d cone and triangular pyramid e cube f triangular pyramid
3 a cylinder b cube c triangular prism d rectangular prism
e hexagonal prism f triangular prism
4 a 9 b 24 c 12 d 5 e 3 f 4
5

Top view	◯	·	◯	⬝

6 triangular pyramid and cone **7** square prism **8** 6 **9** a 4 b if rotated

Unit 107 Page 72

1 a cylinder b cone c sphere d cylinder e cone f cylinder **2**
3 a c b in a circle c in a straight line d sphere e cone f sphere
4 a b c d

f **5** cone

6

	Cone	Cylinder	Sphere	Cube
Top view	·	◯	◯	☐

		Cone	Cylinder	Sphere	Cube
a	**Side view**	triangle	rectangle	circle	square
b	**No. of edges**	1	2	0	12
c	**No. of surfaces**	2	3	1	6
d	**No. of corners**	1	0	0	8
e	**No. of curved surfaces**	1	1	1	0
f	**Does it roll?**	Y	Y	Y	N

7 sphere **8**   **9** cylinders

Unit 108 Page 72

1 a ☐ b c ◯ d e f **2** parallelograms – a, b and e **3** rhombuses – e and f

4 a b c d e f **5** trapezium

6 **7** **8** **9** various

Unit 109 Page 73

1

Triangle	1	2	3	4	5	6	7
		△ △△					
No. of sides	3	a 6	b 9	c 12	d 15	e 18	f 21

2

Pentagons	1	2	3	4	5	6	7
No. of sides	a 5	b 10	15	c 20	d 25	e 30	f 35

3

Octagon	1	2	3	4	5	6	7
No. of sides	a 8	b 16	c 24	d 32	40	e 48	f 56

4 a △, ☐, ◯, △, ☐, ◯
b △, △, ◯, ◯, ☐, ☐, △, △, ◯, ◯, ☐, ☐
c △, ☐, ▽ △, ☐, ▽
d
e

5 number of triangles × 3
6 number of pentagons × 5 **7** number of octagons × 8 **8** **9** rotate 90° to the right about the dot

Unit 110 Page 73

1 a ⊙ b c d e f

2 a the point in the middle b half the inside of a circle
c circles with a common centre d the perimeter of a circle e part of the circumference f an area bound by 2 radii and an arc

3 a 1 cm b 0.5 cm c 0.7 cm d 1.5 cm e 2 cm f 1.2 cm **4** a 0.5 cm b 0.4 cm c 0.6 cm d 0.8 cm e 0.3 cm f 0.7 cm

5 a b c **6** a half of a circle b quarter of a circle c part of the circumference **7** 1.7 cm **8** 0.55 cm

Unit 111 Page 74

1

	Shape	Diagram	No. of edges	No. of vertices	No. of surfaces
a	cube		12	8	6
b	cylinder		2	0	3
c	cone		1	1	2
d	sphere		0	0	1
e	triangular prism		9	6	5
f	rectangular prism		12	8	6

2 a ☐ b ○ c ⊙ d ○ e △ f ▭

3 a triangular pyramid b rectangular prism
c pentangonal prism d triangular prism e pentagonal prism
f square pyramid **4** a no b yes c no d yes e no f no

5

Shape	Diagram	No. of edges	No. of vertices	No. of surfaces
triangular pyramid		6	4	4

6 ▭ **7** hexagonal prism **8** yes

9 octagonal pyramid

Unit 112 Page 74

1 a 6 km b 12 km c 4 km d 1 km e 7 km f 8 km **2** a 30 cm b 60 cm c 20 cm d 5 cm e 35 cn f 40 cm

3 a 12 mm b 4 mm c 2 mm d 6 mm e 2 mm f 1 mm **4**

5 11 km **6** 55 cm **7** 2.5 mm

	Description	Length	Width	Scale	Scale length	Scale width
a	backyard	50 m	30 m	1cm : 5 m	10 cm	6 cm
b	sports ground	200 m	150 m	1 cm : 20 m	10 cm	7.5 cm
c	swimming pool	25 m	10 m	1 cm : 5 m	5 cm	2 cm
d	school ground	900 m	500 m	1 cm : 100 m	9 cm	5 cm
e	park	7500 m	4500 m	1 cm : 500 m	15 cm	9 cm
f	garage	7 m	6 m	1 cm : 1 m	7 cm	6 cm

8

Description	Length	Width	Scale	Scale length	Scale width
courtyard	16 m	8 m	1 cm : 2 m	8 cm	4 cm

9 3 cm 3 cm 4.5 cm

Unit 113 Page 75

1 a 2 m b 4 m c 6 m 2 m d 2 m e 4.8 m 2 m f 8 m 10 m 6 m **2** a 5 × 5 cm b 10 and 10 and 10 cm

c 15 × 5 cm d 5, 5, 5, 5 and 5 cm e 5 × 12 cm f 15, 20 and 25 cm

3 a 400 cm b 30 cm c 80 cm d 300 cm e 70 cm f 40 cm

4 a 24 b 96 c 216 d 600 e 150 f 54 **5**

6 10 × 10 cm **7** 40 cm **8** halves 2 m

9 120 : 480, 12 : 48, 1 : 4

Unit 114 Page 75

1 a yes b no c no d yes e yes f no 2 a 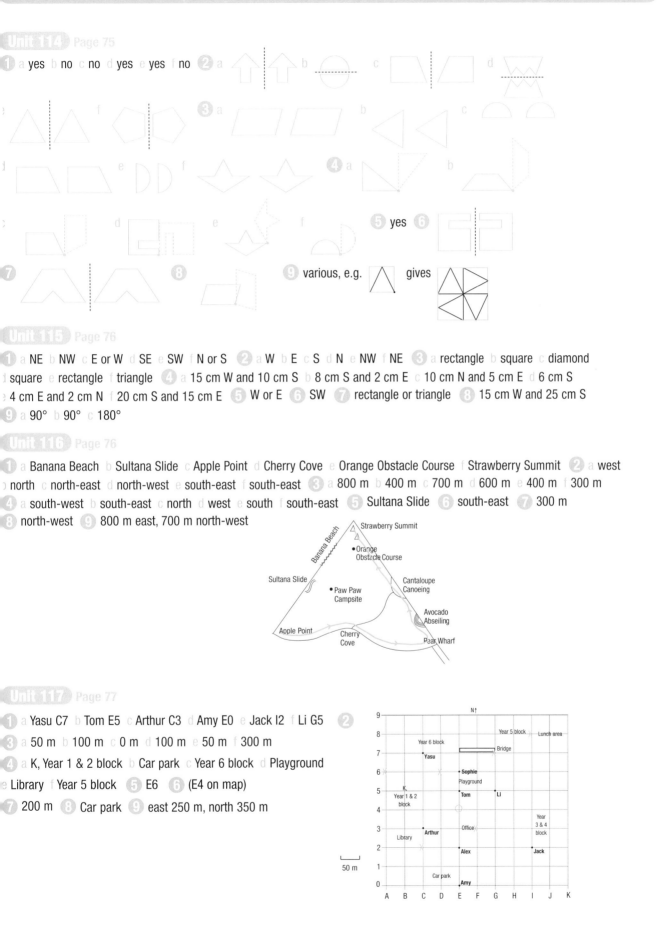 b c d

3 a b c

4 a b

5 yes 6

7 8 9 various, e.g. gives

Unit 115 Page 76

1 a NE b NW c E or W d SE e SW f N or S 2 a W b E c S d N e NW f NE 3 a rectangle b square c diamond
d square e rectangle f triangle 4 a 15 cm W and 10 cm S b 8 cm S and 2 cm E c 10 cm N and 5 cm E d 6 cm S
e 4 cm E and 2 cm N f 20 cm S and 15 cm E 5 W or E 6 SW 7 rectangle or triangle 8 15 cm W and 25 cm S
9 a 90° b 90° c 180°

Unit 116 Page 76

1 a Banana Beach b Sultana Slide c Apple Point d Cherry Cove e Orange Obstacle Course f Strawberry Summit 2 a west
b north c north-east d north-west e south-east f south-east 3 a 800 m b 400 m c 700 m d 600 m e 400 m f 300 m
4 a south-west b south-east c north d west e south f south-east 5 Sultana Slide 6 south-east 7 300 m
8 north-west 9 800 m east, 700 m north-west

Unit 117 Page 77

1 a Yasu C7 b Tom E5 c Arthur C3 d Amy E0 e Jack I2 f Li G5 2
3 a 50 m b 100 m c 0 m d 100 m e 50 m f 300 m
4 a K, Year 1 & 2 block b Car park c Year 6 block d Playground
e Library f Year 5 block 5 E6 6 (E4 on map)
7 200 m 8 Car park 9 east 250 m, north 350 m

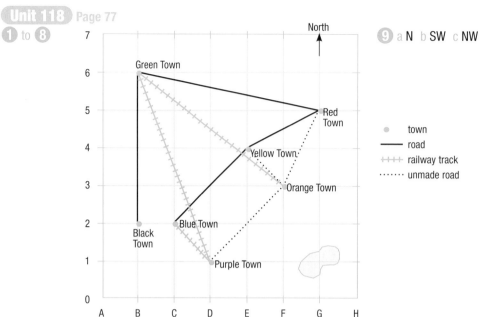

Unit 118 Page 77

1 to 8

9 a N b SW c NW

Legend:
- • town
- —— road
- +++ railway track
- ⋯⋯ unmade road

Unit 119 Page 78

1 a Nebraska b New Mexico c Nevada d Minnesota e Missouri f Wyoming **2** a L7 b C10 c B5 d N8 e K1 f Q2
3 a north b east c north d north e north f west **4** a Oregon b Wisconsin c Mississippi d Tennessee e Idaho f Alabama
5 Colorado **6** N2 **7** south-east **8** Arkansas **9** Arizona, New Mexico, Texas

Unit 120 Page 78

1 a Yumen b Urumqi c Changsha d Xi'an e Burma f Nanning or Hong Kong **2** a D4 b B6 c I3 d J7 e J1 f H5
3 a Golmud b Shijiazhuang c Changchun d Taipei e Guiyang f Yumen **4** a 1000 km b 2000 km c 1000 km d 2000 km
e 1000 km f 2000 km **5** Karamay **6** D2 **7** Xi'an or Yangtze River **8** 3000 km **9** E3, E2, F2, F1, F2, G2, H2, I2, I3

Unit 121 Page 79

1 a b c d e f

2 a b c d e f

3 a 25 minutes past 3

b 10 minutes to 8 c 25 minutes to 11 d 25 minutes past 10 e 7 minutes to 6 f 18 minutes past 2 **4** a 3 hours 15 minutes
b 5 hours 55 minutes c 1 hour 40 minutes d 10 hours 30 minutes e 7 hours 50 minutes f 4 hours 25 minutes

5 **6** **7** 3 minutes past 7 **8** 3 hours 20 minutes **9** 10 minutes past 3 (3:10 pm)

Unit 122 Page 79

1 a 9:22 b 5:49 c 4:56 d 2:17 e 1:34 f 8:37 **2** a before midday b before midday c after midday d before midday
e before midday f after midday **3** a 6:58 am b 7:10 pm c 3:16 pm d 2:11 am e 1:23 pm f 1:06 am
4 a 3 hours 29 minutes b 1 hour 27 minutes c 2 hours 47 minutes d 5 hours 32 minutes e 3 hours 57 minutes
f 6 hours 47 minutes **5** 7:02 **6** after midday **7** 9:27 am **8** 6 hours 19 minutes
9 sample

PM
02:26

Unit 123 Page 80

1 a quarter past 7 b 27 minutes past 3 c 18 minutes to 10 d 5 minutes past 12 e 12 minutes past 11 f 5 minutes to 12

2 a [clock] b [clock] c [clock] d [clock] e [clock] f [clock]

3 a 8:23 b 2:21 c 3:18 d 7:02 e 10:55 f 10:36 **4** a 12:45 b 4:27 c 9:42 d 11:54 e 6:15 f 4:41 **5** 22 minutes past 6

6 [clock] **7** 4:10 **8** 10:34 **9** >

Unit 124 Page 80

1 a 0112 b 0903 c 0552 d 1847 e 1441 f 2323 **2** a 2:37 pm b 11:48 pm c 7:29 am d 3:04 am e 7:15 pm f 1:22 pm
3 a 0316 b 2247 c 1829 d 0453 e 0702 f 2036 **4** a 10:25 am b 8:07 pm c 1:38 am d 4:59 pm e 6:46 am f 12:17 pm
5 1645 **6** 11:26 am **7** 2132 **8** 6:23 pm **9** 8:16 pm

Unit 125 Page 81

1 a 7:53 pm b 6:49 am c 11:16 pm d 4:24 pm e 10:31 pm f 1:05 am **2** a 2326 b 1313 c 0712 d 0448 e 1759 f 0935
3 a 2329 b 0854 c 0317 d 1537 e 1946 f 0506 **4** a 5 hours 8 minutes b 1 hour 15 minutes c 5 hours 41 minutes
d 5 hours 7 minutes e 4 hours 38 minutes f 1 hour 31 minutes **5** 5:52 pm **6** 1936 **7** 0612 **8** 1 hour 53 minutes

9

	Analog time	Digital time	24-hour time
16 minutes to 4 in the afternoon	[clock]	PM 3:44	1544

Unit 126 Page 81

1 a 6 minutes, 24.14 seconds b 13 minutes, 36.40 seconds c 6.29 seconds d 1 minute, 43.05 seconds
e 25 minutes, 13.19 seconds f 47 minutes, 12.63 seconds **2** a time 2 b time 1 c time 2 d time 2 e time 1 f time 1
3 a 0.06 s b 0.11 s c 1.85 s d 9.03 s e 1 min 8.02 s f 1.14 s **4** a 270 b 4500 c 6 d 5 e 60 f 234
5 26 minutes, 9.47 seconds **6** time 1 **7** 0.74 s **8** 1440 minutes **9** 36 hours, 2160 minutes, 129 600 seconds

Unit 127 Page 82

1

```
        a          b  c  d e      f 5
Aug.  Sep.  Oct.  Nov.  Dec.  Jan.  Feb.  Mar.  Apr.
      2004                    2005
```

4

```
      born   sister   started   broke   went   In school   went to
             born     school    arm     to     basketball  Comm.
                                         USA    team        Games
      ↓      ↓        ↓         ↓       ↓      ↓           ↓
      1995   1997     1999      2001    2003   2005        2007
```

2 a 122 days b 16 days c 28 days d 129 days e 64 days
f 13 days

3

```
Raymond  Kerry Sally   Tim        Harvey Vivienne              Will
31   5  10  15  20  25  30   4    9  14  19  24   1    6  11  16
Dec.    January 2005              February            March
```

5 See Q 1 **6** 158 days **7** See Q 3 **8** See Q 4

9
```
   Fuji      Mt. Shasta    Krakatoa     Thera  Mauna Loa
   1707      1786          1883         1956   1984
   ↓         ↓             ↓            ↓      ↓
   1700            1800          1900          2000
```

Unit 128 Page 82

1 a 1107 b 1355 c 1222 d 1132 e 1320 f 1300 **2** a 10:55 am 2 b 12:00 midday c 1:20 pm d 1:51 pm e 11:26 am
f 1:07 pm **3** a 11:17 am b 1:55 pm c 11:07 am and 11:32 am d 11:00 am and 11:25 am e 12:31 pm, 1:26 pm and 1:51 pm
f 12:55 pm and 1:20 pm **4** a 2 b 3 c 5:30 pm d 10:30 am e 8:30 pm f 1:30 pm **5** 1212 **6** 1:25 pm
7 12:12 pm, 1:07 pm and 1:32 pm **8** 2 hours **9** 3:21 pm

Unit 129 Page 83

1 a 1845 b 1455 c 0907 d 1129 e 1546 f 0149 2 a 0245 WST, 0415 CST, 0445 EST b 0745 WST, 0915 CST, 0945 EST c 0920 WST, 1050 CST, 1120 EST d 1300 WST, 1430 CST, 1500 EST e 1655 WST, 1825 CST, 1855 EST f 1910 WST, 2040 CST, 2110 EST 3 a 11:55 am b 11:55 am c 11:25 am d 11:25 am e 9:55 am f 11:55 am

4 a b c d e f 5 2245

6 1735 WST, 1905 CST, 1935 EST 7 2:20 pm 8 9 10:05 pm EST

Unit 130 Page 83

1 a 10 am b 4 pm c 8 pm d 6 am e 2 am f 6 pm 2 a 9 pm b 1 pm c 11 am d 3 pm e 5 am next day f 1 am next day 3 a 8:40 pm b 4:40 pm c 11:20 am d 3:20 am e 12:40 pm f 3:20 pm 4 a 10:40 am b 5:20 am c 4 pm d 4 am e 6:40 am f 9:20 am 5 8 am 6 3 am 7 6 pm 8 5:20 am 9 France, Spain, Algeria, Mali, Burkina, Ghana

Unit 131 Page 84

1 a 50 km/h b 100 km/h c 300 km/h d 135 km/h e 10 m/s f 200 km/min 2 a 560 km b 550 km c 4000 m (4 km) d 120 m e 500 m f 175 km 3 a 2 hours b 40 s c $2\frac{1}{2}$ hours d $43\frac{1}{3}$ s e 45 minutes f $\frac{1}{2}$ hour 4 a 6 m/s b 2 s c 200 m d 0.1 km/min e 2 hours f 240 km 5 40 km/h 6 540 m 7 5 hours 8 700 m 9 70 km/h

Unit 132 Page 84

1 a 3.9 cm b 8.6 cm c 9.1 cm d 4.7 cm e 2.3 cm f 1.4 cm 2 a 42 mm b 89 mm c 77 mm d 12 mm e 105 mm f 136 mm 3 a 19 cm, 19.8 cm, 20 cm, 21 cm b 4.2 cm, 4.6 cm, 5 cm, 5.1 cm c 8 cm, 8.3 cm, 8.6 cm, 8.7 cm d 40 cm, 46 cm, 47.2 cm, 50 cm e 6.8 cm, 6.9 cm, 6.95 cm, 7 cm f 25 cm, 26 cm, 27.3 cm, 29 cm 4 a 45 cm b 73 cm c 82 cm d 2.826 m e 1.006 m or 100.6 cm f 1.222 m or 122.2 cm 5 5.3 cm 6 273 mm 7 210 cm, 250 cm, 260 cm, 270.8 cm 8 227 cm or 2.27 m 9 400 × 12 = 4800 mm or 4.8 m

Unit 133 Page 85

1 a km b cm c mm d m e cm f km 2 a 3.26 m b 4.12 m c 8.91 m d 7.21 m e 8.47 m f 3.36 m 3 a 200 cm b 700 cm c 1200 cm d 469 cm e 834 cm f 576 cm 4 a 4 b 8 c 16 d 8 e 2 f 30 5 mm 6 9.26 m 7 387 cm 8 16 9 various, e.g. skirt, ruler, chair

Unit 134 Page 85

1 a 4000 m b 9000 m c 6000 m d 10 000 m e 14 000 m f 18 000 m 2 a 5 km b 3 km c 7 km d 11 km e 16 km f 20 km 3 a 7.436 km b 2.163 km c 9.105 km d 13.218 km e 16.243 km f 21.785 km 4 a m b km c mm d cm e km f m 5 27 000 m 6 13 km 7 2.143 km 8 m 9 no

Unit 135 Page 86

1 a km b m c cm d m e cm f km 2 a 3.720 km b 4.981 km c 6.342 km d 9.875 km e 14.264 km f 23.871 km 3 a 2310 m b 6845 m c 2800 m d 9761 m e 12 310 m f 16 075 m 4 a 2779 km b 1391 km c 1305 km d 970 km e 2210 km f 2624 km 5 km 6 2.106 km 7 4302 m 8 3852 km 9 Alice Springs and Canberra

Unit 136 Page 86

1 a 4.6 cm b 3.9 cm c 8.1 cm d 12 cm e 14.6 cm f 27.6 cm 2 a 4.61 m b 7.38 m c 9.26 m d 12.84 m e 36.95 m f 21 m 3 a 1.376 km b 4.218 km c 5.798 km d 6.635 km e 9.801 km f 10.635 km 4 a 5500 b 115 c 5.2 d 9.24 e 4700 f 25 5 38.5 cm 6 47.16 m 7 21.763 km 8 265 cm 9 a 4800 m b 4.8 km

Unit 137 Page 87

1 a 9.6 cm b 2.7 cm c 8.3 cm d 12.9 cm e 46.3 cm f 370.2 cm **2** a 1.47 m b 2.18 m c 5.32 m d 81.63 m e 47.90 m
f 34.72 m **3** a 7600 m b 8720 m c 4832 m d 18 715 m e 46 210 m f 29 304 m **4** a 600 mm, 60 cm, 0.6 m
b 46 mm, 4.6 cm, 0.046 m c 830 mm, 83 cm, 0.83 m d 42 mm, 4.2 cm. 0.042 m e 19 mm, 1.9 cm, 0.019 m
f 241 mm, 24.1 cm, 0.241 m **5** 964.1 cm **6** 37.19 m **7** 21 030 m **8** 136 mm, 13.6 cm, 0.136 m **9** various

Unit 138 Page 87

1 a 10 cm b 12 cm c 9 cm d 26 cm e 20 cm f 12 cm **2** a 8 cm b 18 cm c 20 cm d 18 cm e 21 cm f 32 cm
3 a 10 cm b 16 cm c 32 cm d 25 cm e 24 cm f 38 cm **4** a 18 cm b 80 cm c 24 cm d 72 cm e 45 cm f 48 cm
5 27 cm **6** 55 cm **7** 12 cm **8** 120 cm **9** regular

Unit 139 Page 88

1 a 14 cm b 32 cm c 40 m d 19 m e 40 km f 70 km **2** a 28.8 cm b 57 cm c 30 cm d 66 cm e 112 m f 120 m
3 a 24 cm b 40 m c 21 m d 24 m e 33 cm f 30 km **4** a 5 cm b 4 m c 16 km d 25 mm e 36 cm f 24 m **5** 52 cm
6 28 cm **7** 16 m **8** 7 m **9** various, e.g. sides of 15 cm, 15 cm and 10 cm or 10 cm, 10 cm and 20 cm

Unit 140 Page 88

1 a 4 cm, 4 cm, 16 cm² b 6 cm, 2 cm, 12 cm² c 7 cm, 3 cm, 21 cm² d 5 cm, 5 cm, 25 cm² e 2 cm, 1 cm, 2 cm²
f 12 cm, 9 cm, 108 cm² **2** a 10 cm² b 99 cm² c 42 cm² d 18 cm² e 32 cm² f 40 cm² **3** a 6 cm² b 56 cm² c 12 cm²
d 40 cm² e 108 cm² f 30 cm² **4** a 49 cm² b 81 cm² c 121 cm² d 9 cm² e 64 cm² f 36 cm² **5** 9 cm, 3 cm, 27 cm²
6 12 cm² **7** 9 cm² **8** 100 cm² **9** 16 cm² + 12 cm² = 28 cm²

Unit 141 Page 89

1 a 30 m² b 40 m² c 54 m² d 8 m² e 21 m² f 99 m² **2** a 36 m² b 8 m² c 108 m² d 1.5 m² e 12 m² f 81 m²
3 a 12 m² b 18 m² c 150 m² d 80 m² e 5000 m² f 180 m² **4** a 34 m² b 33 m² c 41 m² d 21 m² e 51 m² f 48 m²
5 120 m² **6** 9 m² **7** 5 m² **8** 19 m² **9** various, e.g. 6 m and 7 m

Unit 142 Page 89

1 a 20 cm², 10 cm² b 28 cm², 14 cm² c 20 cm², 10 cm² d 64 cm², 32 cm² e 90 cm², 45 cm² f 12 cm², 6 cm²
2 a 8 cm², 4 cm² b 42 cm², 21 cm² c 32 cm², 16 cm² d 18 cm², 9 cm² e 70 cm², 35 cm² f 18 cm², 9 cm²
3 a 24 cm² b 24.5 cm² c 9 cm² d 15 cm² e 50 cm² f 10 cm² **4** a 3, 9 b 2, 14 c 4, 36 d 5, 30 e 6, 60 f 10, 40
5 32 cm², 16 cm² **6** 48, 24 **7** 6 cm² **8** 6, 42 **9** The area of a triangle is half base by perpendicular height.

Unit 143 Page 90

1 a 15 m² b 10.5 m² c 8 m² d 9 m² e 40 m² f 9 m² **2** a 21 m² b 18 m² c 30 m² d 6 m² e 25 m² f 18 m²
3 a 16 m² b 22.5 m² c 18 m² d 15 m² e 21 m² f 10 m² **4** a 27 cm² b 16 cm² c 100 cm² d 10 m² e 72 m² f 70 m²
5 14 m² **6** 32 m² **7** 54 cm² **8** 45 cm² **9** 120 cm²

Unit 144 Page 90

1 b, d, e **2** a 9 ha b 4 ha c 11 ha d 47 ha e 69 ha f 47.6 ha **3** a 3 ha b 9 ha c 5 ha d 12 ha e 14 ha f 20 ha
4 a 20 000 m² b 60 000 m² c 70 000 m² d 130 000 m² e 150 000 m² f 190 000 m² **5** farm, beach **6** 58.7 ha **7** 15 ha
8 210 000 m² **9** a 40 b 10 c 500

Unit 145 Page 91

1 b, c, f **2** a 200 ha b 500 ha c 800 ha d 1000 ha e 1400 ha f 2500 ha **3** a 4 km² b 7 km² c 3 km² d 12 km²
e 15 km² f 27 km² **4** a 8853 km² b 10 651 km² c 564 620 km² d 148 713 km² e 1 642 060 km² f 824 749 km²
5 national park **6** 1900 ha **7** 30 km² **8** 2 293 885 km² **9** 1 cm², 1 m², 1 ha, 1 km²

Unit 146 Page 91

1 a km² b m² c m² d ha e ha f km² **2** a 3 ha b 5 ha c 9 ha d 11 ha e 19 ha f 24 ha **3** a 4 km² b 8 km² c 1.1 km²
d 4.68 km² e 3.95 km² f 9.61 km² **4** a > b < c < d < e < f > **5** km² **6** 5.2 ha **7** 4.76 km² **8** <
9 1 208 724 km²

Unit 147 Page 92

1 a 412 g b 500 g c 250 g d 841 g e 236 g f 116 g **2** a 1.72 kg b 6.1 kg c 4.25 kg d 5.136 kg e 9.648 kg f 10.985 kg
3 a 3246 g b 1079 g c 4600 g d 8210 g e 9317 g f 5556 g **4** a 2160 g b 3.276 kg c 4.2 kg d 1050 g e 7000 g
f 9.245 kg **5** 720 g **6** 7.226 kg **7** 4109 kg **8** 1025 g **9** 820 g

Unit 148 Page 92

1 a kg b t c kg d g e t f g **2** a 2000 kg b 9000 kg c 4000 kg d 11 000 kg e 15 000 kg f 20 000 kg **3** a 1 t b 5 t
c 8 t d 19 t e 30 t f 52 t **4** a 2100 kg b 7600 kg c 4800 kg d 3215 kg e 9746 kg f 21 080 kg **5** t **6** 27 000 kg
7 27 t **8** 14 302 kg **9** 1 t 630 kg

Unit 149 Page 93

1 a small piece of gold b boy c sugar d truck e bag of apples f suitcase **2** a 7000 kg b 14 000 kg c 3500 kg d 11 500 kg
e 44 250 kg f 1750 kg **3** a 9 t b 21 t c 10.5 t d 7.25 t e 14.75 t f 45.5 t **4** a 6.32 t b 4500 kg c 7812 kg d 3.125 t
e 41.6 t f 5836 kg **5** weighbridge **6** 2500 kg **7** 19.25 t **8** 7250 kg **9** 2 litres

Unit 150 Page 93

1 a 40 cm³ b 90 cm³ c 75 cm³ d 250 cm³ e 440 cm³ f 375 cm³ **2** a 60 mL b 25 mL c 80 mL d 460 mL e 790 mL
f 920 mL **3** a 2000 cm³ b 4000 cm³ c 9000 cm³ d 12 000 cm³ e 17 000 cm³ f 22 000 cm³ **4** a 1 L b 7 L c 8 L d 14 L
e 16 L f 24 L **5** 650 cm³ **6** 240 mL **7** 6000 cm³ **8** 19 L **9** 22 × 125 mL = 2750 mL = 2.75 L

Unit 151 Page 94

1 a 0.927 L b 0.446 L c 0.832 L d 0.042 L e 0.05 L f 0.1 L **2** a 791 mL b 398 mL c 852 mL d 17 mL e 95 mL f 40 mL
3 a 2163 mL b 9487 mL c 8215 mL d 6024 mL e 4117 mL f 2008 mL **4** a 2.375 L b 9.456 L c 4.25 L d 9.701 L
e 4.635 L f 21.785 L **5** 0.35 L **6** 146 mL **7** 7612 mL **8** 31.24 L **9**

Capacity	Volume	Mass
1 mL	1 cm³	1 g
50 mL	50 cm³	50 g
500 mL	500 cm³	500 g

Unit 152 Page 94

1 a 2 kg b 5 kg c 8 kg d 12 kg e 19 kg f 25 kg **2** a 3 L b 7 L c 10 L d 13 L e 15 L f 22 L **3** a 300 g b 10 g c 85 g
d 450 g e 975 g f 260 g **4** a 5 mL b 25 mL c 60 mL d 120 mL e 380 mL f 790 mL
5 15 kg **6** 17 L **7** 620 g **8** 325 mL **9**

Capacity	Volume	Mass
5 mL	5 cm³	5 g
400 mL	400 cm³	400 g
1 L	1000 cm³	1 kg

Unit 153 Page 95

1 a 20 mL b 60 mL c 85 mL d 500 mL e 150 mL f 825 mL **2** a 15 cm³ b 40 cm³ c 75 cm³ d 520 cm³ e 660 cm³
f 975 cm³ **3** a 6 L b 9 L c 3 L d 1 L e 8 L f 7 L **4** a 4000 cm³ b 5000 cm³ c 2000 cm³ d 10 000 cm³ e 14 000 cm³
f 17 000 cm³ **5** 700 mL **6** 850 cm³ **7** 11 L **8** 12 000 cm³ **9** 1 L − 750 mL = 250 mL

Unit 154 Page 95

1

		Length (cm)	Breadth (cm)	Height (cm)	Volume (cm³)
a		2	2	3	12
b		4	1	2	8
c		4	3	6	72
d		5	2	4	40
e		5	3	4	60
f		6	4	2	48

2 a 80 cm³ b 84 cm³ c 450 cm³ d 84 cm³ e 80 cm³
f 128 cm³ **3** a 24 cm³ b 2 cm³ c 12 cm³ d 8 cm³ e 48 cm³
f 105 cm³ **4** a 9 mL b 200 mL c 47 mL d 1000 mL
e 950 mL f 1200 mL

5

		Length (cm)	Breadth (cm)	Height (cm)	Volume (cm³)
		4	2	3	24

6 72 cm³ **7** 16 cm³ **8** 825 mL
9 various, e.g. 5 cm × 2 cm × 1 cm

Unit 155 Page 96

1 a 9 m³ b 14 m³ c 32 m³ d 46 m³ e 85 m³ f 74 m³ **2** a more than 1 m³ b less than 1 m³ c about 1 m³ d more than 1 m³
less than 1 m³ f about 1 m³ **3** a cm³ b m³ c cm³ d m³ e m³ f cm³ **4** a 24 m³ b 96 m³ c 32 m³ d 150 m³ e 60 m³
18 m³ **5** 53 m³ **6** more than 1 m³ **7** cm³ **8** 90 m³ **9** 1 box = 125 000 cm³, 1 m³ = 1 000 000 cm³, so 8 would fit

Unit 156 Page 96

1 a cm³ b cm³ c m³ d m³ e m³ f cm³ **2** a 32 units³ b 24 units³ c 45 units³ d 35 units³ e 20 units³ f 72 units³
3 a 20 b 24 c 32 d 35 e 45 f 72 **4** a 64 cm³ b 126 cm³ c 16 cm³ d 16 cm³ e 2 cm³ f 15 cm³ **5** cm³ **6** 10 unit³
7 12 cm³, 18 cm³, 20 cm³, 23 cm³ **8** 56 cm³ **9**

Volume (cm³)	Length (cm)	Breadth (cm)	Height (cm)
24	2	2	6
24	3	2	4
24	12	1	2

Unit 157 Page 97

1 a marble b golf ball c apple d tennis ball e basketball f watermelon **2** a 27 units³ b 8 units³ c 343 units³ d 216 units³
125 units³ f 1 unit³ **3** a 5 units³ b 5 units³ c 6 units³ d 7 units³ e 12 units³ f 7 units³ **4** a 56 cm³ b 48 cm³ c 480 cm³
100 cm³ e 700 cm³ f 216 cm³ **5** a matchbox b shoe box c cereal box **6** 64 units³ **7** 10 units³ **8** 75 cm³ **9** b 84 units³

Unit 158 Page 97

1 a 1 b 0 c 0.5 d 0.2 e 1 f 0.6 **2** a yes b no c no d yes e yes f yes **3** a 0.25 b 0.5 c 0.125 d 0 e 0.375 f 0.375
4 a 0.25 b 0.5 c 0.375 d 0.25 e 0.5 f 0.25 **5** 0 **6** a yes b yes c no **7** 1 **8** 0 **9** various, e.g. it will rain

Unit 159 Page 98

1 various, e.g. a 0.6 b 0 c 0.5 d 0.8 e 0.9 f 0.1 **2** a $\frac{2}{10} = \frac{1}{5}$ b $\frac{2}{10} = \frac{1}{5}$ c $\frac{1}{10}$ d $\frac{1}{10}$ e $\frac{1}{10}$ f $\frac{1}{10}$ **3** a F b A c D d C e B f E
4 a B and E b C c D d E e D and F f A and F **5** certain **6** 0 **7** E **8** C **9** 66, 65, 64, 63, 62, 61
55, 54, 53, 52, 51
44, 43, 42, 41
33, 32, 31
22, 21
11

Unit 160 Page 98

1 a 26 b 24 c 10 d 6 e 16 f 18 **2** a 160 b 100 c 260 d 180 e 240 f 60 **3** a 20 b 8 c 18 d 18 e 12 f 8
4 a 120 b 80 c 80 d 180 e 160 f 180 **5** 44 **6** 340 **7** 16 **8** 200 **9**

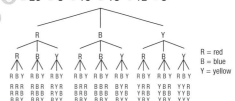

R = red
B = blue
Y = yellow

Unit 161 Page 99

1

Computer use	Tally
email (E)	IIII III
internet (I)	IIII IIII
games (G)	IIII IIII
homework (H)	IIII I

2 a 8 b 6 c 10 d 10 e 18 f 16 **3** a Activity b No. of students c 8 d 10 e 10 f 6 **4** a all b email c internet and games d homework e homework f email and homework **5** 34 **6** 28 **7** Students and computer use **8** 0 **9** various

Unit 162 Page 99

1 a 16 mm b 24 mm c 16 mm d 24 mm e 40 mm f 40 mm **2** a $\frac{16}{80} = \frac{1}{5}$ b $\frac{24}{80} = \frac{3}{10}$ c $\frac{24}{80} = \frac{3}{10}$ d $\frac{16}{80} = \frac{1}{5}$ e 0 f $\frac{32}{80} = \frac{2}{5}$ **3** a 30 b 30 c 20 d 20 e 50 f 40 **4** a $\frac{1.6}{8} = \frac{1}{5}$ b $\frac{1.6}{8} = \frac{1}{5}$ c $\frac{2.4}{8} = \frac{3}{10}$ d $\frac{2.4}{8} = \frac{3}{10}$ e $\frac{1}{2}$ f $\frac{1}{2}$ **5** 56 mm **6** $\frac{40}{80} = \frac{1}{2}$ **7** 70 **8** $\frac{3.2}{8} = \frac{4}{10} = \frac{2}{5}$ **9**

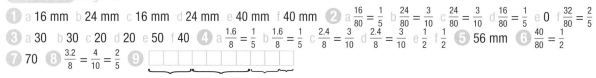

brown   blond   black red

Unit 163 Page 100

1 a $\frac{3}{8}$ b 25 c $\frac{1}{4}$ d 25 e 25 f 50 **2** a $\frac{1}{4}$, 25%, 50 b $\frac{1}{4}$, 25%, 50 c $\frac{1}{8}$, 12.5%, 25 d $\frac{1}{8}$, 12.5%, 25 e $\frac{1}{8}$, 12.5%, 25 f $\frac{1}{8}$, 12.5%, 25 **3** a football b cricket and netball c 50 d same e 50 f 175 **4** a 250 b 200 c 100 d 50 e 200 f 300 **5** $\frac{3}{8} + \frac{1}{4} = \frac{5}{8}$ **6** 25% **7** 300 **8** 250 **9**

Preferred ice-cream flavour	No.	Degrees
chocolate	40	144
vanilla	25	90
strawberry	20	72
caramel	10	36
other	5	18

Unit 164 Page 100

1 a 60 mL b 13 m c 2100 mm d 28°C e 48.5 g f 625 kg **2** a 704.3 b 2912.5 c 5662 d 9554.3 e 24 648 f 45 573.3 **3** 22.5°C a 20°C b 25°C c 15°C d 20°C e 30°C f 25°C **4** a 6 b 7 c 80 d 2.9 e 250 f 470 **5** $4 **6** 658.3 **7** 21.9°C **8** 1413.5 **9** various

Unit 165 Page 101

1 a 200 mL b 300 mL c 500 mL d $\frac{1}{2}$ e $\frac{1}{5}$ f $\frac{3}{10}$ **2** a $\frac{1}{2}$ b $\frac{1}{4}$ c $\frac{1}{12}$ d $\frac{1}{12}$ e $\frac{1}{12}$ f $\frac{2}{12} = \frac{1}{6}$ **3** a 60 b 20 c 20 d 120 e 20 f 80 **4** a 150 b 200 c 100 d 50 e 350 f 150 **5** $\frac{1}{2}$ **6** $\frac{3}{4}$ **7** 80 **8** 300 **9**

oil	detergent		water	

Unit 166 Page 101

1 a 12 hours b 5.5 hours c 2 hours d 10 hours e 1 hour f $4\frac{2}{3}$ hours **2** a 100 km b 300 km c 650 km d 500 km e 300 km f 500 km **3**

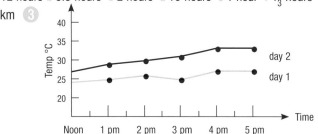

4 a day 2 b day 2 c day 2 d day 1 e day 2 f day 1 **5** 1 hour **6** 400 km **7** example: temperature of two days **8** 5°C

9

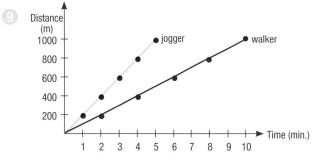

Unit 167 Page 102

1 a !!!! !!! b !!!! c !!!! ! d !! e !!! f !!!! ! g !!!!

2 a 13 b 8 c 14 d rabbit e possum f bird and kangaroo

3 a 18 b 9 c 10.5 d 15 e 19.5 f 16.5 5 6 6 35

7 29 8 21 9

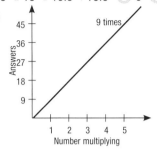

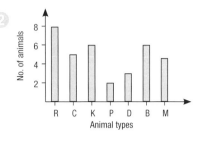

Unit 168 Page 102

1 a 10 b 2 c 4 d grey e brown f brown 2 a 60°F b 88°F c 32°C d 5°C e 70°F f 27°C 3 a playtime and maths
b assembly c reading d writing e assembly f playtime and maths 4 a 25°C b 30°C c 7°C d 10°C e Wednesday f Thursday
5 22 6 same 7 assembly and art 8 17°C 9 various

Unit 169 Page 103

1 a 1912 b 1957 c 1980 d 1921 e 1962 f 2000 2 a 7 million b 15 million c 17 million d 18 million e 14 million
f 1 million 3

	Insect type	Tally	Total
a	butterfly	!!!i !!!!	9
b	ant	!!!i !!!i !!!!	14
c	fly	!!!i !!!	8
d	flea	!!!i !!!i !!!	13
e	grasshopper	!!!i	5
f	beetle	!!!i !	12

4

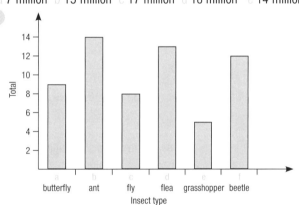

5 greater 6 1975 – 1984 7 61 8 ant 9 various

Unit 170 Page 103

1 a 83 105 b 261 969 c 1 156 291 d 1 945 769 e 5 310 832 f 381 973 2 a 4713 b 8431 c 3517 d 7108 e 113 513
f 274 013 3 a 33 547 b 274 833 c 1 215 215 d 534 997 e 544 250 f 634 737

4 a

```
    5 ¹2 ¹4
  − 3¹ 5 0¹6
  ─────────
    1 6 1 8
```

b

```
    4 ¹0 9 ²2
  − 3 5 6 6
  ─────────
      5 2 6
```

c

```
    9 ¹6 ²2 ¹4 6
  − ¹3 8 5 2 1
  ───────────
    5 7 7 2 5
```

d

```
    4 ¹2 ¹6 8 ¹0
  − 1 9 8 6¹3
  ───────────
    2 2 8 1 7
```

e

```
    1 ¹3 ¹5 7 9
  − ¹ 6¹8 4 9
  ───────────
      6 7 3 0
```

f

```
    2 ¹1 4 9 ¹2
  − 1¹ 8 3 5¹6
  ───────────
      3 1 3 6
```

5 1 347 621 6 38 615 7 512 391

8

```
    4 ¹6 ¹1 ¹0 7
  − 2¹ 9¹ 8¹ 3 0
  ─────────────
    1 6 2 7 7
```

9 increased by: $874 deposit – $755 withdrawal = $119

Unit 171 Page 104

1 a 8760 b 27 640 c 25 560 d 97 440 e 73 450 f 198 960 **2** a $71\frac{5}{12}$ b $15\frac{57}{70}$ c $71\frac{1}{5}$ d $30\frac{3}{5}$ e $208\frac{1}{4}$ f $36\frac{29}{30}$ **3** a 1363 b 1518 c 5022 d 684 e 1056 f 8170 **4** a 9495 b 101 307 c $5264\frac{1}{2}$ d $6240\frac{4}{7}$ e $4220\frac{4}{5}$ f 92 832 **5** 152 460 **6** $62\frac{3}{20}$ **7** 3285 **8** $41493\frac{5}{6}$ **9** 479 × 6 = 2874; 2874 ÷ 3 = 958, therefore 958 boxes in each crate

Unit 172 Page 104

1 a 10 b 30 c 20 d 8 e 8 f 7 **2** a 8 b 36 c 25 d 24 e 18 f 50 **3** a $1\frac{1}{10}$ b $\frac{1}{3}$ c $1\frac{1}{6}$ d $1\frac{1}{6}$ e $1\frac{1}{16}$ f $\frac{1}{2}$ **4** a $\frac{6}{15} = \frac{2}{5}$ b $\frac{8}{30} = \frac{4}{15}$ c $\frac{5}{42}$ d $\frac{15}{32}$ e $\frac{8}{36} = \frac{2}{9}$ f $\frac{2}{14} = \frac{1}{7}$ **5** 3 **6** 24 **7** $1\frac{1}{9}$ **8** $\frac{3}{5}$ **9** 3

Unit 173 Page 105

1 a 7.001 b 11.559 c 20.915 d 31.733 e 41.063 f 58.053 **2** a 2.82 b 1.635 c 0.533 d 6.079 e 4.375 f 0.261 **3** a $12.63 b $58.50 c $33.28 d $19.96 e $22.00 f $13.93 **4** a 0.462 b 0.092 65 c 0.021 48 d 0.123 245 e 4.93 f 0.004 6 **5** 16.646 **6** 3.128 **7** $57.30 **8** 0.010 25 **9** $43.50 + $92 = $135.50

Unit 174 Page 105

1 a 15 b 83 c 65 d 29 e 447 f 384 **2** a 2 b 3 c 11 d 7 e 12 f 5 **3** a 0 b 4 c 5 d 4 e 8 f 66 **4** a 11 b 12 c 53 d 39 e 1000 f 40 **5** 392 **6** 20 **7** 8 **8** 1000 **9** 5

Unit 175 Page 106

1 a lemon tree b carrot seed c 81c d 94c e $12.50 f 43c **2** f **3** a $22.68 b $23.10 c $20.60 d $23.15 e $21.78 f $26.10 **4** a $2.44 b $13.59 c $5.71 d $8.46 e $24.50 f $25.33 **5** $31.40 **6** True **7** a $68.71 b $67.74 c $87.20 **8** $19.79 **9** various

Unit 176 Page 106

1 a 11 b 86 c 37 d 48 e 94 f 128 **2** d **3** a 8 b 16 c 16 d 8 e oranges f pineapples and pears **4** a 4 b 8 c 10 d 16 e 18 f 28 **5** 51 **6** 37.9 cm **7** 475 g **8** 38 **9** 18 nights

Review Tests Units 1 – 6 Page 107

1 A **2** –1 **3** false **4** true **5** three hundred and sixty-eight thousand, five hundred and two **6** 647 853, 6 384 971, 6 395 211, 6 583 942 **7** four hundred and ninety-six thousand and twenty-five **8** 730 460 **9** divide by 5 **10** –3 **11** 972 811, 1 000 000 **12** 164 092 tens

Review Tests Units 7 – 9 Page 107

1 D **2** A **3** true **4** false **5** $12 360 256.31 **6** 1 006 969 **7** 655 **8** $72 217 **9** 7840 christmas trees **10** 18 185 L **11** twelve million, three hundred and sixty thousand, two hundred and fifty-six dollars and 31 cents

12

+	468	110	946	1187	32 345
721	1189	831	1667	1908	33 066

Review Tests Units 10 – 15 Page 108

1 C **2** A **3** true **4** false **5** 1 166 000 **6** $4\ ^16\ \boxed{8}\ ^12$ $-\ ^13\ \boxed{7}\ ^14\ 8$ $=\ 9\ 3\ \boxed{4}$ **7** 8215 **8** 61 764 t **9** $426 – $269 = $157 **11** 732 241 km²

10

–	72	83	107	124	141
56	16	27	51	68	85

12

367 000 → 248 000
– 119 000 | + 119 000
248 000 ── 367 000

Review Tests Units 16 – 18 Page 108

1 D **2** A **3** true **4** false **5** 0 **6** 40, 10 **7** 0 **8** 80 **9** 60 + 15 = $75 **11** > **12** 24 + 84 + 30 = 138 pieces of fruit

10

×	4	7	12	9	8
3	12	21	36	27	24

Review Tests Units 19 – 22 Page 109

1 C 2 B 3 false 4 true 5 4635 6 800 students 7 68 341 8 32 000 9 150, 300, 450, ... increasing by 150 each time
10 320, 3200, 32 000 11 180 × 50 = 9000 12 7770 plants

Review Tests Units 23 – 27 Page 109

1 D 2 B 3 false 4 true 5 2880 + 216 = 3096 6 51 120 7 $2403 8
9 $4500 + $267 = $4767 10 16 × 33 = 528 or 18 × 30 = 540, 540 11 22
12 nothing! i.e. equal

×	6	60	600	6000
8	48	480	4800	48 000

Review Tests Units 28 – 30 Page 110

1 A 2 C 3 false 4 true 5 70 × 90 = 630 6 4, 8, 12, 16, 20, 24, 28, 32 7 460, 230 8 400 × 30 = 12 000
9 > 10 40 × 20 = 800 11 greater than 12 estimated 20 × 70 ≈ 1400

Review Tests Units 31 – 34 Page 110

1 D 2 B 3 true 4 false 5 65 6 $48\frac{2}{3}$ 7 173 8 2 9 8 and 7 pieces remaining 10 81
11 $2473 \div 5 = 494\frac{3}{5}$ 12 0.43

Review Tests Units 35 – 39 Page 111

1 B 2 A 3 true 4 true 5 $12\,072\frac{2}{3}$ 6 26 7 4210.3 8 129.5 or 130 runs 9 140 10 670 11 true
12 $10\frac{8}{14}$ or $10\frac{4}{7}$

Review Tests Units 40 – 43 Page 111

1 B 2 C 3 false 4 true 5
434
430 440 450 460 470
6 $5 7 78.2
8 535 + 385 = 920 not 921
9 1056 + 25 = 1081
10 110 km/h 11 $\frac{29+30+31}{3} = 30$
12 43 × 5 = 215 and
215 ÷ 5 = 43

Review Tests Units 44 – 47 Page 112

1 D 2 B 3 false 4 false 5 112 6 60 7 0 8 16 9 6 10 36 ÷ 9 × (4 + 6) = 40 11 21 + 10 = 31
12 8 × 3 ÷ 6 = 24 ÷ 6 = 4

Review Tests Units 48 – 54 Page 112

1 A 2 B 3 false 4 true 5 4 326 000 6 7 7 × 2 8 (100 − 16) − (4 × 7) = V, V = 56
9 500 × $\frac{1}{5}$:500, 100, 20, 4, $\frac{4}{5}$ 10 1 206 000 11 10 111 − 1100 = 1011 12 95 − (4 × 19.65) = $16.40

Review Tests Units 55 – 59 Page 113

1 D 2 B 3 false 4 false 5 21 6 6.8, 2.2 7 8 8 $\frac{x}{6} = 12 \therefore x = 72$ 9 not correct 10 one and one quarter
11 nine multiplied by ten, subtract seven multiplied by twelve is six 12 $\sqrt{(x + 5) \times 11} - (3 + 2) = 6$
$\sqrt{(x + 5) \times 11} = 11$
$(x + 5) \times 11 = 121 \therefore x = 6$

Review Tests Units 60 – 64 Page 113

1 D 2 A 3 false 4 false 5 −6, −4, −2, −1, 0, 1, 3, 5, 8 6 17 + 3 = 20 or 13 + 7 = 20
7 example: 176
                4 × 44
            2 × 2 × 11 × 4
                  2 × 2
8 20 m 9 144 − 16 = 128 10 −10 11 111, 112, 114, 115, 116, 117, 118, 119
12 The total is 5, 13, 25, 41, 61, 85. So the differences are 8, 12, 16, 20, 24.
The differences increase by 4 each time.

Review Tests Units 65 – 71 Page 114

1 D 2 C 3 true 4 true 5 3 6 > 7 $\frac{27}{8}$ 8 12 9 ●●○○○○○ / ●●○○○○○ / ●●●○○○○ 10 e.g. $\frac{2}{3} = \frac{4}{6} = \frac{6}{9} = \frac{10}{15}$
11 $\frac{14}{8}, \frac{15}{8}, \frac{16}{8}, \frac{20}{8} \therefore$ largest fraction is $\frac{10}{4}$ 12 3

Review Tests Units 72 – 75 Page 114

1 B 2 C 3 true 4 true 5 $\frac{9}{5} = 1\frac{4}{5}$ 6 $\frac{1}{2}$ 7 $\frac{21}{8} = 2\frac{5}{8}$ 8 $\frac{1}{6} + \frac{1}{4} = \frac{5}{12}$ 9 $\frac{3}{4}$ 10 $\frac{6}{5} = 1\frac{1}{5}$
0   $\frac{2}{5}$ 1 $1\frac{1}{5}$
11 $\frac{1}{2} < \frac{3}{5}$ 12 $\frac{2}{8} + \frac{6}{8} - \frac{1}{8} = \frac{7}{8}$

ANSWERS: Review Tests Units 76 – 120

Review Tests Units 76 – 79 Page 115

① B ② C ③ true ④ true ⑤ $\frac{7}{8}$ ⑥ $\frac{3}{5}$ ⑦ $2\frac{2}{3} > 1\frac{1}{6}$ ⑧ 8 ⑨ $\frac{2}{5}$ ⑩ 2, 30 ⑪ 165 red, 220 blue, 275 other ⑫ 0.42 t

Review Tests Units 80 – 86 Page 115

① B ② C ③ false ④ true ⑤ 7.65 ⑥ 14.05 m ⑦ 29.62 ⑧ 64.29 ⑨ twenty-one and forty-six thousandths
⑩ 38.85 + 19.32 = $58.17 ⑪ $3.75 ÷ 4 = 94c and $4.98 ÷ 6 = 83c (cheaper!)
⑫ × 10: right by 1 decimal place
× 100: right by 2 decimal places
× 1000: right by 3 decimal places

Review Tests Units 87 – 94 Page 116

① D ② A ③ true ④ false ⑤ 36% ⑥ 12 children ⑦ $15.22 = $15.20 ⑧ HK$168 ⑨ $7.92 and change is $2.08
⑩ 80 − 16 = $64 ⑪ 0.75, 75% ⑫ or

Review Tests Units 95 – 98 Page 116

① A ② A ③ true ④ false ⑤ ⑥ ⑦ 11 ⑧

⑨ various, e.g. ⑩ perpendicular ⑪ a no b no c yes d yes e no ⑫ M E X W

Review Tests Units 99 – 103 Page 117

① C ② A ③ false ④ true ⑤ 115° ⑥ 195° ⑦ protractor ⑧ ⑨ A no B no C yes
⑩ 300° ⑪ 60° ⑫ 60°

Review Tests Units 104 – 108 Page 117

① B ② C ③ false ④ true ⑤ 5 faces, 9 edges, 6 vertices ⑥ B ⑦ ⑧ ⑨ 8
⑩ true ⑪ A ⑫

Review Tests Units 109 – 114 Page 118

① C ② A ③ false ④ true ⑤

No. of hexagons	1	2	3	4
No. of sides	6	12	18	24

⑥ ⑦

⑧ multiplied by 4, i.e. 9 × 4 = 36 ⑨ radius ⑩ translated ⑪ ⑫

Review Tests Units 115 – 120 Page 118

① B ② C ③ false ④ true ⑤ ⑥ north-east ⑦ east ⑧ north-west ⑨ no ⑩ (1, 1)

⑪ (A, 2), (C, 2), (B, 4) ⑫ north-east

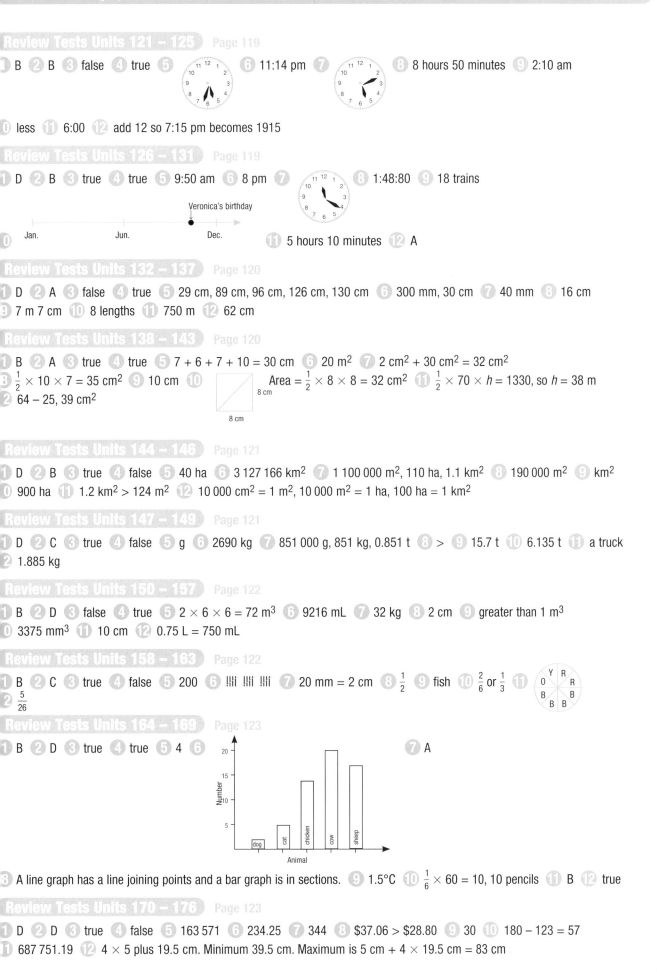

Review Tests Units 121 – 125 Page 119

1 B 2 B 3 false 4 true 5 [clock showing approx 6:33] 6 11:14 pm 7 [clock showing approx 1:20] 8 8 hours 50 minutes 9 2:10 am

10 less 11 6:00 12 add 12 so 7:15 pm becomes 1915

Review Tests Units 126 – 131 Page 119

1 D 2 B 3 true 4 true 5 9:50 am 6 8 pm 7 [clock showing approx 4:05] 8 1:48:80 9 18 trains

10 [timeline from Jan. to Dec. with Veronica's birthday marked] 11 5 hours 10 minutes 12 A

Review Tests Units 132 – 137 Page 120

1 D 2 A 3 false 4 true 5 29 cm, 89 cm, 96 cm, 126 cm, 130 cm 6 300 mm, 30 cm 7 40 mm 8 16 cm

9 7 m 7 cm 10 8 lengths 11 750 m 12 62 cm

Review Tests Units 138 – 143 Page 120

1 B 2 A 3 true 4 true 5 $7 + 6 + 7 + 10 = 30$ cm 6 20 m² 7 2 cm² + 30 cm² = 32 cm²

8 $\frac{1}{2} \times 10 \times 7 = 35$ cm² 9 10 cm 10 [square with diagonal, labeled 8 cm on side and 8 cm below] Area $= \frac{1}{2} \times 8 \times 8 = 32$ cm² 11 $\frac{1}{2} \times 70 \times h = 1330$, so $h = 38$ m

12 64 − 25, 39 cm²

Review Tests Units 144 – 146 Page 121

1 D 2 B 3 true 4 false 5 40 ha 6 3 127 166 km² 7 1 100 000 m², 110 ha, 1.1 km² 8 190 000 m² 9 km²

10 900 ha 11 1.2 km² > 124 m² 12 10 000 cm² = 1 m², 10 000 m² = 1 ha, 100 ha = 1 km²

Review Tests Units 147 – 149 Page 121

1 D 2 C 3 true 4 false 5 g 6 2690 kg 7 851 000 g, 851 kg, 0.851 t 8 > 9 15.7 t 10 6.135 t 11 a truck

12 1.885 kg

Review Tests Units 150 – 157 Page 122

1 B 2 D 3 false 4 true 5 $2 \times 6 \times 6 = 72$ m³ 6 9216 mL 7 32 kg 8 2 cm 9 greater than 1 m³

10 3375 mm³ 11 10 cm 12 0.75 L = 750 mL

Review Tests Units 158 – 163 Page 122

1 B 2 C 3 true 4 false 5 200 6 |||| |||| |||| 7 20 mm = 2 cm 8 $\frac{1}{2}$ 9 fish 10 $\frac{2}{6}$ or $\frac{1}{3}$ 11 [spinner diagram with sections Y, R, R, B, B, B, B, O]

12 $\frac{5}{26}$

Review Tests Units 164 – 169 Page 123

1 B 2 D 3 true 4 true 5 4 6 [bar graph: Number vs Animal — dog, cat, chicken, cow, sheep] 7 A

8 A line graph has a line joining points and a bar graph is in sections. 9 1.5°C 10 $\frac{1}{6} \times 60 = 10$, 10 pencils 11 B 12 true

Review Tests Units 170 – 176 Page 123

1 D 2 D 3 true 4 false 5 163 571 6 234.25 7 344 8 $37.06 > $28.80 9 30 10 180 − 123 = 57

11 687 751.19 12 4 × 5 plus 19.5 cm. Minimum 39.5 cm. Maximum is 5 cm + 4 × 19.5 cm = 83 cm

© 2007 Pascal Press
Reprinted 2008, 2009 (twice), 2010, 2011

Updated in 2012 for the Australian Curriculum

Reprinted 2014, 2015, 2016, 2018, 2019, 2020

ISBN: 978 1 74125 264 4

Pascal Press
PO Box 250
Glebe NSW 2037
(02) 8585 4044
www. pascalpress.com.au

Publisher: Vivienne Joannou
Project editor: Mark Dixon
Edited by May McCool, Jeremy Billington and Rosemary Peers
Typeset by Typecellars Pty Ltd and lj Design (Julianne Billington)
Answers checked by Peter Little
Cover by DiZign Pty Ltd
Printed by Vivar Printing/Green Giant Press